D1593314

studies in jazz

Institute of Jazz Studies
Rutgers—The State University of New Jersey
General Editors: Dan Morgenstern and Edward Berger

1. BENNY CARTER: A Life in American Music, *by Morroe Berger, Edward Berger, and James Patrick, 1982*
2. ART TATUM: A Guide to His Recorded Music, *by Arnold Laubich and Ray Spencer, 1982*
3. ERROLL GARNER: The Most Happy Piano, *by James M. Doran, 1995*
4. JAMES P. JOHNSON: A Case of Mistaken Identity, *by Scott E. Brown;* Discography 1917–1950, *by Robert Hilbert, 1986*
5. PEE WEE ERWIN: This Horn for Hire, *as told to Warren W. Vaché, Sr., 1987*
6. BENNY GOODMAN: Listen to His Legacy, *by D. Russell Connor, 1988*
7. ELLINGTONIA: The Recorded Music of Duke Ellington and His Sidemen, *by W. E. Timner, 1988; 4th ed., 1996*
8. THE GLENN MILLER ARMY AIR FORCE BAND: Sustineo Alas / I Sustain the Wings, *by Edward F. Polic;* Foreword *by George T. Simon, 1989*
9. SWING LEGACY, *by Chip Deffaa, 1989*
10. REMINISCING IN TEMPO: The Life and Times of a Jazz Hustler, *by Teddy Reig, with Edward Berger, 1990*
11. IN THE MAINSTREAM: 18 Portraits in Jazz, *by Chip Deffaa, 1992*
12. BUDDY DeFRANCO: A Biographical Portrait and Discography, *by John Kuehn and Arne Astrup, 1993*
13. PEE WEE SPEAKS: A Discography of Pee Wee Russell, *by Robert Hilbert, with David Niven, 1992*
14. SYLVESTER AHOLA: The Gloucester Gabriel, *by Dick Hill, 1993*
15. THE POLICE CARD DISCORD, *by Maxwell T. Cohen, 1993*
16. TRADITIONALISTS AND REVIVALISTS IN JAZZ, *by Chip Deffaa, 1993*
17. BASSICALLY SPEAKING: An Oral History of George Duvivier, *by Edward Berger;* Musical Analysis *by David Chevan, 1993*
18. TRAM: The Frank Trumbauer Story, *by Philip R. Evans and Larry F. Kiner, with William Trumbauer, 1994*
19. TOMMY DORSEY: On the Side, *by Robert L. Stockdale, 1995*
20. JOHN COLTRANE: A Discography and Musical Biography, *by Yasuhiro Fujioka, with Lewis Porter and Yoh-ichi Hamada, 1995*
21. RED HEAD: A Chronological Survey of "Red" Nichols and His Five Pennies, *by Stephen M. Stroff, 1996*

HOT JAZZ

From Harlem to Storyville

David Griffiths

Studies in Jazz
No. 28

The Scarecrow Press, Inc.
Lanham, Maryland, & London
and
Institute of Jazz Studies
Rutgers—The State University of New Jersey
1998

SCARECROW PRESS, INC.

Published in the United States of America
by Scarecrow Press, Inc.
4720 Boston Way
Lanham, Maryland 20706

4 Pleydell Gardens, Folkestone
Kent CT20 2DN, England

British Library Cataloguing in Publication Information Available

Library of Congress Cataloging-in-Publication Data

Griffiths, David, 1939–
   Hot jazz : from Harlem to Storyville / David Griffiths.
     p. cm.—(Studies in jazz ; no. 28)
   Includes index.
   ISBN 0-8108-3415-4 (cloth : alk. paper)
   1. Jazz musicians—Interviews. I. Title. II. Series.
ML 394.G84   1998
781.65′092′2—dc21   98-28624
[B]   CIP
                                 MN

Contents

Foreword

For some years David Griffiths has enjoyed a considerable reputation in Britain for his writings on jazz, and now with the publication of *Hot Jazz: From Harlem to Storyville* his following is certain to become international.

Although David's knowledge of jazz history is superfine he never flaunts it during his interviews; instead he allows the subjects to talk relaxedly and in doing so gleans many details that would certainly elude a more bombastic approach. His accompanying observations are full of insight and information.

This book makes it obvious that Griffiths shares the full confidence of those whose careers he skilfully traces, and we, the jazz readers, are richer because of this. His writings shed light on areas of research that have generally been neglected, in fact, several of the musicians covered in this work only gave one detailed interview during their entire lifetime—and that was to David Griffiths.

Not all of the thirty or so of David's subjects are famous jazz names, but (as is often the case) those who are not blinded by the spotlight see things more clearly and in better perspective than "the stars of the show." Anyone who is interested in the human background to the endeavours and achievements of jazz musicians will greatly enjoy this fascinating book.

John Chilton, 1998

Series Editor's Foreword

During its lifespan (from 1965 to 1995; far above average for highly specialized jazz periodicals), Britain's *Storyville* was the primary source for new information about what its editor, Laurie Wright, was fond of calling "the vintage years." This meant, more or less, the music of the first three decades of the twentieth century, with occasional forays into the fourth. From its 162 issues, a reader could mine no end of nuggets, biographical, discographical, and sociohistorical.

Among *Storyville*'s distinguished regular contributors was David Griffiths, who specialized in profiles of lesser known musicians. His pieces consistently shed light on the contributions of what might be called the foot soldiers of jazz, players without whom the well-documented stars would not have been able to accomplish what they did.

A Griffiths article was always based on painstaking research, mostly gleaned straight from the source, by way of interviews or extensive correspondence and exchange of tapes. These mostly first-person stories had much to tell, not only of successes and satisfactions, but also of the struggle to remain in a profession buffeted by changing tastes and mores. A surprising number of players managed to hang in by crossing over to Latin bands, which benefited from an audience of dancers far longer than their jazz (or swing) counterparts.

If not for the dedication of researchers like David Griffiths, the stories of these men and women would only have been heard by their colleagues, friends, and families. Studies in Jazz is very pleased to collect and re-introduce these illuminating narratives.

Dan Morgenstern
Director
Institute of Jazz Studies
Rutgers University, Newark

Preface and Acknowledgments

An important and sometimes overlooked musician was the side-man in the big bands of the thirties and early forties. It was because of this fact that I started out interviewing and writing to these jazz musicians in order to provide a better appreciation of them by the jazz student. The majority of these interviews first appeared in *Storyville* magazine. The Editor, Laurie Wright, was a forthright campaigner for the "great years of classic jazz and blues," and I felt that he had a sympathetic readership who would derive much interest from these life story reminiscences, many of which revolved around the swing era. The interviews are almost verbatim, with little editing, as most interviewees expressed their stories and opinions quite frankly.

Many of the musicians interviewed were elderly, and not all of their memories were infallible. My principal difficulty was in getting their stories into chronological order. In most cases, I believe I succeeded, but there were a few who omitted dates and gaps in their careers that I have been unable to fill. At times, it was like piecing together a jigsaw puzzle, but unfortunately such missing pieces of information are unlikely, with the passing years, to be uncovered.

During the years I have been involved in this research many of the older jazz musicians have passed away. Nearly all of those I interviewed, or was in correspondence with, sadly are no longer alive. Some kept their own musical scrapbooks; these were a godsend for a researcher, as there were always newspaper clippings, which, if you were lucky enough, still retained their dates. Occasionally, photographs were dated by the musicians, and all these tidbits of information enabled some sort of order to be established in their careers.

Upon their deaths, I do not know what may have happened to

these scrapbooks; although in monetary value they may be considered worthless, in research and archival value many of them are almost priceless. I suspect that the families of some musicians may well have disposed of these books without realizing how valuable they are to researchers, so they will be lost forever.

The interviews provide a dose of social history as the musicians describe the life of touring musicians and their working conditions, particularly from the mid-twenties through the thirties and into the early forties. The changes that have taken place since the Second World War were major influences on musicians and their music. Although the subjects compose only a very small percentage of musicians, they are representative of the entire jazz music scene of the time. In the main, they were born and based in the United States, but several musicians born and living outside of America are included as well.

Acknowledgments

Throughout the years I have spent working on this project, there have been many people whose assistance, generosity, and friendship have been invaluable.

I am indebted to everyone I interviewed and those who took the trouble to write and answer my queries. I would like to extend my gratitude to: Freddie Skerritt, Leslie Johnakins, Roger Boyd, Harvey Davis, Walter Bishop Sr., Bobby Booker, Bobby Woodlen, George Hancock, Greely Walton, Barclay Draper, Sal Dentici, Earle Howard, Herbie Cowens, Memphis Slim, Josh White, Lester Boone, Cliff Olson, Lizzie Miles, George Guesnon, Emanuel Sayles, Emanuel Paul, Kid Thomas Valentine, Kid Sheik Cola, Curtis Jones, Earle Roberts, Floyd Johnson, Blanche Finlay, Floyd Campbell, Jasper Taylor, Eddie Dawson, August Lanoix, Bill Dillard, Charles I. Williams, and Eddie Craig. Many of these people are now deceased; this book can only serve as a memorial to them and their music.

I would also like to extend my deep appreciation to the following people who, although they are not the principal subjects of this book, were so generous in sharing their recollections with me: Clyde Bernhardt, Tommy Benford, Franc Williams, George Winfield, Doc Cheatham, Andy Kirk, Bill Coleman, Preston Love,

Rudy Powell, Russell Procope, Charlie Holmes, Billy Butler, Bobby Williams, Arthur Bowie, and Dill Jones.

My thanks also go to others who were so generous with their support, time, and knowledge: Frank Driggs, Karl Gert zur Heide, Bertrand Demeusy, Wim Van Eyle, Peter Carr, Lily Coleman, John Chilton, Mia Howard and family, Carline Ray, Ginny Goodwin, Bob Wilber, Sheldon Harris, Gwyn Lewis, Theo Zwicky and Delilah Jackson.

Finally, my most grateful thanks must go to Dr. Albert Vollmer and his family, and Johnny and Liza Simmen. If it had not been for these people, this project would never have been accomplished. Johnny Simmen is one of the greatest writers on jazz and one for whom I have so much admiration. He and his wife have encouraged me to continue with my work when at times I have felt like calling it a day. Their friendship over many years I have valued enormously.

Doctor Albert Vollmer and his family not only allowed me to be a guest at their home in Larchmont, New York, on many occasions, but also were responsible for assisting me in reaching many of the New York musicians. This book would never have been possible, if it had not been for their constant, deeply appreciated assistance.

Introduction: In the Beginning

My interest in jazz started well before I had left school at the age of sixteen. In my late teens, I edited and published a small mimeographed magazine, which at first I called "Dave's Jazz Mag," but subsequently renamed "New Orleans Jazz Rag," as the majority of its short articles were devoted to musicians of the Crescent City.

An early decision to try and get some exclusive material for the magazine resulted in brief interviews with trumpeter Pat Halcox and flautist Johnny Scott. What either of them must have thought of my interviewing technique at that time, I shudder to think, but their kindness and patience in enduring my questions led me ever onward.

In April 1961, I learned that clarinetist Monty Sunshine, who had just left Chris Barber's band and formed his own outfit, was going out with a touring package show that included folk singers Robin Hall and Jimmie McGregor and blues singer Memphis Slim. A rehearsal of this particular show took place in the basement of a striptease club in London's Soho, and I took the opportunity to seek out Memphis Slim for an interview. At his suggestion, we waited until after the rehearsal and then walked back to his hotel so that we could hold the interview in his room. On our way to the hotel Memphis Slim spotted and introduced me to Josh White, who was staying in the same hotel. Memphis Slim had in his room a portable record-player and a number of his own albums, just released, which he played throughout most of the interview.

He told me that he was already playing piano at the age of eight or nine and at seventeen had started working professionally. Although "Beer Drinkin' Woman," which he recorded for the Bluebird label in October 1940, had sold over half a million copies, he had been paid only $60 for making it. He went on to

1

say that the "Blues In The Mississippi Night" album (with Big Bill Broonzy and Sonny Boy Williamson) was actually recorded at the Decca Studios in New York City in 1947, following a concert at the Town Hall. He recalled Sam Chatman as a very fine singer but said that he was not related to him (Memphis Slim had started life as John Lee Chatman, but later changed his Christian name to Peter). Memphis was the manager of Arbee Stidham and was hoping to get him over to tour Britain. He was responsible for getting Roosevelt Sykes to come to Britain. Jazz Gillum was then driving a jeep around, and Memphis maintained that, although many of the other blues singers had given up and gone into other work, he had no plans to do so.

He ventured that you should always use your own name in copyrighting your compositions to avoid problems in collecting royalties. He talked about the possibility of bringing his band (Matthew Murphy, guitar; John Calvin Jr., tenor saxophone; Sam Chatman, bass; and Billy Stepney, drums) to Britain, as he thought that we would enjoy them. His plans were that he might tour the U.S. with the band starting in New York. (A year after this 1961 interview with him, he had settled permanently in Europe, and such plans never materialized.)

We must have spent more than one hour talking, but he suddenly realized that another British writer was due to visit him and so I had to depart. Just as I was leaving, Memphis Slim suggested that I ask the hotel desk to ring Josh White's room to see if he might be available to do an interview with me. To my amazement, Josh White kindly invited me to his room for a bout of my questions. The difficulty arose that I knew hardly anything about his musical career, and I was worried that my inexperience as an interviewer would be exposed. Happily, Josh White sat me down and talked about his early days and put me perfectly at ease. I regret that in those days, the indispensable cassette tape recorder was not around, as it would have been so nice to have captured this interview on tape.

Josh White was born in Greenville, South Carolina, on February 11, 1915, and was christened Joshua Daniel White. His was a very religious family, and his parents wanted him to take up religion. While he was still at school, he met a blind musician walking across the street who played "Joshua" for him. The musician wanted young Josh to accompany him as his guide. He asked

Josh's mother whether she would allow this, and she said that she would have to pray on it. After three days she agreed to let Josh go with him. (According to Sheldon Harris's splendid *Blues Who's Who*, I assume that the musician who Josh was talking about would have been either Blind John Henry Arnold or Blind Joe Taggart.)

Josh travelled all over America, guiding, he recalled, fifty-six different blind men, including Blind Willie Johnson and Columbus Williams. He said that Blind Lemon Jefferson was the only blind guitarist who taught him new ideas on the guitar, though he said Jefferson played little on the guitar and was primarily a singer, pouring out his soul in the blues numbers. White's first recordings were made in Chicago when he was fourteen years old with Joe Taggart for the Paramount label. Subsequently, he returned to Greenville for two years, where he broke his leg playing football.

He moved to New York City in 1932 and was given $100 when he went into the recording studios and made twenty-eight sides over two days, but he did not receive any royalties for them. On the second day in the studio, a man heard him and arranged for him to go on air in the radio program "Harlem Fantasy" with Clarence Williams's Southernaires and Eva Taylor on vocals. This program lasted for some eight months. Then he met his wife-to-be, Carol, in a New York church; they were married in 1934. Around this period, his right hand was paralyzed for six years, but suddenly it recovered, although he admitted that he faked a lot now and did not play guitar as well as he did before. He used the pseudonym of Pinewood Tom, so his mother would not know what was happening. She associated blues singing with drinking. He thought that his mother might know about what he was doing, but she never let on to him that she did.

White credited the musical *John Henry*, in which he appeared with Paul Robeson in Philadelphia and New York City, with bringing him to public notice; after this show, he met and swapped songs with many leading folk singers, including Burl Ives. He played with Leadbelly for some twenty-six weeks, frequently at the Village Vanguard in New York City, and he considered him "quite a man." He met Big Bill Broonzy and they got to become buddies. He told me that the last time he had seen Bill, he did not even recognize him, but he thought he was a great singer.

At this point Josh White called a halt to our talk, as he had to get ready for an evening performance. I never did get another opportunity to contact him. At the time I was too naive to ask him for his address in order that I could write to him for additional background material. Now I know better.

These two interviews with Memphis Slim and Josh White were to become curtain-raisers for a series of interviews that I would conduct with musicians in the coming years. During the 1960s, many of the older New Orleans musicians, who had worked in the Storyville district of that city, toured the United Kingdom and it was in that period that I was able to interview Emanuel Paul, "Kid" Thomas, and "Kid" Sheik Cola. By the mid-1970s, with a little money in the bank, I was able to afford an annual holiday trip to New York City, and, with the much appreciated assistance of Dr. Albert Vollmer, I was able to meet and interview in depth more than a dozen of the veteran musicians based in the Big Apple. All of these interviews took place over an eight-year period between 1974 and 1982.

Eleven of these interviews that I conducted were published as life story articles by *Storyville* magazine, based in Chigwell, Essex, United Kingdom. They were: Freddie Skerritt (66), Leslie Johnakins (70), Roger Boyd (85), George Hancock (85), Bobby Woodlen (85), Barclay Draper (87), Earl "Nappy" Howard (88), Walter Bishop Sr. (91), Bobby Booker (101), Greely Walton (107) and Harvard "Harvey" Davis (115). The number in parentheses after each musician's name refers to the issue number of *Storyville* magazine. These articles were nearly all profusely illustrated with photographs from Frank Driggs' collection.

Sal Dentici's life story appeared in *Doctor Jazz* magazine (No. 97) published in the Netherlands, as well as *The Mississippi Rag* (September 1981). Earle Roberts' life story was published in *The Mississippi Rag* (September 1989) and Floyd "Candy" Johnson's life story was published in *Jazz Journal* (March 1980).

All of these life story articles, some with additional material, are included in this book, but the rest of the pieces are published here for the first time. Some of those people I interviewed were more articulate, and not all of the memories are infallible. This is why you will find a couple of chapters are written in the third person rather than the first person, as I had to carry out my own research to supplement their life stories.

Lester Boone

I was born in Tuskegee, Alabama, on August 12, 1904. I went to school in Atlanta, Georgia, and Chicago, Illinois. I came to Chicago in 1922 and became interested in music after going around to different places, such as the Lincoln Gardens, the Sunset Cafe, the Plantation Cafe, and the Entertainers' Cafe, and listening to the music. This was around 1925 or 1926.

Joe Oliver was playing at the Lincoln Gardens then and, I think, Sammy Stewart's Band was playing at the Sunset, while Jimmy Wade's Band was in the Entertainers' Cafe on 35th and Indiana Avenue. I used to go and hear the Erskine Tate Orchestra at the Vendome Theatre on State Street with Buster Bailey, clarinet; Reuben Reeves, Louis Armstrong, trumpets; Teddy Weatherford, piano; Jimmy Bertrand, drums; later on Stumpy Evans also joined them on saxophone.

Well, after listening to all those fine musicians, the musical bug bit me. There happened to be some fellows who used to practice next door to where I lived in Chicago. They had a piano, trombone, and drums, and they spoke to me about getting a saxophone, and I went to Wurlitzer's and bought myself a C-Melody saxophone.

I enrolled at the Illinois College of Music, which was situated on the West Side of Chicago. I studied under Professor Tuttle, and after a few months I began to practice with some of the other fellows I met, including Leon Scott, trumpet; Fred Avendorph, drums; George Thigpen, trumpet; Lucille Price, piano; and Edwin Duff, saxophone.

Eventually, I obtained a job with a three-piece group at a place called the Tuxedo Cafe at 31st and Indiana Avenue. I also studied with Horace Eubanks; he was from St. Louis and played with Lottie Hightower's Orchestra at a dancing class at 39th and State

Street. Eubanks played the C-Melody saxophone, and I liked the way he played.

I played with various small combos, such as Hughie Hoskins's group and the violinist Detroit Shannon's group. I also worked in Mame Ponce's place, across from the Vendome Theatre, with Glover Compton's trio. Glover was on piano, "Snags" was on drums, and I replaced a fellow called Slocum on the clarinet. He left and went to Europe. For a while in November, 1928, I played with Irene Eddy; she was later Teddy Wilson's wife. Sidney Catlett and, at other times, Lloyd Shaw were on drums and we played at a place on 25th and South Parkway called the Book Store Cafe. It was next door to the Plantation where Joe Oliver was playing.

Finally, I had a break and joined the fast company. The first band I played in was led by Alexander Calamese at the Jeffrey Tavern on Chicago's South Side. Calamese had followed Hugh Swift's Orchestra in there. Later I played with Charlie Elgar's Orchestra at the Savoy, and I also substituted in Carroll Dickerson's Orchestra when Louis Armstrong was fronting it. I subbed for Richard Curry when he was sick and whenever Jimmy Strong was sick or out. Early in 1929, I went with Earl Hines' Orchestra, who I worked with for over a year. We opened at the Grand Terrace on December 28, 1928, and I recorded with them for the Victor label in February 1929.

After I left Earl Hines, I joined Jerome Carrington at the Regal Theatre in Chicago. I took Darnell Howard's place, and he took my place in the Hines Orchestra. From there, I went to the Grand Theatre and worked in the pit orchestra, under the direction of the drummer and leader, Billy Butler. Then I joined Lucky Millinder, but later I went to the Williams Hotel in Grand Rapids, Michigan, with my own combo—Thomas "Tick" Gray on trumpet, Oliver Bibbs on drums, Francis Riley on piano, Charlie Buchanan on guitar, and I played the saxophone and clarinet.

Around March of 1931, I joined Louis Armstrong's own orchestra. I had known Louis personally for many years and he invited me to join the band. We left Chicago and headed for New Orleans for a three-month engagement at the Suburban Gardens, and we were met by quite a few people at the train station when we arrived in New Orleans, and there were a couple of bands, as well. Everyone was glad to see Louis.

We left the station and went to the Pelican Restaurant, and there

we had a banquet which was arranged by the Elks Club. We settled in down there and I was staying at the Patterson Hotel. Louis
was also there, but some of the other fellows were living in different places. We began our engagement at the Suburban Gardens
playing six nights a week. It was very nice and the people of New
Orleans were very hospitable. An incident happened while we
were broadcasting on WSMB, a local radio station. Louis announced "Tiger Rag" and then said, "We're going to take this tiger
like Grant took Richmond," and they cut us off the air.

After we closed in New Orleans, we went practically all
throughout Texas. We had an incident in Texas when we played
a dance there and they had a rope down the middle of the hall
separating the Blacks from the Whites. Everyone was feeling
good due to Louis's playing, and the rope fell on the floor, and
everyone started mixing, and they forgot all about that mess. The
troopers came in and made them stop that dance, because the
people were so mixed up by then. Everyone was having a ball.

On the road, many incidents would happen, and I think this
happened in Waco, Texas. We were playing in an upstairs dance
hall. The place was jam-packed and people started to fight and
throw soda pop bottles. The policemen came in and one stood up
on the stage and spoke through the loudspeaker. He held his
hands up and everyone became nice and quiet.

We came back to New York and joined the RKO theatre circuit.
We played the Lafayette Theatre for one week—I think Blanche
Calloway was there the week before us—and then we went on to
the Paramount Theatre in New Haven, Connecticut, for one week
and the Metropolitan Theatre in Boston for a further week. We
played a "Battle of Jazz" with the Casa Loma Orchestra on the
outskirts of Boston. Then we went to the Pearl Theatre in Philadelphia before coming back to New York, where the band broke
up in March of 1932.

I worked with drummer Kaiser Marshall's band in Washington, D.C., during May of 1932. It included Samuel Utterback,
trumpet; Ulysses Scott, alto saxophone; Earres Price, piano; and
Ralph Escudero, bass. Then I started to play with Billy Maple's
Orchestra at the Silver Slipper at 48th and Broadway, and from
there I worked with Charlie Skeet's Band at the Circle Ballroom,
that was a dancing school, for a while.

Early in 1934, I joined Eubie Blake's *Shuffle Along* orchestra. We
went on tour and also played the Illinois Theatre in Chicago for
about eight weeks. Then they broke the show down and con-

densed it, and we went out on the road. We played Wisconsin, Minneapolis, the Fox Theatre in St. Louis.

When I came back I led a band on tour under the name of Jean Calloway's Band. At that time the name of Calloway was very popular, with both Cab and his sister, Blanche, leading their own bands. This band was billed with the word Calloway in big letters and the name Jean, who was not related to them, in very small letters, if at all.

Around this period, I also worked with the Mills Blue Rhythm Band, under the direction of Lucky Millinder. I took Buster Bailey's place, as he had left to join Fletcher Henderson's Orchestra, as "Smack" was reorganizing his band again. *[This would date it as around November 1935, but 1933 may be correct. The Mills Blue Rhythm Band personnels are worthy of much more research, as discographic information in the past has been sketchy—D.G.]* I was not in the band too long, and I did not make any recordings with them. We played some dates down in North or South Carolina, tobacco warehouses and places like that.

Then I worked with the Napoleons Of Rhythm at the Savoy Ballroom. Napoleon left the band and trombonist Hy Clark took the band over, I played tenor saxophone with them *[1935]*. I was with Kaiser Marshall at the Ubangi Club in Harlem. I also worked with Jelly Roll Morton, Hot Lips Page's band, Don Redman's second band, Benny Carter, and also with Eddie South's band at the Blue Angel Cafe in New York. We had Everett Barksdale on guitar, Zinky Cohn on piano, and Ed Burke on trombone.

[I attempted to detail Lester Boone's career in correct chronological order from this period on with little success. Throughout the thirties, musicians were switching from group to group and regular lengthy engagements were sometimes few and far between. Any definite dates I have inserted in brackets—D.G.]

I worked at the Kit Kat Club with Bobby Hargraves's band. I also worked with drummer Freddie Moore's band at the Victoria Cafe at 141st Street and 7th Avenue and, previous to this, I had also worked with Fred at the Hot-Cha Club at 135th Street and 7th Avenue, next door to Small's Paradise. With Leon Abbey and his group, Joe Turner's band at the Swanee Club, 125th Street and Lenox—it was upstairs over the Empire Cafeteria. Joe had about four or five pieces. Also worked with Cliff Jackson's Krazy Kats *[1937]* at the Radium Club on 143rd Street and Lenox—that was next door to the Cotton Club. I also worked with Willie Bryant's band; that was when they were broadcasting over WJZ in New York every Thursday night in a program called "Harlem Night" or something like that.

I also had my own combo and played at various locations such as The Village, the Black Cat Cafe, Swing Rendezvous, the Place, the Spot, the Pepperpot, and George's Tavern. I worked out at Sunnyside Horse Shoe Bar and Grill at Sunnyside, Long Island. Louis Bacon, trumpet; Don Abney, piano; Bill Mason, drums; Woodley, bass—they all worked with me there. I also worked with Louis Metcalfe and Billie Holiday's band at one time in Brooklyn. Then with Garvin Bushell and Sonny White and his group at Tony Pastor's Cafe in the Village. Also worked with Lucky Robert's group, Ford Dabney, Peek-A-Boo Jimmy and Sonny Thompson's group doing club dates in New York.

Then on to Kelly's Stables on 51st Street with my own combo, Skinny Brown, tenor saxophone, and Earres Price, piano. We were there with Coleman Hawkins, Billie Holiday, and the King Cole Trio. From there, I went to the Yeah Man's Cafe in Harlem with my own trio and after that [December 1938 to January 1939] to Small's Paradise with a nine-piece group that included Eddie Heywood, piano; Cedric Wallace, bass; Joe Smith, drums; Leslie Johnakins, Sammy Davis, and myself, saxophones; Robert "Cookie" Mason and Gene Price, trumpets; James Bradley, trombone. Benny Carter took Eddie away from me for his own band.

I also worked with violinist Leon Abbey and played with him at the Apollo Theatre and other dates. Worked with Corky Williams at Pod and Jerry's at 133rd Street and 7th Avenue.

I opened up the Hollywood Cafe with my own group with Jack Carter, the drummer who went to Europe. Jimmy Reynolds was on piano, Gene Brooks later on drums, and a fellow named Page on trumpet. Around this time [1940] I also worked with Elmer Snowden at the Saratoga Club.

I went to Lucky's Bar in Brooklyn leading my own trio from 1948 until September of 1969. I had Bill Mason on drums and Jimmy Reynolds on piano and quite a few other fellows over the years.

When I was playing, I always liked to swing the melody. In the early days you could always tell what they were playing, but now the fellows' styles are way out.

Cliff Olson

My birth-date was December 8, 1916, in Superior, Wisconsin. I was born at home, a lusty, bawling, long-winded Norwegian. Recently, a relative back in the Midwest had a study made of the Olson family tree, which meant going back through the records on my father's side to the fjords of the Trondheim, Norway, area. When it was accomplished they sent me a copy of their findings. It seems that I sprung from true Viking stock, from the "bow hunters" back in the eleventh century.

We had a family orchestra. Now there was a group! We were all involved in that endeavour, my father saw to that. He was a trumpet player in the city band of Ironwood, Michigan, in his younger days and never got over it, so that when he ended up a very married man with four kids to raise, he still managed, by a miracle, on his low enough paycheck as a railroad worker, to buy a beautiful rose mahogany victorola wind-up phonograph and buy all the John Philip Sousa band records—Red Seal Victors they were—all of the Enrico Caruso operatic aria records, most all of the available symphony orchestra recordings of that time, the works of Victor Herbert, and, of course, a wide selection of the works of the old masters, Beethoven, Mozart and the like.

He managed many miracles for each of us. A fine old upright piano for my sister to play, along with a full set of orchestra bells, those long silver bars, like a set of vibes, that folded up into a wooden case, with sturdy handle . . . and weighed a ton, at least! We had to carry that thing every place we played, a real killer.

My older brother, Ray, started on violin at the age of eight and did very well with it. He took up the trombone at ten and joined the first-rate school orchestra and band, then the symphony orchestra, by the time he was fifteen, just as I did two years later.

Dad played trumpet and guitar and me on clarinet, and after

10

much rehearsing and trying to sound as full as we could, my father offered our services to every lodge and church function in my home town for free. No money involved and with no car, we lugged all our stuff by hand and sheer will power all over my home town, through snow and rain, wind and hail. Everything that Mother Nature could throw at us, but we were of "Viking" stock and therefore we were born tough and, to my knowledge, we never once missed a gig. Dad wouldn't hear of it, no matter what the excuse. At first, we'd complain now and then about the money, part of the agreement to appear, but Dad would say, "Stop your complaining, there will be cake, cookies and fruit punch for you kids, and if you play real extra good, they may even see fit to give you seconds, but don't ask for it, wait until they offer it."

During the six years from the age of nine until I was fifteen, I had basically formal training, including joining the symphony orchestra on clarinet at fifteen, but then I happened to hear some things done by people like Coleman Hawkins and Duke Ellington, and this was a different ball game and had a great affect on me. By that time, my father was fairly lenient about music. I think his attitude was: I don't care what he is playing as long as he is playing.

At that point in time, a friend of mine had a tenor saxophone and he had played away at it for several months, but he was not getting anywhere with it. He wanted to form a little orchestra in high school and so he said to me, "You've got to play it." So I fumbled around with that tenor, and after playing clarinet, I found the saxophone quite easy. It's easier to play the clarinet first and then switch to the saxophone, so I was off and running.

Before I was sixteen, I had an opportunity to play in a deep, dark, lower reputation nightclub with four Black musicians. I was going to high school, then playing from nine to two in the morning, running home, sleeping fast and going to school. That's learning, and they taught me a lot. In the area where I lived there were very few Black musicians, but they were treated as something very special, but be sure to go and hear them play.

In 1933, when I was a junior in high school, the Tony Nuzzo Orchestra from Chicago heard me play play tenor saxophone when they came through my home town. By then, I had played it for less than a year, but already I was getting a definite handle on playing it like Coleman Hawkins, so that is where I joined up with them and played all summer and into the fall season. We played theaters, state fairs, auditoriums; it was a big show with entertainers and dancers, a whole production.

We went to Chicago to the Century Of Progress World's Fair and came home at the end of October. I barely got accepted back in my high school in order to finish my senior year and graduate with my class the following June, but it was tough because I had to make up all of the work that I had missed from the first eight weeks of school.

I left my home town again, for good, the very next day after I got out of school, this time to head my first band, a quintet, in a very raunchy night club in Hurley, Wisconsin. It was quite a place, in that it was actually remote enough in the wooded section of northeastern Wisconsin to make it the perfect place for many of the Chicago gangsters to hide out, and this included some of Al Capone's men and even John Dillinger and his gang, all of whom took over that place, "The Little Bohemia." Two days after I closed, they staged a terrible gun battle with the FBI men in which several men, including a couple of J. Edgar Hoover's FBI men, were killed in that bloody battle. Somehow, John Dillinger escaped. I left that job, just in time. Chalk one up to my guardian angel.

That was when the staff orchestra job came through, just in time to save my hide, and I travelled to WNAX, Yankton, South Dakota, a CBS affiliate station that beamed out to about ten states in the Midwest. So you see it was a very powerful station to be able to do that, and we, staff musicians, knowing that the performing standards were of the very highest caliber, really had to be sharp at all times just to keep our jobs, and therefore we all improved rapidly.

They had me playing several programs each day, plus announcing a four-hour evening shift five days a week. And upon hearing me sing, they gave me my own show as a vocalist, every Tuesday and Thursday from 3:30 until 4:00 P.M. Doing my own announcing, writing the script and I was backed by a pianist and rhythm section. Good experience for a nineteen-year-old kid.

We had a staff of about twenty-eight musicians. In one program we would be a bohemian kind of orchestra and then semi-classical, and we would do popular band music as well.

Now, sometime in the spring or summer of 1937, I am thinking of making a move to something new and upon hearing that a trumpeter and a trombone player were leaving the Lawrence Welk Band to start one of their own, I hooked up with the two of them and began touring all over the Midwest with the new unit called the Leo Terry Orchestra. Nine men in all and capable of playing a lot of very danceable music. The band became very popular in a short time, and by then I was doing a lot of feature work as a clarinet soloist and vocalist with them.

One night, when we finished a job near Des Moines, Iowa, an early one (we were all done by midnight), the leader said, "Earl Hines and his band from the Grand Terrace in Chicago are playing at the big ballroom downtown, so let's go over there. They are playing until about 1:30. Our trombone player and leader had a conversation with Earl during a break and mentioned me as "being a hot young clarinet player," and the next thing I knew Hines asked me to get my horn and sit in on a few songs. I was a bit nervous, but I agreed and what a treat. It was great and I played my heart out with that great band until closing time. With a very powerful rhythm section like that to back me, I couldn't do less than my best.

A year later, the very fine Henry Halstead Band from the famous Park Central Hotel came through on a nationwide tour and an offer to join up with them came my way, so I readily accepted that one. From then on, we played nothing but the top spots, major hotels, and played a lot on the major radio networks—NBC, CBS, ABC, and Mutual stations. It was as a result of that exposure that I achieved national recognition by the time I was barely 22 years old, both as a player and vocalist and now as an arranger and composer for full orchestra.

One of the most memorable experiences of my big band days took place after we closed a month's engagement at one of the major hotels in Chicago. We had been featured on NBC Network five nights a week at 11 o'clock, so we were then booked for twenty-one one-nighters to take full advantage of all that great publicity.

It was mid-January, we headed west in a chartered Greyhound bus and got as far as the western plains of Nebraska. In the middle of the night we found ourselves hopelessly snowed in by a raging blizzard. Along the road for miles past, we had seen snow mounds that were abandoned automobiles. God forbid that there were still people in some of them. (We learned later that five people froze to death in some of those cars during that bitter cold night.)

Bert, our very trusted and well seasoned bus driver took over at that point, saying that he couldn't keep the bus warm and we'd have to leave. He knew every foot of that ground and said that there was a small town off to the right about two miles away and we'd have to bundle up as best we could and head out across the fields. He had a long rope and instructed each of us to loop it around a wrist, form a line, and follow him through the waist high snowdrifts, which we did. We made it to the town by 4 A.M. and awakened the sleepy owner of the little hotel. As he had no rooms available, he rigged up cots in the basement storage area, turned up the water heater and seventeen frozen musicians shared three shower stalls at the same time. Glad to be alive and warm and safe. We slept into the afternoon the next day and then ate like cannibals.

The storm had abated somewhat by late afternoon, but no one had any plans to venture outside into the bitter cold winds that whipped across the plains. We read old magazines, some of the men played cards to pass the time. The big fireplace was such a comfort to everyone and the food was wholesome and plentiful.

During our stay, we heard a conversation between two other hotel guests, it went like this: "Isn't it too bad about Henry and Bernice, today being their sixty-fifth wedding anniversary, and they had planned to go to their son's place in Denver for the big celebration tonight. Wish there was something to do for them here in town, under the circumstances."

There was something we could do, so we got together with the townspeople and became a part of it four hours later. They had some volunteers to go out to our bus, get our instruments, bring them back to us, and we headed over to the town hall just a block or two away, fired up the big pot bellied stove, unpacked, set up on the stage, and by now people were decorating the hall with streamers. The wives and mothers of the town brought tons of warm food and even found time to make a few decorated cakes, then went over to Henry and Bernice's home. They hustled them over to the town hall, and we played our hearts out that night, and everybody danced their shoes off, and we all had the most fun and the damndest best party anywhere. We finally managed to continue on our westward tour after the roads were cleared the following day. We were all filled with warm and sweet memories of that little town in Western Nebraska.

After we played the last of an engagement at a major hotel in Kansas City, I had some time off from that band, but I kept on playing. This time, some guest appearances with the powerful and exciting Gene Krupa musicians at a very popular jazz club in Kansas City, which was a major music city, one of the top spots. for sure, here in the U.S.A.

Shortly after that in 1939, I left the Halstead Band in Dallas and headed for Hollywood, arriving there with my horns, my one piece of luggage, and a total of seven dollars in my pocket. I didn't know one single soul, but I had three things going for me—guts, ambition, and a very strong drive to survive. It took a lot of work to get around and play for free for everybody and anybody who would listen, but I made it work and never missed a meal.

I played at the new West Coast Cafe Society in San Francisco's Fillmore section with a fine group backing Billie Holiday. The band was headed by Al Golden, a studio and radio trumpet player, it was a six-piece combo consisting of Al on trumpet, myself and Julie Kinsler on saxophones, Les Burnett on piano, Johnny Cyr on drums, and Al Woodbury on bass. The boss of Cafe Society was George "Red" McCullen, who also inaugurated Hollywood's Famous Door.

We opened on October 1, 1941, and closed three weeks later. Billie Holiday was wonderful and phenomenal. I can remember the rehearsal for opening night. It was just one of those things where everyone in the group was highly qualified to do this with her, or we wouldn't have been there. She walked in, and we started the rehearsal, it was one time only. We went through a lot of music with her. An interesting thing was that all of her own charts were very basic and that, to me, is the mark of real fine entertainers. They do not depend upon the music behind them to put them over with the audience in front of them. They know it is up to themselves.

Anyway, the rehearsal went very smoothly and, as we finished, her manager came over and told us that Billie would like to speak with us all for a minute. She came over and without changing her expression said, "I just want you gentlemen to know that I have been on tour all over the country, and there were so many places I went to where them musicians couldn't play my music, so it feels mighty good to have it done right now."

We had a great time and it was interesting because you'd look out and the lights were low and they'd shoot a spot right on Billie's face and the gardenia that was always there in her hair, and we would peer out at the audience and would see Orson Welles and all of the big people in the film industry, and they were there every night.

Hollywood memories. . . . Marlene Dietrich, my, what a lady she was. I toured with her doing the army camp shows in 1941. The Hollywood Caravan Show was a big success with the GIs, as we had Jack Benny, Red Skelton, George Burns, Jane Russell, and many more. It was a great show.

Sitting on a sofa with Judy Garland at Jackie Cooper's home in Beverly Hills on a December evening, as Judy helped Jack's mother, Mrs. Bigelow, trim the tree and wrap the presents. I never remember seeing Judy smile much. I don't think that she ever found much happiness. The reason I was there was because Jack played drums in a little jazz group we formed. We played at The Racquet Club in Palm Springs, yes, the famous place owned by actor Charlie Farrell, who costarred with Shirley Temple a lot in former years.

One of the real highlights came as a result of saying yes to a request for me to play with my newly formed L.A. Sextet for a benefit for the Crippled Children's Society of Los Angeles. It took place on a Sunday afternoon at a big estate up in the hills of Hollywood and ran for six hours, but we alternated with another band, which just happened to be the Benny Goodman Orchestra with Teddy Wilson, Lionel Hampton, and Charlie Christian. What a day that was, as I was heard under the very best of circumstances and as a result of that job, I had a major break two days later. I was signed up as first saxophonist with the big studio orchestra at MGM Studios doing the soundtracks for the big musicals.

Then a little later on working with the Nat King Cole Trio, as the fourth man at The Radio Room on Vine Street. For two years, I was one of the very busiest men in town, playing with far too many groups to mention here.

I can recall the occasion that Art Tatum played a private concert for me and another saxophone player for five hours from 2 A.M. until 7 A.M. at the home of a prominent Black attorney and his wife in their beautiful Victorian home, located two doors down from Nat King Cole, in the Hancock Park area of Los Angeles. What a night!

Then came the Army and four years, mostly as a GI band leader. During that period, Stan Kenton brought his whole band out to the Army Hospital, Barnes General, in Vancouver, Washington, when I asked him to cover for me, as I had to take my own band for military duty one Thursday afternoon and wouldn't be available to do it. He was a great guy and good old friend from years back.

Finally, home from the service at war's end, and fortunately I was asked to reconnect in Hollywood exactly where I had left off four years before. Now a married man with a new home and a baby on the way, I had to get work in a hurry. I rejoined the very fine orchestra at the Earl Carroll Theater playing for the big musical productions at night. My days were spent arranging music for many different singers and stage acts, as well as recording sessions.

I joined Ray Noble in 1950. He was the "prince of the business." I did the Edgar Bergen-Charlie McCarthy Show with Ray Noble's Band, and then we went to Las Vegas for the grand opening of the Desert Inn. After hours, I had a jazz quartet at the Pink Flamingo. In Las Vegas, at that time, the places were coming thick and fast all along the Strip; it was great because there was music at all hours. If you didn't bother sleeping, you could get around and hear some great music at anytime of the day or night. Around the same time, I also did some work in television with the Artie Shaw Band on the Chrysler Show, and also shows with the NBC Orchestra with Skitch Henderson conducting.

Far too many things went on musically from this point on and so I'll deal with the highlights as best I can.

Playing with Dave Brubeck and Paul Desmond at the Blackhawk in San Francisco. Songwriting in 1955 and getting some of my own songs out on records and being reviewed and played all over the U.S.A. and doing some cowriting with the pianist from Jimmy Dorsey's Band. Recording the soundtracks at Paramount Studios, as well as 20th Century Fox and Warner Brothers. I moved to the San Francisco area and headed a company doing radio and television commercials for national products including Goodyear tires, Del Monte, and Safeway Meats.

In 1967, I was appointed by the State of California to be the Director of Music at San Quentin Prison. This offer came from the State Offices in Sacramento, quite an honor to be singled out for this appointment. In the Music Department, I had around four hundred and fifty students a week.

I resigned from my position at San Quentin in March of 1972, as I wanted to spend more time with my family. The day started at noon and sometimes I didn't get home until midnight. And five years is a long time there. I then began teaching music, playing with my own band and doing some arranging in Redding, California.

More recently, in 1989, I played in the Bahamas, and then in

Figure 1. West Coast clarinetist Cliff Olson (left).

1990 I worked in Czechoslovakia. Then in 1992 and 1993, I toured Great Britain with my own trio.

Up to this day, I am very busy with my own music publishing and record companies, playing and touring and more work coming up all the time. I have recently recorded with the Dallas Symphony Orchestra and hopefully there is the likelihood of some producers in Nashville putting my music on record. No rest for the wicked, as they say, but I am having a lot of fun, sinning, if that be the case.

Lizzie Miles

[Lizzie Miles and I corresponded for several years prior to her death, and the following is a compilation drawn from her letters during that period.]

My maiden name was Elizabeth Landreaux and I was born in New Orleans on March 31, 1895. Lizzie Miles is my stage name. My entire family spoke French, my mother and father read and wrote in French. My father was a penman; he made calling cards by hand—beautiful cards. They also spoke Creole (broken French), but not my grandmother. My grandmother on my father's side was an Indian and she spoke French. She was an American Indian. My mother's mother came from San Dominique. My mother knew many Creole songs, but I would never learn them.

I don't guess there's no one who can tell you how that ragtime "raddy" music started, because I started singing ragtime when I was five and my mother used to be always singing and there was ragtime then. That name "jazz" and "dixieland" is just names that people gave it, but it's pure ragtime music played by all races in their way, as New Orleans was a town full of all kinds of people, so who can tell how it all started where and when.

Sidney Bechet was my neighbor and school playmate of mine. He is younger than I. As kids we'd play together in the evenings when work was done. He owned a little nickel tin flute, that's what he'd play. I'd sing and another neighbor, Wilhelmina Barth, would play piano. I knew his whole family, mother, father, sister and four brothers, Homer, Leonard, Albert Joseph, Sidney, and Bertha. Homer is living, but I don't know if his sister is. He was around 61 or 62 years, he was younger than me and Wilhelmina.

I sang with Bunk Johnson when I was twelve years old, but I've been travelling since I was fifteen. I've been in every city in

America and lots of the small towns as I travelled with a circus for four years, then with two minstrel shows under canvas.

King Oliver was the best trumpet man in New Orleans. One time, he was what we called a "raddy" trumpet man—in words of today, you'd say "hot." The best band was around 1910 when Oliver and Ory was together. Ory used to be a sweet trombone, he and George Fields, they played pretty music. I haven't heard Ory play in person since 1910, only on his records. I had only seen Ory in action in New Orleans, nowhere else.

I sang with King Oliver here in New Orleans, then in Chicago. That's right, I sang with King and Louie [*Armstrong*] when Louie first came to Chicago. I knew Lil [*Hardin*] before I knew Louie. I don't known when Ed Garland left Chicago, but he was with King at Dreamland. It was 1922 and Garland and Lil was with King before Louie came. When I was working in Chicago at Dreamland—that was a nightly cabaret with King Oliver and Band—that's when Louie came from New Orleans. I didn't know Louie and had never seen him before, as he was in the Boys' Home when I left New Orleans to travel with the shows. Then I left there to go to New York to make records. But I worked often with King in New Orleans when it was the Oliver and Ory band, because they played for most of the concerts and balls.

Fred Keppard was the first great jazz cornet to leave New Orleans with a hot group and he could play. That was long before Louie Armstrong and King Oliver. Buddy Petit was a great cornet man; I sold him his last gold Buscher cornet with pearl valves. He was the greatest until Oliver and Louie.

A. J. Piron was a jazz violinist who could play classics, ragtime. He was great, a cripple, one leg shorter than the other. In those days, that's how all the orchestras played—led by violin, not piano. When they started leading orchestras with a piano some violins stayed on, but most were dropped. We had some fine violins here.

I'm not sure, but I think that Manuel Perez took the first dixieland band from here to Chicago. A real dixieland band should not have a saxophone in it. The old style featured violin, cornet, trombone, clarinet, bass, guitar, and drums. Never used a piano. All these other instruments was added in later years when they dropped the violin, which they should never have done.

Only time that I sang with Amos White was on minstrel shows.

I was told by Amos White when I first met him, he was a "Geeche" from South Carolina of the Jenkins Boys' Home, and he drifted to New Orleans after the war. I saw him in New Orleans and also worked with him and Manuel Manetta's band in Bucktown in New Orleans. Then he drifted to California, but as a printer. When I was out there and saw him, he had no band. Manuel Manetta is an old-timer around here. Manuel was a violin and piano player, I never heard his violin, but he was a cabaret piano man. I don't think he had done any show work. He used to play in Storyville, but he gives lessons now, I'm told.

Back in those days, I knew Wilbur De Paris's family. They had a family band once, which used to travel with the medicine shows. His mother and father was playing in the band, with sister and, I think, three brothers.

In 1922, I left New Orleans for New York to make some records. *[It was reported that she worked as a soloist at Dashy's Inn Golf Club, Bronx, N.Y., and had recorded "Muscle Shoal Blues," written by George W. Thomas of Chicago.—(news item dated May 13, 1922)—D.G.]*

I worked with Willie "The Lion" Smith at the Capitol Palace Cabaret, along with Fats Waller and Cliff Jackson, a fine piano man. *[Tommy Benford recalled that at the Capitol Cabaret, Lenox Avenue between 139th and 140th Streets in New York, that Smith, piano; Bubber Miley, cornet; Garvin Bushell, clarinet; Charlie Irvis, trombone; Bill Benford, tuba; and Dewey Beasley, drums, accompanied Lizzie Miles. He said that it would have been around 1923 or 1924. The Capitol closed either in 1926 or 1927.—D.G.]*

At that time, the best band I liked to sing with was Charlie Taylor's Southernaires, out of Philadelphia. I could sing with them forever. They gave an introduction that got under your voice so that the patrons could hear every word you sang, and they were playing. It done my soul good to sing with them. One night, a coffee man from Brazil gave me a gold fifty-dollar bill to sing his favorite song with them. He was there every night while he was in New York. That band would make even a dummy sing, they were great. Charlie Taylor played the violin, Reynolds played the piano, he's the fellow who wrote "I'm Confessin'."

I sure didn't like Duke Ellington's playing. He used to play in Willie "The Lion" Smith's lunchtime, when he first came to New York from Washington. He couldn't send me like Willie or Reynolds. After their working hours, Duke Ellington and Fletcher

Henderson used to come and listen to Charlie Taylor's piano man, Reynolds. Charlie also had a very good trumpet man named [?] Wheeler. Charlie Taylor looked like an Indian or Spanish, small and short, but a violin player. Jazz history has left out the most real good ones with all the lies it tells.

[*The* New York Age *of November 5, 1924, reported that Lizzie Miles was planning a foreign trip: In a few weeks, she was to sail for Paris. She had impressed members of the Jilbachish [sic] Russian Opera Company, who paid repeated visits to Herman's Inn Club in New York.—D.G.*]

I lived in Paris for one year, working at Chez Mitchell, 61, Rue Blanche on Rue Pigalle and Rue Fontaine. Sidney Bechet wrote some very fine songs, including "Do That Thing" when I worked there with a troupe called "Alexander Starjinsky." [*A report calls them Nine Russian Singers and Dancers under the direction of Alexander Schayinsky. I have been unable to trace the correct spelling of this group, which has also appeared as Shargenski.—D.G.*]

I was to have visited London, but I had a better offer to return to America, as salaries were much better there. Upon my return, I made my record with King Oliver, "You're Such a Cruel Papa to Me." King Oliver didn't go over so big in New York. Those Eastern musicians didn't care so much for the New Orleans musicians those days and gave them a hard way to go. King was having trouble with the union so he didn't use his name, but it was Clarence Williams on piano, Buddy Christian on either guitar or banjo, and King on trumpet. I only made one record with King Oliver and two or three with Jelly Roll Morton and one with Lil Armstrong.

Jelly loved to make pretty runs, then turn and look at you to see if you thought them great. He had a run he used to make in most of his pieces that I used to love to watch him make. I've heard no one yet make it like him—sort of double syncopation. Never any arrangements, just a rehearsal, if I knew the song. That's one thing most musicians don't like to do. That's why so much stuff is not done as good as it could be—not enough rehearsals. Jelly was a real bragger. Anybody that could do something, well, Jelly would say that he'd put them in the business. In New Orleans, we called him "Whining Boy" because he used to crook his mouth and whine, but he was a fine dresser. He had one of the modern offices on Broadway. His wife, Mildred, used to work at the same night club that I did in the Bronx. They both had diamonds in their teeth.

I made a recording for Victor called "Man Of War," it was a double meaning song. You had to know the tactics of war to get it, but it was my biggest tip-getter when I worked at the Nest Club in Harlem.

I'm no blues singer, I'm a popular song singer. I sang more popular songs than I did blues. I never cared for low-down blues, I never cared to be complaining about "my man" all the time. Well, Bessie Smith was more of a moaner than a singer. They call me a blues singer, but I sang more popular tunes than blues. More ballads, I never sang many blues, I guess it's cause I had a loud, heavy voice.

From 1938 to 1939, I was in New Orleans taking care of my sick mother. I went to Chicago in 1939 and stayed there until 1942. During that period, I recorded for Frank Melrose. [*Regrettably, I did not question Lizzie Miles further on this recording session, which took place on October 7, 1939, as no personnel information is known about it, although trumpeter Guy Kelly's presence is likely.—D.G.*] "Keep Knocking but You Can't Come In" was one of the titles that we recorded and when I was a little girl, we used to sing that, but called it "The Bucket's Got a Hole in It, Can't Buy No Beer." In New Orleans, for years you could get two and one-half cents of beer or wine in a bucket, that's how that song got started.

Then I had to return to my sick mother, so from 1942 I stayed until now in New Orleans. I couldn't get an audition in 1951, but instead I got a date, and I've been stepping out ever since. Then I returned to Bourbon Street. Joe Robichaux was my piano man for three years at Davilla's Mardi Gras Lounge. I worked with Sharkey Bonano and Tony Almerico at the Parisian Room on Rue Royale, that's why Emory Cook called me Queen Mother of Rue Royale, that's where we made his albums.

In 1952, I recorded "Salty Dog" for Capitol Records. "Salty Dog" is New Orleans slang and is a sort of piece like "Chopsticks" that most of the kids could play on a piano as a child. So, one recording day, Sharkey Bonano was playing it on the piano, and each one of us said a verse to the melody of "Salty Dog," so it was recorded right there and then. You could go on and on with verses, there is no end to them.

Those Emory Cook "Sounds Of Our Times" recordings that I

Figure 2. Lizzie Miles from New Orleans (mid-1950s).

made with Tony Almerico's Parisian Room Band and pianist Red
Camp are my best. Emory Cook is the only one who gave me a
decent recording. Until then, I never thought that my recordings
sounded like me, but on some of those Cook let me sing soft and
not hollering and shouting like a fish peddler. They would have
been better, if Red Camp had known them better, but Emory
Cook likes his playing and I guess he did the best he could. I
recorded once for Cook from almost two or three in the afternoon
till 3 or 4 A.M. Mr. Cook kept asking me if I was tired. We made
all those numbers on those records in two recordings. Although
one album was titled *Torchy Lullabies My Mother Sang Me* in fact
my mother never taught me anything about singing! That song
"Animal Ball," I started singing it when I was fifteen years old. I
learned it from that grand entertainer and piano man, Tony Jackson. Jelly Roll and Tony Jackson each had a different style of inter-
preting the music and between Jelly and Tony, Tony was the
best—the best player and singer.

One night, I was just having fun in the Mardi Gras Lounge, as
there was no one in the place, I started singing in creole for my
own amusement. A customer came in and said, "Keep it up, it
sounds good." Later I found out that he was the owner of one of
the Bourbon Street clubs called Blacksmith Shoppee, his name
was Tom Caplinger. I have three songs in French on records, "Bill
Bailey," "Good Man," and "Basin Street Blues." I never sang in
French while I was in Paris, but I talked to them in French.

*[In March of 1959 Lizzie Miles was sixty-four and was determined
to continue working—D.G.]* I'm living in hopes of coming over [to
Britain] once to make one concert before my voice leaves me. It's
still good and powerful. It's one of the reasons people think that
I am not telling them my right age, 'cause they can't understand
how I can bellow the way I do. But I will stop when my voice
starts cracking, but as long as it's all right, I want to keep singing,
as I love to sing and the people love it.

*[Around September/October, 1959, Lizzie Miles retired from profes-
sional singing and steadfastly committed herself to her religious inter-
ests.—D.G.]* I've been on tour for four weeks, I got home on Saturday, and this will be my last trip away from home, as everything
has changed, even the people. It's only money, money, and no
service of any kind for it.

This tour will make me call it a day. The worst I've ever witnessed. I had my first auto accident, these wild cowboys ride like they're crazy. Going home one morning, a car ran out of an alley into our car, which was badly damaged, no one was hurt. During the last Saturday of the engagement, the neon light caught fire and caused everyone to leave the place. At Monterey, I had to sing just with a piano man who was drunk. Thank God, my voice was fine. I took three encores and sang about ten or fifteen songs.

No, I've made up my mind to call it a day, as this was the worst trip that I have had in my forty years of travelling. My last trip started Labor Day in Columbus, Ohio, and finished in Sacramento, California. No more singing or travelling.

Don't believe any of the reports that you hear, especially on jazz, because most of them are loud and wrong. I never read so much wrong stuff as I have read on jazz, and most of the writers weren't born and are now writing about something they never heard.

Jazz is just one of the names that was given to ole American ragtime music mostly played by ear, instead of reading music, and when it was played like that they say, today, "mellow" and "in the groove." We called it "raddy music," and nowhere have I heard raddy music like they played in New Orleans in the twenties and thirties, believe me!

They will never know the origin of jazz, as it's the old ragtime music and someone in every race played it at one time or another. I read a story on this ole trumpet man, Buddy Bolden, by a man—I could be his mother—and I didn't know Bolden or heard him, but my uncle, who is 82, did. They write things people tell them, but don't know whether it's right or wrong.

Here in America, it's not what you can do, but who you know and how much money you have. A lot of personal favoritism, so if you don't get with the right people shame on you. We have a lot of prejudice in America and it seems to be getting worse, but New Orleans has always been an exception to everywhere else in America. It was once called the Paris of America and that's why it was really good ole New Orleans.

George Guesnon

[George Guesnon was a banjo player, who was born in New Orleans on May 25, 1907. His musical career was mainly spent in New Orleans and he died at his home in that city on May 5, 1968. His story is not only about his jazz activities, but also throws some light on the characters and places of New Orleans that were hitherto relatively unknown. The son of a plasterer, Guesnon originally started work as a plasterer's apprentice, although he had bought himself a ukelele, which he taught himself to play.]

Around 1914–1915, Johnny Prudence led a band, consisting of Joe Nicholas, trumpet; George Stewart, clarinet; Ambroose, trombone; Arthur Ogle, drums; Jules Levernay, guitar; and Prudence, bass. In 1917 Israel Gorman replaced George Stewart on clarinet. The band played on a boat that ran from New Orleans to Mandeville named the *Camelia*, and thus they became known as the Camelia Band.

I played my first job in 1927, not 1929 as rumor has it, with "Kid" Clayton's Happy Pals (Jimmy "Kid" Clayton, trumpet; Peter Badie, alto saxophone; Tink Baptiste, piano; George Williams, drums; and Earl Stockmeyer, banjo) at the Humming Bird Cabaret, which was managed by Professor Sherman Cook and was situated on the corner of Bienville and Marais Streets in New Orleans.

I became friendly with the guys in the band and was allowed to play in Earl's place when he took off. While working there, I began playing the banjo, uke-style, then I studied with John Marrero, who became my teacher and whose fine work I have tried to carry on with distinction and pride. In a short while I was able to turn over to the tenor style of playing, which was the right way and became very good at it. So good, in fact, that when John

Marrero left Celestin's Tuxedo Orchestra, I was called in to take
his place. Trumpeter Guy Kelly and I were the two new men in
the band at that time.

With this band, I worked a little over a year and left to go on a
regular job with Willie Pajeaud, Wilhelmina Barth, and Ernest
Trepagnier in a jitney dance at the Alamo Dance Hall on Canal
and Burgundy Streets. I worked with this group about ten
months, and then, in the middle of 1929, I joined the Sam Morgan
Jazz Band, my first gig with them being an excursion to Chicago.
I stayed a little over six years with them. I still say, in my opinion,
the Sam Morgan Jazz Band was the greatest of the New Orleans
jazz bands, and they did record for Columbia Records, here in
New Orleans, two years before I joined the band. When Sam Morgan suffered his stroke, I joined Lou Johnson's Californians from
Monroe, but this band broke up shortly afterwards.

There were some fabulous characters in New Orleans in those
days. The pimps, for instance, each were known by their own
trademark of distinction: Thomas Wade alias "Clerk," the Diamond King of Storyville; Bob Row and Sidney Severan, the Fashion Plates of the Red Light District; and, in my book, the most
polished and colorful of them all, Morris Moore, the guy who had
everything—well read, versed on any subject, a lover of musicians, the arts, but above all a ladies' man.

Another legendary figure was Joe Sheep, who ran a small sandwich shop on Dumaine, near North Claiborne Avenue, and
whose five- and ten-cent sandwiches were such a delicacy; he was
the talk of the town. All through the night, the streetcar conduc-
tors would have their cars parked six and eight deep in line waiting to get the Sheep's tasty sandwiches, and for musicians it was
a meeting place to chat and chew. Doctors, lawyers, teachers, just
about everybody who was anybody in downtown New Orleans
and of every color, race, and creed under the sun, at one time or
another ate at Sheep's—the House of Creole Goodness. You could
bet that whenever the great Louis Armstrong came to town, it
wouldn't be long before he'd be heading for Sheep's to get his
favorite blood sausage. Today, there is no more Sheep's, but, in
my book, the memory lingers on.

Though not as famous as Joe Sheep, Joe Weiner was another
legendary character of the red light district. He was the sandwich
man. He had an indescribable contraption built in the form of a

stove to keep the bread warm and weiners and smoked sausage piping hot, that being the only kind of sandwiches which he sold, and words could never describe what a treat it was to eat one. His beat was strictly the district, and his trade came mostly from pimps, hustlers, gamblers, and whores.

Today, standing direct in the center of Orleans Street at North Claiborne Avenue facing the front of town, one can see five blocks away the Municipal Auditorium at St. Claude Avenue. Erased by time and progress are two famous New Orleans landmarks, the Treme Market and Tower. The Tower stood in the center of Orleans Street between Claiborne and Robertson and the Market ran from North Robertson to Liberty Street. It was an amazing sight to behold with its cobblestone floor and lined inside on both sides with stands that sold meats and seafoods of every known land and description, lined on the outside, in the same formation, the vegetable stands with beautiful fresh fruit and every kind of rare spice known.

On Saturday nights people came to do their marketing in droves and it was truly a meeting place for friends, the slogan was "I'll see you in the Treme." The Tower was a tall beautiful structure with handwoven lace work and resembled in many ways the famous Eiffel Tower in Paris. Today, these things are just memories and another closed chapter of a forgotten past.

In 1935, I left New Orleans to join Little Brother Montgomery in Jackson, Mississippi, and while there I alternated with his band and the small orchestra of Joe White, the great drummer-man of the F.S. Wolcott's Rabbit Foot Minstrels. In Little Brother Montgomery's band we had Doc Parmley, trumpet; Rosser Emerson, Lucien Johnson, saxophones; Luke Parmley, brass bass; and Henry Ross, drums. I was with the Minstrels for two years—1936 and 1937. Then from 1938 to 1939, I was back in New Orleans, gigging with about everybody who was anybody. *[On April 4, 1940, George Guesnon recorded four titles for Decca Records in New York City.—D.G.]*

When the War started with Japan, I joined the Merchant Marine and stayed in the service from 1941 to 1947. *[In 1946, George Guesnon was again in New York City recording two titles for the Lissen label. These sessions in New York were never touched upon in the correspondence between George and myself, so I can throw no more light on either of them.—D.G.]*

In 1955, I played New York, San Francisco, and Los Angeles and recorded for Blue Note Records with George Lewis's band. With this band, I worked at Childs' Paramount Restaurant and the Diamond Jazz Jubilee, which was held in Los Angeles. When I was in Los Angeles, there was one fellow who used to come in every night and sit right in front of the bandstand with his eyes glued on me. One night he called me down for a drink and said to me, "You know, I've been coming here night after night, do you know why?" I told him "No." He said, "I've been waiting for you to make one mistake or one bad chord. If there is such a thing as a perfect machine, you're it." At this, I just smiled, because what he didn't know was that this was the major reason why I am the choice of every bandleader in New Orleans, a musician's musician, and that's been going on for years. First is because I have a wrist of iron, second I add to a band a fire and a drive it never had before.

On August 11, 1958, I took part in a movie made at WDSU TV Station for Art Ford's Jazz Party with eighteen other New Orleans musicians, including Peter Bocage, Kid Punch Miller, and Percy Humphrey.

At present [December 1959], I am playing with Percy Humphrey's Orchestra. We have a very good band, as follows: Percy Humphrey, trumpet; Jim Robinson, trombone; Manuel Paul, tenor sax; Emma Barrett, piano; myself, banjo; Josiah Frazier, drums; and Richard Alexis, bass. There isn't too much work, but we are playing a few spot jobs about as much as any, but we now live in a rock and roll world and we are just about forgotten with the exception of a chosen few. *[Shortly after George Guesnon wrote these words, there was a great deal of interest in the New Orleans traditional jazz music scene with both Riverside Records and Atlantic Records visiting to record veteran musicians. Many smaller recording companies, including Ken Grayson Mills's Icon label, Barry Martyn's MONO label, George Buck's GHB label and others were busily engaged in recording the music. In the period from 1960 to 1965, George Guesnon played on more recording sessions than he had done during any other period of his working life.—D.G.]*

My Creole Blues [Icon LP-1] recording seems to be well liked, it is the unanimous choice of all my friends, but it's the same old story, plenty of raves and flattery, but no loot, but that's the way it is and always has been with the New Orleans musicians.

[On July 19, 1964, Guesnon wrote] I made two half-hour programs about the roots of jazz, which were filmed by producer Karl Genus. One I was playing with Alvin Alcorn's Band and the other one just speaking about the life of my good friend, Jelly Roll Morton.

[In December 1966, with his health deteriorating, he wrote] I haven't touched my banjo since the 24th of June, 1965, the last gig I played and I don't think I shall ever again. Of course, being sick and not hardly feeling well could be attributed as the main cause, but again, another one is that there is so little appreciation, and such a coldness and attitude of indifference towards the New Orleans jazzman and his music, no matter how well he can play it. Down here in the South that one has to see that they are only fools to continue beating their brains out for nothing and quitting seemed to be the best thing to do. I received a copy yesterday of the last record I made with Kid Thomas, for Jazz Crusade, in April of 1965, which has just been released, it's very good.

[George Guesnon had a very proud temperament, but with health and weight problems to contend with, he was unable to get out much anymore. Unlike some of the other New Orleans veterans, he never really received his due musical recognition. The title of his Icon LP-9 album seems to sum it up completely: Endless the Trek, Endless the Search.*—D.G.]*

Emanuel Sayles

As Told by David Griffiths

Unlike George Guesnon, Emanuel Sayles was still musically active until his death in 1986 and reaped some of the benefits of the New Orleans jazz revival of the 1960s. A banjoist, guitarist, and composer, he was born in Donaldsonville, Louisiana, on January 31, 1905, the son of a famous New Orleans guitarist, George Sayles.

He began playing early in life and studied under Dave Perkins, who was one of the important music teachers in New Orleans. According to Emanuel, Abby "Chinee" Foster replaced his cousin, Peter Raphael, on drums in the Pensacola Jazzin' Band in 1925, and it was with this outfit that Emanuel went to Jacksonville, Florida. Their personnel was Thomas Mack, trumpet and leader; George Morris, trombone; Edmond Hall, clarinet; Al Morgan, bass; Ed Washington, B-flat alto; Helen Jackson, piano; Emanuel Sayles, banjo; and Chinee Foster, drums. They spent three months in Jacksonville, then went to Pensacola and Mobile, Alabama.

In 1928, Emanuel Sayles took Willie Foster's place with Fate Marable and his Cotton Pickers' Orchestra aboard the S.S. *Capitol*. The lineup comprised of Albert Snaer and Louis Acerhart, trumpets; Jacob Frazier, trombone; Horace Millinder, William Rollins, and Norman Mason, saxophones; Fate Marable, piano; Sayles, banjo and guitar; Al Morgan, brass and string bass.

Around this period, he was working with William "Bebe" Ridgley's Tuxedo Orchestra, as well as the Lee Collins's band. Trumpeter Lee Collins and tenor saxophonist David Jones began working at the Astoria Ballroom on South Rampart Street in New Orleans, and Victor Records was persuaded by Ray Bauduc to

record this band under the title of Jones And Collins Astoria Hot
Eight. On November 15, 1929, they went into the recording studio
with Emanuel Sayles (who had replaced Rene Hall on banjo) as
cowriter of "Damp Weather Blues," one of the tunes that was
recorded. Clarinetist Sidney Arodin was added to the personnel
for that date.

Eventually, Emanuel Sayles left this group, with his place being
taken by Danny Barker. Throughout the thirties and forties,
Emanuel Sayles was sadly neglected, and it has been assumed
that he resided in Chicago from 1933 to 1949. He worked with
Sidney Desvigne's Southern Syncopators at the Knights of Pyth-
ias Roof Garden in New Orleans and on the riverboats. The personnel was Sidney Desvigne and Gene Ware, trumpets; Louis
Nelson, trombone; Tats Alexander, Gene Porter, and Ted Purnell,
saxophones; Adolph DuComgé, piano; Sayles, banjo and guitar;
Ransom Knowling, brass and string bass; and Ward Cosby,
drums (according to a photograph taken aboard the S.S. *Capitol*).
He also worked with Armand Piron's band.

Sayles wrote the author about this period:

> You said some truthful words when you mentioned how I was
> badly neglected back there in the thirties and forties. Fellows who
> knew way less than I did were pushed ahead of me. Mostly friend-
> ship, jealousy, others envied me because I played my instrument
> too good for them. With every band or combo I played with, I did
> my best to help make the guys play better and for that I made many
> enemies.

The only concrete evidence that he was in Chicago comes
through a recording session he made with Roosevelt Sykes's
band, but throughout our correspondence, he never discussed
this period further.

During the early part of the 1950s, Emanuel was leading his
own trio at the Paddock Lounge in New Orleans. Then in 1960,
trumpeter Charlie Love and drummer Albert Jiles put together
and rehearsed a concert of ragtime and pre–World War I jazz for
the Tulane University Fine Arts Festival. The majority of music
performed by them was taken from the full-band orchestrations
published as *The Red Back Books of Standard Rags,* and, following
the concert, a recording was made of them by Bill Russell. Eman-

uel wrote, "That was one of the big thrills of my life when I rehearsed and recorded those Scott Joplin tunes." Riverside Records released this recording in their *New Orleans: The Living
Legends* series, as well as a session that Emanuel Sayles made with
"Sweet Emma" Barrett and her Dixieland Boys recorded in January 1961.

With the opening of Preservation Hall in June 1961, Emanuel
began getting increasingly more work and in June 1962, he wrote:

> At present, we have three concert halls running in New Orleans:
> Preservation Hall (Sandra and Allan Jaffe, Managers), Dixieland
> Hall (Al Clark, Manager) and Icon Hall (Ken Mills, Manager). Two
> weeks before Mardi Gras Day, all the halls were packed with tour-
> ists. Some of them even had concerts in the day time. It proves to
> them that the tourists really come here to see and hear real New
> Orleans style music.

In July, 1962, he described recordings supervised by Nesuhi
Ertegun:

> Atlantic Records have been here a whole week. I recorded with Paul
> Barbarin, Jim Robinson, Punch Miller, and George Lewis. All of the
> recordings were made at Cosimo Studio with all the modern stereo
> equipment (engineer was Cosimo Matassa). That was my first re-
> cording with Paul and George and I made sure and did a good job
> on the banjo. Have found Mr. Nesuhi Ertegun a swell fellow to
> work for, I must say that he really knows how to get the best out of
> musicians at a recording session.

By November 1962, the flurry of recording activity seemed to
have died down and Emanuel was reporting that "No one has
heard from Ken Mills [of Icon Records and Icon Hall] since he left
here some four or six weeks ago, I have asked many of his friends
about him. Maybe he's busy pressing and printing his albums
that he recorded here last summer. I was only on one session—
John Casimir—and was able to sneak in some banjo solos." In
fact, Emanuel also recorded with Avery "Kid" Howard's La Vida
Band and can be heard on some of the tracks on *Afraid To Stay
Here, Afraid To Leave This Town* (Icon LP-4). Emanuel Sayles played
tenor banjo, but in February 1962, he was recorded by Barry Mar-

tyn's MONO label playing guitar with Peter Bocage's Creole Serenaders.

There had been so much interest in the New Orleans music
scene that he wrote:

> I have been inspired to compose some New Orleans style tunes—
> "Struttin' Down Bourbon Street," "726 Saint Peter Street," "Eureka
> Band on Parade," "Manny With the Banjo," and "Gimme That
> Good New Orleans Jazz"!
>
> Here's a good one, I spent two weeks with "Sweet Emma's"
> Band during which we played a birthday party for a teenager. They
> looked at the band and were somewhat displeased. We were play
> ing for about forty-five minutes before they could get the feel of the
> band. They were looking for the "Twist" music, so the band played
> one and I sang. After that we had them twisting to our kind of
> music and they liked it. Some of the kids remembered me from the
> Halls, but most of their young friends had never danced to our kind
> of music, but we made them like it.
>
> To tell you the truth, the public loves to see a banjo and hear a
> musician who can take solos, but some of the band leaders are very
> jealous, they always try to hide a banjo.
>
> On December 3, 1962, George Buck recorded me as a leader—
> Sayles' Silver Leaf Ragtimers—I used the musicians from George
> Lewis's old band. The tunes were: "Gimme That Good New Or
> leans Jazz," "Tailgate Ramble," "If Ever I Cease To Love," "Tipper
> ary," "Ting A Ling," "Do Lord," and "Winin' Boy." Then on Janu
> ary 7, 1963, Sweet Emma will use me with her band in a trip to New
> York City. Some big debutante party being given by Mrs. Grace
> Jones of Hanes Hosiery Company.
>
> Our Japanese tour, from September to November 1963, was a big
> success. We played about thirty different cities—two-hour concerts
> in each. There were always from three to six thousand people in
> attendance at each concert. At all the concerts, the audiences under
> stood and highly appreciated our traditional New Orleans jazz. We
> made some television shows, recorded for King Record Company,
> and George Buck Jr. had a Mr. Takashi Hiramatsu tape a concert
> for which we were paid here in New Orleans.
>
> Eighty percent of the concert jazz fans were young Japanese, the
> remaining twenty percent being from thirty to forty years in age.
> The Japanese musicians can play our traditional and dixieland jazz,
> but they say "we originate jazz" in New Orleans and I thank them
> very much.

The George Lewis and his New Orleans All-Stars Tour of Japan, to which Emanuel refers, was so popular that they were invited back for another three-month tour the following year. He later wrote:

> On September 24 and 25, 1964, I was at Disneyland with "Sweet Emma's" band, but Louis Armstrong headlined the program. He tried to get Emma to fly back home in Disneyland's private airplane, but she did not go.
>
> Since January 18, 1965, I have been working at Bill and Ruth Reinhardt's Jazz Ltd. in Chicago. They originally opened for business in 1947 when I was living in Chicago. Bill is the leader of the band and the clarinet player. The band members are Don Ingle, trumpet; Dave Rasbury, trombone; Earl Washington, piano; myself, banjo and guitar; Quinn Wilson, tuba, bass, and violin; and Freddy Kohlman, drums. I was called from New Orleans to play in Mike McKendrick's place, who was sick but finally died in March. Since my stay here, I have missed out on some recordings in New Orleans.

For the next couple of years, Emanuel Sayles worked at Jazz Ltd. before returning home to New Orleans. In October 1969, he did a solo tour of Great Britain, backed by Barry Martyn's Band. From September to October 1971, he was a member of Kid Thomas's Preservation Hall Jazz Band which did a world tour, including Australia and Japan (although Emanuel Sayles did not play in Japan as he had no working visa) and ended with a visit to London in November 1971.

The New Orleans Video Access Center made a two-hour documentary on Emanuel Sayles. This was for an educational program shown on American television during the summer of 1977.

Al Clark of Nobility Records had this to say about Emanuel:

> His *Banjos on Bourbon* album will always be a favorite of mine, because it was the first Nobility album. It was designed to present the New Orleans banjo as a solo instrument and I don't think any other album has been made with that purpose. Emanuel Sayles and Narvin Kimball are the banjoists and Jerry Green is the bass man. This is the definitive New Orleans banjo.

Emanuel Paul

[Tenor saxophonist Emanuel Paul was from the 1950s onwards, a long-standing member of the Eureka Brass Band of New Orleans, as well as a sideman in Kid Thomas Valentine's Creole Jazz Band. What follows is an insight into his early days of his jazz career following an interview with me in the middle of 1964.]

My name is Manuel Paul. I was born on February 2, 1904, in the Carrollton District of New Orleans. I started around in the music line when I was seventeen years old, that would be around 1921, that was when I played the violin.

During that time, I was associated with the church. We built up a religious band, as the pastor of that church thought that it would be something interesting for the young folk, whose ages ranged from eighteen to twenty, and would keep them in the church. He helped us to get our instruments as he bought the instruments and gave each member of the group one. He had a Professor Taylor to teach us, then later a Professor Correa, both of them were good violinists. Later the people started dropping off, so small that the group gave up altogether. Out of the whole group, only two of us were still playing, and the other fellow's name was Sam Dutrey. You've heard of him; he's still playing clarinet and tenor saxophone.

I went on and still fooled with the violin, we used to play at parties, small groups—piano, violin and drums. Finally, it was keeping me out so much at night that the "Miss" did not like it too much, so she pulled me in. I had to put the violin to one side for a while. She thought that something was missing, though, and so she said, "Why not try to like some other instrument," so she thought of the banjo. Well, it had to be a string instrument, as I didn't want any blowing instrument, which I didn't think that I would ever do. I bought a banjo and learned to play it myself.

A few months later, a cousin of mine, named James Paul, he played piano, asked me to come out and play with him. From him I went to different other groups, and at one time we had a little fellow called Shelley Lemelle. He was a wonderful trumpet player. Now his brother-in-law, Wills, he was a good trumpet player as well, but discontinued playing. We all had an orchestra. We had a fellow by the name of Emanuel Pere, he played the saxophone and there were others, whose names I cannot recall.

We used to have a rehearsal every Sunday, getting together to form the band, but that band kind of broke up with the fellows pulling out and playing with other groups. There were so many different bands that I played with during the twenties.

I continued with the banjo up to around 1934 and then I gave it up. I had worked at the Marine Bank and the Canal Bank from 1923 to 1933, but then came the Depression and I had to seek other work, I had no time for music. I had to make a living for myself and my family.

In 1935, I joined the E.R.A. Band, being led by Louis Dumaine. Then in 1936, the W.P.A., a relief organization, formed a band, that was how I fell into that. At that time, I didn't have an instrument, so I borrowed one from a friend of mine. Then when he needed it, I borrowed another instrument from another friend and so on. I played soprano saxophone, guitar, banjo, different instruments. Later I purchased my own instrument, a soprano saxophone, and so I played that in the W.P.A. Band.

I stayed in that band a long while, but later I left, because they had some kind of theory instruction, and questions were given for different fellows to answer, and we were kind of too clever for them, so we lost our work. Later I worked on private construction work, until that work ran out, and then I was just jobbing around.

Finally, the W.P.A. called back. They wanted me as a tenor saxophone player. Well, at that time I had no tenor, so I borrowed a cousin's tenor. Being laid up, the condition of it was so bad that I had to have it repaired, and later I started back playing with them. A month after I began playing, my cousin found he wanted to use the tenor, so that left me in another pickle. I had a tough time then. Sammy Lee helped me to find a tenor saxophone, it cost $72.00. The neck was bent up, but it was useful. You know I still have that tenor at my house. I used it for a long time. It had a good tone, but I could not get a goose neck to fit it. Later on, I found another old horn a kid had, it was one of the first tenors they had made. I used the goose neck off of that instrument and let the rest go for scrap. From then on, I played with different fellows around.

I played at Shadowland with Albert French and Sam Mossey on drums, just the three of us. We played at the Shadowland during the wartime, and we used to pack that place out. Our tips used to be as high as $30.00. Albert played banjo and guitar and used to sing many songs. At that time we were not in the union, so one day this fellow, Victor (the owner) he managed to get us into the union and then he wanted a larger band. Later we left Victor and went to a place on St. Charles Avenue, I forget the name now.

Our group was made up of Anderson Minor, Specks Robinson, drummer Alvin Clements, Dominique "T-Boy" Remy was the trumpet player, and he had a girlfriend who used to go around with him. This girl used to play some piano, wonderful piano player, I cannot recall her name though; she left New Orleans and went to California. Then after she left, they had this fellow from across the river, Benny Turner. He played the piano with us and we stayed there about three months. Our tips were so much then that Minor would take about half an hour to count the tips while we were still playing. We used to make good money there. Then along came some tax troubles, so we quit that job. We stayed about six months before we quit.

"T-Boy" found another place out on Napoleon Avenue, near the river. We made up a new outfit there. Now this girl, Ruby Thompson, she played piano with us, she's dead now. She was a school teacher, and she was very critical about who she would play with, but she liked to play with us. We had "T-Boy," Minor, and a nonunion drummer from across the river, and that was when "T-Boy" asked me around 1945 to play with the Eureka Brass Band. Before that I had played with Kid Howard, and the first funeral I ever played was with Kid Howard—that was before the Eureka Brass Band. I was on alto saxophone with Howard, and the funeral was over in Algiers.

Since then, most of you know my story and of my connections with the Eureka Brass Band and Kid Thomas's band, so much so, that I will not go into that for the present, that remains to be told later.

"Kid" Thomas and "Kid" Sheik

As Told to David Griffiths

["Kid" Thomas and "Kid" Sheik both spent the majority of their trumpet playing careers in New Orleans, although, during their later years, both were to tour abroad on a number of occasions. The following interviews with both trumpeters took place in Britain in the mid-sixties when New Orleans' musicians were making regular visits to Europe.]

"Kid" Thomas Valentine

[Born in the parish of St. John Reserve, Louisiana, on February 3, 1896, he started to learn the valve trombone before switching to trumpet. In 1915, he was invited to join the Marshall Lawrence band. Seven years later, he moved to New Orleans.—D.G.]

When I first came to New Orleans, there was this boy, a trumpet player, Johnny Rigg, he came from further up Reserve than I came from. He came down to play with this band managed by banjoist Elton Theodore, and each night, after they had finished playing at their place, they called in at another place, and they were asked if they would play a number or two, which they did. The man liked their band, and he wanted to hire them and fire the band that he had already.

They didn't want to do it, as they already had jobs. Anyway, the man kept ringing them up and writing to them, so finally they took the job. Then, one of the fellows who had been working there before with the other band came along with some liquor. He asked the fellows in the band if they wanted to have a drink. Now Elton, he was a funny fellow, when you offered him something to drink, he always wanted to have a taste of it first. He was not much of a drinker. He tasted it and told the other fellows in the band, it was bad, he wouldn't drink it. This trumpet player, Johnny Rigg, didn't take any notice. He reckoned it was good. He drank all the liquor, and though it didn't affect him at the time, by the time he reached Rampart Street and was sat on his trumpet case waiting for the streetcar, he died right there on the street.

Elton Theodore knew a fellow from my home by the name of Larry Bragnell, he told Elton that if you don't have a trumpet player, I know a fellow who plays the trumpet. He sent a letter to me, and in his letter he told me how to cross the river to reach Algiers, to get on a ferry with a ten-cent ticket and reach his home.

This would have been around 1922 or 1923 when I came to New Orleans. We then started to get the band together, and we would rehearse maybe three or four times a week. Six of us altogether, we had Tommy Henderson, drums; "Tete" Rouchon, bass; Albert Jackson, trombone; Steve Angrum, clarinet; and myself. We had jobs, and the bass player asked me what my name was. I replied Kid Thomas, so we called ourselves the Kid Thomas Band. We just rehearsed until we were heard by others.

They decided to hold a two-band contest, just for kicks you know. "Sonny" Allen [*Henry "Red" Allen*] had a band, so there was one fellow for us, the other for "Sonny," and they put up the money. Anyway, you couldn't get in the place where it was held, it was so packed, so "Sonny" had the main bandstand and we had the bandstand by the front entrance. "Sonny" played one song, we'd play one, and so on. Now, we were coming to the end, and "Sonny" said, "We play for the prize." I decided on something different, and I picked out a beautiful waltz that I had played with a band in the country. I played it, everyone applauded as they had never heard a waltz like that before. Then "Sonny" played his song for the prize, which was a briefcase, but that waltz won the prize for me. They didn't want to give us that prize, I was a stranger, so they wanted to give it to the hometown boy, "Sonny." A policeman who was there said that we had won it fair, so I was given the briefcase, which I kept for a long time.

As a result of that, I made a lot of enemies in Algiers, and we were not hired anymore, although we had a better band than "Sonny."

We were the first band that ever went down to an island in the Gulf. The only way you could go down there was on the boat. A fellow used to come every Saturday, and we used to go down on his boat. He bought a great big boat from the Governor; it had two decks. The top deck was $2 a head for passengers, the bottom deck, everyone used to gamble down there. Most of the big shots would go along.

We played Saturday and Sunday nights and came back to New Orleans on Monday. Now, you can go down there by road, but while they were building that road, we got stuck in the mud while pushing the car. In those days, the people with money would go on the boats. They were the nicest people to play for, and we had a nice house to live in while we were down there. Our drummer, Johnny Thomas at that time, used to like to kid people and told us that he saw smoke. We thought he was kidding, but it was our house on fire, so we had to sleep elsewhere.

During the Depression, we were getting more jobs than before it. We were making no less that $50 a week per man. Then sometime after the Depression, there was a fellow, his father was a judge, and he wanted to get acquainted with us. At the time, we had a truck, and we'd used to come to the ferry, meet it, and then play for the people as they came off the ferry. Then go around the town before returning to the ferry.

I gave this fellow my card and he became our manager, he got us plenty of jobs and we would play at the best hotels, the fraternities, the schools, and he never wanted a dime. Later he became a good lawyer. He was a real nice person.

[Over the next ten years, Kid Thomas and his band played dance music at the hotels, but by 1936, Kid Thomas was back working on the south bank of the river in various places owned by "Specs" Rodriguez. Over the next twenty years, Kid Thomas employed many of the leading New Orleans musicians in his band and they were the house band at The Moulin Rouge dance hall in Marrero for some years until it became a gambling casino in 1956. With the opening of the Kitty Halls in New Orleans in the early sixties Kid Thomas had regular and steady work.— D.G.]

George "Kid Sheik" Cola

"Kid Sheik" Colar *[it was discovered that his surname was in fact spelled Cola.—D.G.],* but everyone knows me as "Sheik." I was born in New Orleans on September 15, 1908, and when I was about sixteen years old, I went to Wooden Joe Nicholas for some instructions in playing the trumpet.

Later, I followed Chris Kelly around, because I liked the way he played. When he played the blues, it always knocked me out. Everywhere we went, though, Chris would be drinking, and I had to drink to keep up with him. I'd go to Chris's house for a lesson, then we'd start to drink and there'd be no lesson.

Then I started going around New Orleans playing with Wooden Joe's band and would spend an evening with Joe at his home. I started to go around to Joe's home in order to get more technique on the horn. I visited Joe's home two or three times a week. Joe would play the soprano saxophone, and I would play the horn. If I did something wrong, he would stop and show me the right way. I got good experience. Joe would drink, but he would not drink too much.

Following Chris so much, I got his style of playing. I fooled around with piano playing, then the drums, but listening to Chris was how I became interested in the trumpet. I liked the way he could play the blues and use that "wa-wa" mute.

We used to go out to Milenberg, all the fellows used to play out there, Buddy Petit, Sam Morgan, Punch Miller, Chris Kelly, this was when I was about seventeen.

When I was about eighteen, I formed my own group. I had Eddie Sommers on trombone (I had met Eddie when I was about sixteen years old, and I have been playing with him the whole of my life); George Davis, clarinet (he does not play anymore); Willie Baptiste, banjo; Leo Montrell, saxophone; Joe Morris on bass; sometimes Brother Joe Thomas, he would play with us too.

I went out on the road around 1927 or 1928, me and Joe Howard were together. I was with a fellow, Dan Moody, he had a band. He came to New Orleans to get musicians, he had me and Joe Howard. Dan was a good trombone player. Even back in the twenties, I was playing with brass bands. Different bands with different fellows, they would make up a band like the Pacific Band.

Figure 3. Trumpeter George "Kid Sheik" Cola from New Orleans.

In the early forties, I was playing at the Paddock Bar, but in 1943 I left the Paddock, and they put Percy Humphrey in my place. I went into the services and, when I came out in 1945, I was just playing around with different fellows, and then I started my own band again. In 1952, I became a member of the Eureka Brass

Band and have played with them ever since. When I am not playing trumpet, I have spent my spare time sewing sacks that will
contain sugar down on the waterfront. Work is scarce now down
there, and there is not much to be had.

My first recording on my own for the MONO label was made
in 1961, although I had recorded with the brass brands previously. Cleveland was the biggest thrill of my life, my Storyville
Ramblers opened there at the Tudor Arms Hotel in September
1961. We had John Handy, clarinet; Albert Warner, trombone;
Louis Gallaud, piano; John Joseph, bass; and Josiah "Cie" Frazier,
drums.

Curtis Jones

Yes, it is true, things are pretty tough for me right through these periods of time, but my birth sign is August 18, 1906 [Naples, Texas] and, come what may, I won't give up, I will fight to the end.

As far as music was concerned, we had music in school back home down in the country, but I preferred to learn my way, so whenever the teacher would have recess, I would make a break for the piano or organ and play the blues or the boogie, or some other blues song that I heard and liked very much. Until some of my schoolmates would tell the teacher that I was playing the blues or the boogie. Then it was a scold or a whipping, you see I got mine the hard way. The teachers didn't mind me playing the instrument, but they didn't want me to play the blues or the boogie, and I was just the other way because I loved that music. The stuff they wanted me to put down didn't move me at all, it was church songs and hymns. Even today, I still don't want to be worried with nothing like that.

I have been in the music world since I was sixteen years old. My first recording was in the middle twenties. I was on the vocal part as a whole and a dear old-time friend of mine, his nickname was Papa Chittlins [Alexander Moore] furnished the piano music. I forget the drummer's name. This was in 1925, I never did know for what record company I made that recording, since I never did hear any of the tunes that were released. Anyway, the name that I used at that time was Curtis Jones and his Texas Wonders. If the tunes were ever released, I never did hear any of them.

Papa Chittlins was a very happy guy. Now and then we would meet at different roadhouses and he would be wailing away on the piano or some woman would have a bottle of home brew in one hand. He could play some pretty piano for me, and as far as

I know he had a wonderful personality. Everybody that knew him gave him nice and warm respect, and I learned a lot from him. I haven't seen or heard from him since 1928. *[Dallas blues pianist Alex Moore, who was born in 1899, remained an active musician on the Texas scene until his death in 1989.—D.G.]*

In the year of 1929, before whisky was legalized in the U.S.A., I was a bootlegger operating in Dallas, Texas. I got caught and was put up for forty-seven days in Dallas County Jail for whiskey without license. Facing my cell was a bullpen, where they let you out long enough to scrub and clean the cell you slept in. On each side of me was a dope addict, who kept me awake every night howling like wolves for their habits, which learned me a lesson about dope. Something I have never used and never will for the rest of my life after having seen how they suffer.

So when they had my trial, the judge told me that I had suffered so long without a trial and as also this was my first offense, my fine was one dollar, so I paid it, and he told me not to come back anymore.

Five days later, I was in Wichita, Kansas, working at the Broad View Hotel as a bellhop until I was able to find some nightclub work to do in the west part of town. Then a short while thereafter I landed in Kansas City, Missouri, where I met fame in the music world.

I was in Kansas City around 1930, I rode the freight trains out west to Reno, Nevada. Big Joe Williams and I met back in the thirties in St. Louis, Missouri, and a few other small places in the deep South. Somehow, it has been so long that I don't recall in my memories, at the present moment, exactly where or when, but it was way back in my early tour of the South, where I met so many different guys, and it has been so long, I don't remember who or exactly where.

I know a lot of cats out of New Orleans, in which I lived for nine months and played piano for a politician, by the name of Beanzie, at the Astoria Hotel in the year of 1933. That good gumbo I ate down there still tastes good to me, no kidding, and the people sure was nice to me.

It was on July 3, 1936, that I landed in Chicago, a great city, but I only had sixty-five cents, so I began pulling doors, catching as catch can, so eventually by not giving up all hope, I was successful enough to record four tunes—"Lonesome Bedroom Blues,"

"You Got Good Business Blues," "Decoration Day Blues," and "Trouble Blues," with Willie B. James on the guitar and Fred Williams on the drums, and both of them are dead now.

On most of those 1937–1941 recordings, as far as I can remember, while most of the sessions were rehearsed, some of the others were not. The majority of the musicians were in the know, like the great New Orleans bass player, Ransom Knowling. I had met Fred Williams in Chicago and Willie B., he did not need all of those rehearsals. Guitarist Hot Box Johnson, it has been some fifteen or sixteen years since I last saw him, although he is still in my memories. I really do wish I could lay my eyes on him once more. He recorded many a session with me, he sure could play the blues on his guitar.

I made one recording with Jazz Gillum on harmonica, and the great Mr. G. Gant *[Moses Gant?—D.G.]* on his tenor saxophone on "Low Down Dirty Shame Blues." Mostly we seeked to get the best that we could get from the skeleton part and put it in good shape. Then we did our very best to take advantage of it for the betterment of our products. I never made any recording dates with Big Bill Broonzy, although we did quite a few engagements.

I worked quite often with trumpeter Lee Collins at the Olympic Hotel at 1015 North Clark Street, nightly, and the Victory Club, 664 North Clark Street. Around this period, in the year of 1953, I had a ten-week engagement in Toledo, Ohio, in a White club, a three-piece combo, drums, saxophone, and piano. Do you remember Eddie Morand *[this must be Herb Morand—D.G.]*, a trumpet player from New Orleans. He and Ransom Knowling, those cats played in my band here in Chicago for quite sometime. I think he is dead, but Ransom is still wailing around here.

[In the years between 1953 and 1960, Curtis Jones, in his letters to me, found it very tough going. Then, in the early sixties, the revival of interest in the blues seemed to reach a peak both in the U.S.A. and Britain; blues singers and musicians were not only recording, but touring as well. It was at this period that Curtis Jones's career regained momentum.—D.G.]

I have some great news: myself and five other musicians left Chicago on November 6, 1960, about 9:30 A.M. in a Cadillac. We arrived at the Alvin Hotel, 223 West 52nd Street, New York City, early on November 7 at 6.00 A.M., having met a snow storm between the two cities, but no accidents, nor trouble on the highway.

On November 9, 1960, I went into the recording studios at 1 P.M. and recorded twelve selections (*Trouble Blues* was the title of the album on Prestige Bluesville BVLP 1022). Five of us altogether were on some of the titles, but on some of the cuts, I only used three musicians. I used organ, bass, drums, guitar and the piano with my vocalizing. All were strange faces to me, except for guitarist, Johnny "Moose John" Walker. Speaking of Johnny Walker, he also plays the piano too and sings. He also recorded for the same company at the time we were in New York, but I have not seen him since, although I've known him for about six years or more and we have played some engagements together in the city and suburbs, but we had never recorded together before. The rest of the musicians live in New York. (Roberts Banks, organ; Leonard Gaskin, bass; and Belton Evans, drums). I haven't seen or heard from them since.

We recorded a variety of blues, boogie, and novelties, and everyone who was there and had listened to the program gave me tremendous praise until I was real surprised with myself. Even the company that I cut the records for came out and took my right hand and gave me compliments. Words from his mouth saying it was the greatest that has happened there in quite some time. It really was a nice one. We returned home by TWA Skyway on November 11.

I continue to work with Lawrence Hall on trumpet and Jasper Edwards, now working at the post office. Jasper Edwards is a concert musician; he has had combos of his own on the road long before I met him. Lawrence "Trumpet" Hall is arranging for different cats, as well as for me, also he uses my piano.

On December 12, 1960, I was invited to do some piano and vocalizing for Mr. John Steiner, Paramount Phonograph Records Sound Recording Service at the Bird House, located at Dearborn Street and Division Street, Chicago, and I met with many musicians, some of the very best, some from Europe and many other parts of the world. They put everybody's music on tape, to be shipped across the sea, where to, I don't know.

The Blind Pig at 343 West North Avenue, Chicago, is a very popular place on the North Side. I don't know how long it has been in progress. Only just since Christmas 1960, it has been available for colored musicians, but they only have one night for them. Last Tuesday night, July 18, 1961, Ransom Knowling on the bass and Big Joe Williams with his nine-string guitar, whom I have known for so long, played there. I worked it again on August 8 and by popular demand I am booked there again on August 29. *[This all ended, according to Curtis, on September 29, 1961, when the poor Blind Pig died! Curtis Jones played The Blind Pig–type first session at the Gate of Horn, Chicago, on January 29, 1962.—D.G.]*

I began working in Zurich, Switzerland, in February 1962. Champion Jack Dupree was my sponsor of my plane ticket, one way from Chicago to Zurich. He and I have the same manager. I left Chicago on February 3, 1962, and arrived in Zurich to be met by Jack Dupree and his wife and friends, then I had to go to work that same night.

[Despite settling in Europe and regular touring and club work throughout the Continent, Curtis Jones did not seem to gain in financial or musical terms. I recall meeting him in London while he was working with Chris Barber's Band, and he was already expressing terms of dissatisfaction about his career. He suffered heart failure and died in Munich on September 11, 1971. His grave in Germany was sold in 1979 because no one paid for its upkeep.—D.G.]

Earle Roberts

As Told by David Griffiths

[In 1988, Dr. John Latham, a jazz clarinetist and senior lecturer in international economic history at University College at Swansea, Wales, was working at the University of Illinois in Urbana-Champaign. He sat in with some local musicians and, as a result, brought the banjo player, Earle Roberts, to my attention.]

Earle Roberts's grandparents came from Wales, but he cannot remember exactly where their original home was. He was born in Chicago on July 26, 1902. In 1920, he launched his musical career when he played banjo for a grammar school dance. He earned $1 that night and promptly decided that music would be a good career.

His first really important gig was with Jack Johnson's band playing at the Samovar Cafe on South Michigan Avenue, Chicago, in 1924. The Jack Johnson band played popular hits of the day and also the old jazz standards (e.g., "Darktown Strutters' Ball") without much improvisation.

The twenties were a busy period for Roberts. He recorded in Chicago with Frank Westphal's Orchestra (1922 and 1923) and Art Kahn (October 1923 to July 1926). Around 1930, he played bass with Bud Freeman for a couple of years. Freeman was another Chicago boy, and, of course, Earle knew all the guys from Austin High School. Another was Jimmy McPartland, for whom Roberts played guitar from time to time.

During the mid-thirties, Roberts did a great deal of radio work, including a regular broadcast with the Sinclair Minstrels. This was aired by NBC from 1936 to 1938. The sponsor was Sinclair Oil. Roberts had to play a banjo solo each week. He played on the

Don McNeal breakfast show, also for NBC. There is a good photograph of him from this period surrounded by his instruments, including banjo, guitar, cello, bass, baritone saxophone, and Chinese moon banjo. This latter instrument he needed for a Pat Barnes weekly radio serial, in which a Chinese character called for appropriate music. Roberts bought a moon banjo in Chicago's Chinatown, where a store employee taught him a few tunes.

Roberts tells of playing a vibraharp solo in a Chicago cafe when a slightly inebriated fellow asked "Do you have to play that?" "Yes, I'm getting $1 for playing it," Roberts answered. "Well, here's $2 to quit," replied the drunk, which proves that you cannot please everyone all the time.

Roberts held down a plum job as a studio musician with NBC in Chicago. He held this job until 1940 when, he says, "they found out what had been wrong with the orchestra over all those years!" and sacked him.

In 1949, at forty-seven, Roberts enrolled in a school of music to work for a B.S. in music education, while teaching forty music pupils in Danville, Illinois, and maintaining his own six-piece orchestra, a speedboat, and a private pilot's license for his Piper Cub.

During the fifties, he made several trips from Cincinnati to New Orleans on the Delta Queen steamboat, which carried about two hundred passengers. He played cello in the dinner hour group and banjo with the evening dance group, enjoyed status as a crew member privileged to visit the pilot house and accommodations on the boat while it was berthed in New Orleans.

He saw little stylistic differences between New Orleans banjo players and other banjoists. Difference depended on individual conceptions or on the leader of his group, whoever was the stronger-minded.

For a short while, he also played on the Mark Twain steamboat, which made short runs, lasting about two hours, from its home port of Hannibal, Missouri.

He later played with the South Rampart Street Paraders in Danville, Illinois. The personnel was: Bill Zercher, drums/leader; Greg Helgersen, trumpet; John Hutchins, clarinet/soprano/ tenor; Barry Wagner, trombone; Woody Woodward, piano; Doc Cunningham, bass; and Roberts, banjo.

When Roberts started playing, the old plectrum banjo tuning was already going out of fashion, and he adapted guitar tuning

Figure 4. Guitarist, banjoist, and multi-instrumentalist Earle Roberts.

on his banjo. He played a Viga banjo (Viga is a Boston Company), which he bought in 1935, considering them the best in the world. Roberts stressed technique, believing that professionals should be able to sight-read in a flash without a second look. The best banjo player he ever heard was Eddie Peabody, both as a technician and an all-round musician.

Floyd "Candy" Johnson

As Told By David Griffiths

The years between the middle thirties and the middle forties were
known as "The Big Band Era." During that time a number of great
tenor saxophone men developed. Candy Johnson was one of them.
Candy joined my band near the close of that era, and I enjoyed him
and his playing very much. He has a big sounding tone, which was
very noticeable, especially when he was playing solo on one of the
ballads. His approach to jazz was fresh and pleasing. He really did
fit nicely in the band, and I missed him when he left. Today, I am
happy to have him as one of my friends.

—Andy Kirk

Candy Johnson was one of the many lesser-known musicians in
the United States who rarely get the public notice they deserve. I
was quite unaware of his excellent tenor saxophone work until
that famous alto saxophonist, the late Rudy Powell, introduced
Candy's work to me. Rudy had a marvellous ear for good talent
and recommended that I listen to albums on the French Black
and Blue label on which Candy was featured. Subsequently, I
contacted Candy and learned a little more about his career.

Candy Johnson was born in Madison, Illinois, on May 21, 1922.
His musical career commenced prior to leaving school when he
learned to play the drums. He later took up the tenor saxophone,
and the first group he played with was that led by Chick Finney
in St. Louis. At the age of eighteen, he decided on a college career
and entered Wilberforce University, but later had to leave college
in order to join the army. He played with an Army Band and,
while stationed in Louisiana, visited various towns with his own
small group.

During 1942, he played with a band led by A.B. Townsend and later was a member of Ernie Field's Big Band. Later in 1943 he joined the band of Tiny Bradshaw and from there moved on to join the Andy Kirk Orchestra, sharing tenor saxophone duties with Jimmy Forrest and recording a number of titles for Decca Records. He left Kirk in 1947, moved to Cincinnati, where he picked up his nickname of "Candy."

> I was with a group of musicians who used to pass around a bottle of booze during performances. I didn't drink, but did spend a lot of time at a candy store. One night the bottle wound up near me and the trumpet player was so bombed he forgot my name. He shouted over, "Hey, candy." I didn't know what he wanted. The trumpet player didn't want candy, but he decided to call me "Candy" thereafter.

Later on, moving from Cincinnati to Detroit, he formed his own group, "The Peppermint Sticks." They became very popular in Detroit's Paradise Valley where they played at The Rage, the Parrot Lounge, and Club 666. In the latter part of 1951, Candy joined Count Basie's Orchestra and in the following January, they cut eight titles for Norman Granz's Clef label. (Candy can be heard taking a solo on one number, "Fawncy Meetin' You," although his solo is not typical of his later work.) By July of 1952, he had left Count Basie and was replaced by Eddie "Lockjaw" Davis. He then returned to Detroit, where he continued to lead his own small group.

In March 1958, he commenced a fruitful partnership with organist Bill Doggett and his group. On their first recording date, they had a hit with the number "Blip Bop" (this tune, written by Candy, was originally entitled "Candy's Mood" and was first cut on the ALB label). Candy was featured regularly as a soloist with Bill Doggett on both tenor and occasionally baritone saxophones. "Honky Tonk" was another recording which became very popular, but perhaps their most famous recording was "Night Train." He remained with Doggett until the early sixties, playing mainly one-nighters up and down the country, but Candy noticed that work was getting more scarce, and in 1964 he decided that it would be wiser for him to return to college.

He commenced studying music at Bowling Green State Univer-

sity and in 1968 he received his bachelor's degree. Later in that
same year he joined Spencer-Sharples High School as their music
teacher and introduced a new music program. Although he spent
more time thereafter in colleges and high schools, Candy did not
neglect his jazz audience.

In 1971, he played a series of concerts in Europe, and then in
the summer of 1973, he made a return trip to Europe touring with
the Kansas City All Stars. While on this tour, they recorded a
program for French television and also appeared at the San Se-
bastian Festival. It was during this trip that Candy made the
aforementioned albums for the French Black and Blue label.

During 1974, he was kept very busy with musical appearances
at many high schools and universities throughout the United
States. He was featured in a concert by Duke Ellington's Orchestra which was held at Bowling Green State University in February
of that year. Later in March, he played a concert with a friend
from his St. Louis boyhood days, Clark Terry, and in April played
a date with Count Basie's Orchestra. He headlined and organized
an even more popular concert in November, featuring his own
group, "The Peppermint Sticks" (personnel on that date was
Candy Johnson, tenor saxophone/leader; John O'Connor, trumpet; Leonard White, bass; Alvin "Al" Johnson, drums; and Ruth
O'Connor, vocals—all musicians from the Detroit area). Also on
the bill that night were the New McKinney's Cotton Pickers and
Milt Buckner. The evening was quite an occasion, as it was the
first time in forty years that Dave Wilborn, Ted Buckner, and Milt
Buckner had played together.

The following year, 1975, was a hectic one for Candy, as far as
his academic career was concerned, and he graduated with a
M.A. Degree from Bowling Green State University, an honor for
which he had worked so hard over the years. In July, he took a
short holiday in New York City and besides looking up old
friends, he also sat in on sessions with Roy Eldridge and Helen
Humes.

By June of 1976, he broadcast regularly with his own jazz program, and he also did a live television show, *The Music Stand* with
his own group, which was transmitted over Toledo's Channel 30.
His sidemen that day were Herb Williams, trumpet; Randy
Knisely, trombone; Claude Black, piano; Leonard White, bass;
and Al Johnson, drums. The following month saw him in Detroit

Figure 5. Tenor saxophonist Floyd "Candy" Johnson.

playing a big jazz reunion concert including Kenny Burrell and Tommy Flanagan. Candy went on to Davenport, Iowa, for the famous Bix Beiderbecke Festival, where he played with the New McKinney's Cotton Pickers. The following month, he was invited to play a special tribute concert to Duke Ellington, which was held at Grant Park in Chicago, and his performance that day of "Body And Soul" and "Things Ain't What They Used To Be" proved to be one of the program's highlights.

March, 1977, saw him, to the delight of his many European friends, touring Switzerland, France, Belgium and Holland with Jay McShann and Claude Williams. During the trip, he made a number of recordings, including "Kansas City On My Mind" for Black and Blue Records. A very sad occasion took place in August 1977, when Candy played at the funeral of his long-standing friend and fellow musician, Milt Buckner, which was held in Defiance, OH.

In 1978, he played with the Commodores, the United States Navy Band, at their first International Saxophone Symposium, which was held in Washington. Later he appeared regularly at the Paradise Theatre and Orchestra Hall in Detroit. These concerts, which have been very well received, returned vaudeville and the big band jazz era to that theatre.

Candy states that his greatest influence as far as tenor saxophone playing goes was Ben Webster and, like Ben, he admits that he enjoys playing ballads best of all: "Frankly, I enjoy the ballads best, as maybe I put a little more in it when I'm playing, or I want to sound as beautiful as Ben Webster always did."

The *Midnight Slows, Vol. 3* album on Black and Blue demonstrates this. Candy solos on three titles and is joined by Arnett Cobb on three others. Both men get immaculate support from the late Milt Buckner on organ. This is an album for anyone who enjoys listening to good music played really well.

During 1979, Candy Johnson's tenor saxophone was in continual demand, and he played regular engagements in the Detroit, Cleveland, and Toledo areas. In that summer, he was teaching music at a two week jazz studies course held by the Schoolcraft College Summer Music School. He also played with the Mercer Ellington Band on an engagement in Detroit in July.

Blanche Finlay

[The Brecon Jazz Festival, inaugurated in 1984, produced some notable jazz successes. The 1986 Festival produced a surprise star, a female vocalist who was not even scheduled to appear. Manchester-based Blanche Finlay, who had been vacationing in the area, guested with the Speakeasy Jazzband from Swansea at their outdoor Sunday afternoon session. The crowds that thronged around the bandstand cheered her professional delivery of full-throated jazz vocals.]

My father was a very keen musician; he had an army background and played both the upright string bass and bassoon in a military band. Most of the music which I know came about through sitting on his knees and listening to his favorites. He adored Lena Horne, Billie Holiday, Sarah Vaughan, and Ella Fitzgerald, and loved Basie and Ellington. He played in a nightclub, did broadcasts, and taught music. His life was music, and he encouraged the whole family to develop our musical appreciation talents. We all received classical training, and my two sisters, my brother, and I sang as a group called the Parkins Kids.

We mainly did charity work, concerts, and hospitals, and later we started broadcasting and entering lots of competitions. We did all the big Christmas and Easter shows while we were in Jamaica. We were all quite young at the time, none of us was teenagers.

When my brother's voice broke, we three sisters continued our vocal harmony as the Parkins Sisters. We had an absolutely marvellous blend with our voices, one of my sisters was a soprano, I ranged between mezzo and contralto, and my other sister was a mezzo. We also had the same speaking voices, so we were a real close harmony group. My father was enchanted with the Andrews Sisters, and I think that we went through their entire repertoire, but we also did sacred and gospel songs. Later as we grew

61

older and married, we all continued to sing, and in fact the last time that we sang together was at our father's requiem two years ago in New York when the whole family came together as a choir. Both my parents are Americans and most of my family live there.

I arrived in Britain in 1955 and began training as a nurse. I sort of veered into the musical scene over here; it was completely by accident. A supervisor at work who had heard me singing said that she had a friend who owned a club and that she would like him to hear me sing. She took me along to this club called the Green Dolphin in Preston. The band there was fantastic. We were all youngsters looking for the moon, I guess. They adopted us at the club, we worked there, three or four times a week.

Many people, including other club owners, came along to hear me, it was the time of the real nightclubs with first class combos in every location. Everyone was looking for good singers and musicians. Well, that was where it all started, I went up to Blackpool for auditions, and I obtained a great deal of work there. That was the place where people really heard you in venues like the Winter Gardens and the Rainbow Room.

I think it was Billy Bevan who heard me singing at the Green Dolphin Club and offered me a job singing with his band at the Floral Hall in Southport. We also did the rounds working in town halls, as well as doing the residency. Around this time I was singing with various bands, and it was on one of these occasions that the Jackson-Bradshaw traditional jazz band heard me at a concert in Preston Town Hall in 1957 and invited me to join them, which I did. They really introduced me to the music of Bessie Smith and the other classical jazz performers. Together the band and I won many jazz awards and trophies. We were very successful. They had residencies in both Blackburn and Preston, but we also did some big gigs travelling all over Britain.

After eight years of success, I started out on a solo career doing most of the cabaret clubs. My manager at the time sent me down to London to audition for the famous bandleader, Chico Arnez. I remember going along there and only singing four bars, just four bars of music, and he offered me a twenty-five-year contract with a retainer—that meant whether I worked or not, I was paid. Within a fortnight, I was starring with Chico's Band. I was top of the bill, and most of my featured club work when I worked with him was in the West End of London—the Blue Angel, Dolce Vita,

Figure 6. Manchester-based vocalist Blanche Finlay.

Astor Club, Hatchett Restaurant, and the Adelphi Theatre. We did many broadcasting and record dates. We also worked all those American bases, where you were given the red-carpet treatment.

Chico Arnez became my manager, and I think that this period was the nicest part of my career in the popular music world, because he was such a wonderful person, he was just like a father to me. Unfortunately, due to circumstances beyond my control, I was forced to break my contract. I have continued to sing, but never with such brilliant musicians as I did in those early years. I have never seen Chico since then, although I have tried to seek him out during the course of my travels.

During those days in the mid-sixties, while I was living in Chorley but working in Manchester, Ernie Garside used to bring in American musicians (he still does). I worked for Ernie a great deal, both at his Club 43 and the Manchester Sports Guild, usually singing with the support bands. This also gave me an opportunity of listening to the famous stars who were also appearing. I got to know Jimmy Witherspoon while working for Ernie; he is a superlative blues singer. I heard Ella Fitzgerald, Duke Ellington's Orchestra, Count Basie, Sonny Boy Williamson, Sarah Vaughan, Dakota Staton, and many others. At Manchester's Free Trade Hall you also had access to meeting them personally, as each time they came over you would meet informally sitting backstage in the dressing room in between sets. It was so special for me, getting so close to people who I had admired and looked up to all of those years. Duke Ellington used to really unwind between performances. He was so relaxed, it was like some form of meditation after which he was completely refreshed.

Where Ella was concerned, we talked as one artiste to another. She would want to know what I was doing. At one time I was working with a very good congo and bongo player called Cy Coburn in cabaret, and I told her about him. She heard some tapes I had made and was really knocked out by his playing. She wanted to pack him up in her luggage and take him back to the States. He was absolutely magnificent.

What was so nice was that after their concerts, they would come along to the club where I was singing later that night and listen. One night the entire Count Basie Orchestra turned up. This was at the Bossa Nova Club where I was playing, and actually backed me on stage. That was an unforgettable experience, when you are so young, you do not realize that these opportunities are not going to come back again. They told me that I should be working in the States with them and that is a memory to treasure.

I used to sing with the Gordon Robinson Big Band. Some of the other big bands I was featured with were the Alan Hare Orchestra, the Wally McKenzie Orchestra, and Derek Hilton's Orchestra.

After this period of my musical career, I decided to concentrate on pursuing my academic career, and, after much studying, I am a graduate of Manchester and Oxford Universities, as well as Manchester School of Music, and a trained social worker.

I continued to do the occasional television spot, and in 1974 I formed a really good group called The Prophets. They were all former members of the Manchester Youth Stage Band for whom I had been featured vocalist on some continental tours. We did a summer season in the Isle of Man at the Gaiety Theatre, which was a real high spot for the group.

My connections with South Wales arose from doing cabaret in Cardiff and holidaying in Saundersfoot and Tenby. I did a summer season at Pendine in 1978 and met up with the local traditional jazz band, the Memphis Seven, and I travelled with them to various venues, including their old residency at the Temple Bar Inn in Carmel. We also appeared at the Welsh Jazz Festival in that same year and the subsequent two years. I have continued to return to Wales on holiday, and it was a result of my love for South Wales that found me appearing at the Brecon Jazz Festival with the popular group, the Speakeasy Jazzband, because my friend, trombonist Mark Tattersall, plays in this band.

Currently, I do at least six concerts per month and am on the Granada Action Desk. I also do a great deal of unpaid charity concerts for them, as well. Twenty years ago stardom was in my hand. Unfortunately I had to give it up. Now I have no stars in my eyes, but music makes me happy and above all I have formed good and lasting friendships through my voice. I just look out for the opportunity of singing to an appreciative audience.

Floyd Campbell and Jasper Taylor

[Neither Floyd Campbell nor Jasper Taylor were born in Chicago, but both eventually made that city their home. What follows was as a result of correspondence between myself and these two drummers. Both of them gave me a little insight into the early days of their jazz careers, and neither of them dwelt on details of their musical life after the early 1930s.]

Floyd Campbell

My name is Floyd Campbell, and I was born on September 17, 1901. I was surprised to know that you knew I was from Helena, Arkansas, the first stop on the Mississippi River going south from Memphis, Tennessee.

My father had a barber shop and pool room. W.C. Handy (the Father of the Blues) and his band used to play on a palatial riverboat named *Kate Adams* that plied the Mississippi River between Memphis and New Orleans. When the boat stopped in Helena, the musicians often gathered to set up and play in the barber shop, as well as getting their haircuts. My father being a piano player himself always made traveling musicians welcome, so I had early contact with these musicians.

In 1922, my mother died, then a man sent to Memphis for a set of drums for me providing that I stayed in Helena, which I did. Zilner Randolph taught me to read drum music, and we formed a five-piece band with Peter Paterson on the banjo and Cranston Hamilton on the piano. Then Zilner Randolph and Pete Paterson migrated to St. Louis in 1923, after our band broke up in Helena. I went to Memphis and moved up to St. Louis in 1924. (Perhaps you have heard that Pete Paterson was burned to death in a fire in 1979 in St. Louis. They said careless smoking was the cause of the fire.)

In St. Louis I got the opportunity to play in Charlie Creath's band. The band recorded for the Okeh Recording Company, and the players on those dates were Charlie Creath and Leonard Davis on trumpets, Charles Lawson on trombone, Williams Rollins played alto sax, Sammy Long, tenor, and Thornton Blue, clarinet, Pete Paterson on banjo, Pops Foster on bass, and me on the drums and the vocals. My recording of "Market Street Blues" in March 1924 is supposed to be the first male voice recording of the blues. The only composition of mine recorded by Charlie Creath was "Bell Bottom Britches." However I did sing "Cold in Hand Blues" and "My Baby Rocks Me with One Steady Roll."

Shortly after recording those six numbers with Charlie Creath, Leonard Davis, Sam Long and I left the band. Davis going to New York, Long and I going to New Orleans to play on the Steamer Capitol with Dewey Jackson, who was succeeded by Fate Marable as leader in 1926. Zutty Singleton drummed on all the other Creath records.

Jelly Roll Morton came to St. Louis after we left and used various musicians in his recordings, and I am quite sure that this is one of his pick-up bands on that "St. Louis Levee" record.

I also recorded several blues with Dewey Jackson's band in St. Louis in 1926 or 1927. In those days, the record companies were only interested in colored bands playing blues and original numbers. The band had rehearsed and was prepared to record just three numbers. When they said they wanted another number, I had that "Poor Me" number in my head. So without any music or rehearsal, Dewey Jackson, Burroughs Lovingood, and I got together quickly and came up with that number.

During the fall of 1927, I organized my own orchestra. Clifton Byrdlong played third alto in my band at St. Louis in 1928 and 1929. He was a very ordinary third alto player, who never took a solo. I left St. Louis in late 1929, but on several return trips to St. Louis, I visited a tavern owned by Birdlong in the West End Hotel. The last I heard of him, he had left St. Louis, and I don't know where he went. *[An obituary of January 1980 stated that Clifton Byrdlong was buried in Seattle, Washington, and that he and his wife had moved to the West Coast five years ago after retirement. It added that Byrdlong had played the riverboats with such outstanding*

Figure 7. Chicago drummer and bandleader Floyd Campbell.

leaders as Charlie Creath, Harvey Langford, Buggs Roberts, Floyd Campbell and many others during the twenties, thirties and early forties.—D.G.]

I settled in Chicago in 1930 where there was plenty of work, much better than St. Louis. I was there only two days when I got a job with the Freddie Williams Orchestra at a North Side nightspot. Later I worked with trumpeter Jabbo Smith for almost a year at the Showboat at Lake and Dearborn. Jabbo Smith and I had a very happy relationship while playing together in those early thirties.

After we closed at the Showboat, we went to Milwaukee to work at the Wisconsin Roof Garden. Then in January 1933, Jabbo and I returned to Chicago, and we worked at the Panama Cafe night-club for two years.

[Floyd Campbell continued to lead his own band for many years after this period. In 1940, he recorded a couple of titles for the Bluebird label, but these were his final recordings.—D.G.]

Jasper Taylor

I'm Jasper Taylor and was born in Texarkana, Texas, on January 1, 1894, and I reached the ripe old age of three score and ten this January (1964). I am so happy over it all, that sometimes I feel like going out and getting drunk, but I ain't going to do that.

When I was just a tot, my mother would put me to bed, then begin on a flat top piano to play church hymns, popular tunes and chords. I grew up with those chords. At the age of nine down on Laurell Street in Texarkana, I used to sit on the front porch and listen to Scott Joplin play ragtime on his piano. Dude Howard and his string band used to play and sing and sound just like the Beatles do today, and that was sixty years ago.

In 1911, I sang, danced, and played drums in a band with Buffalo Bill's Wild West Show. The following year, I was the drummer with Dandy Dixie Minstrels.

Then in 1913, I played drums with W.C. Handy's band in Memphis, Tennessee. During 1914 and 1915, I worked at the Booker Washington Theatre in St. Louis, Missouri, then in 1916, I was back with W.C. Handy in Memphis. I moved to Chicago in 1917 and joined Clarence Jones at the Owl Theatre. Then for the next two years, I served in France with the 365th United States Army Band. I came back to Chicago in 1920.

In 1909, W.C. Handy wrote "Memphis Blues" with a syncopated break in the middle, very few White musicians could make that break clean. To my mind, "Memphis Blues" was the first jazz to be put on paper.

In Chicago in the year of 1900, Joe Jordan wrote "Teasing Rag." In New Orleans, musicians changed the name of this composition to the "Dixieland One Step."

These days, I am a civil service employee for the City of Chicago and still going strong. Musically, I am writing a book, "A

Pictorial History of Negro Jazz,'' dealing with those who danced jazz, sang jazz, and played jazz.

[Sadly, just eight months after Jasper Taylor contacted me, he passed away in Chicago on November 7, 1964. What happened to his proposed book I have no idea and presumably it will never see the light of day.— D.G.]

Eddie Dawson and August Lanoix

[New Orleans bass players seemed to have a longevity compared with musicians who played other instruments. Perhaps lugging around their string basses was a physical asset to them in keeping fit and healthy in later life. Eddie Dawson certainly outlived many of his contemporaries, as he was born in New Orleans on July 24, 1884, and passed away on August 12, 1972. August Lanoix was also born in New Orleans on August 13, 1902, and was still musically active into the mid-1960s. Both of their life stories reveal how in their teens they became involved in the Crescent City music scene.]

Eddie Dawson (As Told By David Griffiths)

Eddie Dawson began playing in his teens, and his first instruments were the guitar and tenor banjo. Later at the age of thirty-three, he taught himself to play the bass, and this instrument became his tool of trade right up to his death.

In 1906, the young Eddie Dawson was playing at the 101 Ranch, situated at Franklin and Iberville Streets, with Professor Manuel Manetta and the old Willie Humphrey Band. The place was run by Harry Parker and Charlie Parker, and during this period, it was a violation of the law to play a brass instrument in the district.

One night, Freddie Keppard came by with his cornet, and Eddie Dawson managed to persuade him to play a number with the group. The following day, Mr. Parker went to the mayor and obtained a permit allowing Freddie Keppard to play with the band. Thus, Eddie Dawson became the first man to put a cornet in the district.

During 1908, Dawson was playing at Tom Anderson's place, at Basin and Ibeville Streets, with guitarist and mandolin player Tom Brown and the Moran Band. He was a member of the Chris Kelly band in 1910 and, two years later, he played with Hyppolite Charles's Saxophone Orchestra.

He was working with the Kid Rena Band in 1917, but three years later in 1920, he was playing at the Pelican Night Club on Rampart and Gravier Streets with the Percy Humphrey Band.

Then came 1929 and the Depression and things were really bad. Eddie Dawson managed to get by with the money he had saved over the years and occasionally by playing a spot job. Many musicians joined the W.P.A. Navy Band.

By 1939 times were better, and he was playing regular dates thereafter with the Andrew Jefferson and Andrew Morgan Band at Mama Lou's Club and with the Albert Jiles band at the Happy Landing. During the fifties he regularly worked at Mama Lou's with Peter Bocage.

In the mid-sixties, he was a member of Peter Bocage's Creole Serenaders, and he considered them one of the best bands that he had ever played in, mainly because there were all good musicians in it. The lineup was Peter Bocage, trumpet; Wilfred Bocage, tenor saxophone; Louis Cotrell, clarinet; Homer Eugene, trombone; Charlie Hamilton, piano; Sidney Pflueger, electric guitar; Eddie Dawson, bass; and Emile Maurice, drums.

On May 24, 1970, while on a visit to New Orleans, I heard Eddie Dawson at Preservation Hall playing with an all-star group which included Punch Miller, Paul Crawford, and Harry Shields. This was the only occasion I heard him play in person, as on the other nights I was there, Chester Zardis occupied the bass chair.

Incidentally, Eddie Dawson was nicknamed "Rat" by Alphonse Picou, and the name stuck with all the musicians. Although it is claimed Eddie Dawson was a favorite of King Oliver in the pre-World War I years, Eddie never mentioned this in his letters to me.

Despite the fact that Eddie Dawson played in New Orleans for all those years, he made very few recordings. In 1954 he recorded a dance set with Peter Bocage, Emile Barnes, and Albert Jiles, under the supervision of Jim McGarrell. He also recorded for Icon Records in 1962 with the Kid Howard Band.

He was still active in late 1965 with trumpeter Thomas Jefferson's group playing in Metairie, a suburb of New Orleans, with Albert Delone, alto saxophone; Lars Edegran, piano; and Andrew Jefferson, drums.

August Lanoix

[This is the life history of August Lanoix, born August 13, 1902, in the garden district of New Orleans: Height 5 feet, 11 inches, weight 200 pounds, member of St. Catherine's Roman Catholic Church.—D.G.]

My father died when I was six years of age. I attended Thomy Lafons grammar school, and stopped at sixth grade to help my widowed mother. My first job was delivering ice, milk, bread, and oysters for Joseph Kohler at Milan and South Liberty for $3.00 weekly.

After this job, I obtained several others, each at an increase in salary; my second job was Larose ice man; my third, drug store delivery boy at Octavia and Prytania Streets; fourth, Otis Mahogany Mill at Peters Ave and River; fifth, Crescent Bed Company, Broad and Gravier Streets; sixth, Louisiana Copper Company at Dorgenois and St. Louis Streets.

I joined a pleasure club and there I met my future wife, Alberta Gabriel, who lived at such a distance that I could not get to work on time. In 1919, I was fired from the last job, but obtained another at 328 Bourbon Street working at Mayer Bernstein Tailor Shop. My salary began at $8.00 weekly and went up to $15.00 weekly. I then got married.

At this time, I became interested in music. My wife's cousin, Albert Gabriel, played clarinet. Her father, Martin Gabriel, played cornet, her brother played drums, and she played the piano. Albert told me where I could buy a violin.

I began taking violin lessons from James B. Humphrey and playing with the student band until violins became unpopular in jazz bands. My wife helped me with the notes. In 1924, I switched to the trombone, then to the string bass. My instructors were Wendel McNeil and Henry Kimball.

I was a member of the following bands: Martin Gabriel National Jazz Band (six pieces), Manny Gabriel Trio (three pieces), Oriental Serenaders led by Peter Depass (six pieces), Black Diamond Orchestra led by Leo and Harold Dejan (ten pieces), James Kid Clayton Jazz Band (I played bass horn—six pieces), Henry Kid Rena Band (again, bass horn—eight pieces), Remy's Golden Leaf Orchestra (bass horn—ten pieces), Gilbert Young's Rhythm Kings (eight pieces), Sidney Desvignes Southern Syncopators (twelve pieces), Piron's String Ensemble (four pieces), Herbert Leary's Society Syncopators (twelve pieces), Ray Ancors Orchestra led by Oscar Rousseau (ten pieces), Peter Bocage's Creole Serenaders (six pieces), and Toppers Orchestra managed by Sidney Cates (twelve pieces). *[Herbert Leary's Society Syncopators played at the Rhythm Club in New Orleans in 1940. A photograph taken at the time shows a fourteen-piece big band with two bass players.—D.G.]*

August Lanoix was a member of the Charlie Love-Albert Jiles Ragtime Orchestra, which was put together to play a concert of ragtime and pre-World War I jazz during the 1960 Tulane University Fine Arts Festival. [Subsequently, Riverside Records released one side of an album under the title of New Orleans: The Living Legends—Peter Bocage *which was made shortly after the concert in Tulane University. It was reported in May of 1966 that August Lanoix was recovering from a mild stroke which affected his right hand. He seems to have been musically inactive following this illness.—D.G.]*

Bill Dillard

[*Trumpeter Bill Dillard was born in Philadelphia, Pennsylvania, on July 20, 1911. On his twelfth birthday, his father gave him a cornet, and he received tuition from Clarence Smith. He came to Britain in 1937 as a member of Teddy Hill's Orchestra accompanying the Cotton Club Revue and then returned in 1981 to appear at the Cambridge Theatre in London as part of the musical* One Mo' Time.

The in-depth interview which follows was conducted by Sheldon Harris, Dr. Albert Vollmer, and myself on May 20, 1976. A week previously, Bill Dillard had granted me an informal interview and all of the material collected during these two interviews has been collated and placed in chronological order, but there are probably some out-of-sequence events, particularly in the early thirties, as Bill Dillard was unable to give precise dates for the majority of these working engagements.]

When I was a little boy just learning to play I heard of Johnny Dunn. I was around fourteen at the time and it seemed that he had just gone to Europe in those days.

I used to play against Doc Hyder when I was with Linwood Johnson's band. Another band I also worked with was Madame Keene's in Philadelphia. In those days, they mostly had two bands in a ballroom and usually there would be a battle going on between them.

I forget the name of the restaurant in Camden, New Jersey, where Barney Alexander's band played. We had five men in the band over there, Bumps Goldston was playing piano, Tommy [?] was the drummer, he sang very well, a Philadelphia boy. Barney, myself, and I think a tuba player completed the group.

We worked in this restaurant for two or three years, it must have been 1927 and 1928, just before I came to New York. We did play in a speakeasy in Wildwood, New Jersey, during the summer of 1928 called the Blue Heaven. Those speakeasy places were for dancing.

Jelly Roll Morton came by Philadelphia to get me, I think to bring me to New York. By then I had a pretty good reputation around Philadelphia with Josh Saddler and Madame Keene, but I had left earlier that same summer of 1929 for New York. My wife was still there, and she told him that I was already in New York. I later saw Jelly Roll in New York and would go on tours with him up in the coal-mining areas like Wilkes-Barre, mostly in the summer of 1930, I think.

Jelly Roll Morton would get most of the men from the Rhythm Club when something came up. His recording guys he used to take to Camden, seemed like he booked them from the Rhythm Club. In the afternoons or evenings, that is where we all went and if anybody needed someone that's where they would get them. They usually had a piano there and someone usually playing. When somebody new came into town that was one way he had of displaying what he could do. They used to have battles there, especially trumpet players.

Louis Armstrong had come to New York, and he was playing so high and so much trumpet compared to what the average trumpet player had been playing. They were all fascinated with his E's and F's and they were trying to get shallower mouthpieces and trying to match him, so trumpet became an instrument just for challenge. We had some pretty good battles, and I remember Roy Eldridge and Rex Stewart, they played a fast style, not your usual trumpet style.

We had a fellow named Cuban Bennett. He died so young, too soon, because he drank so much whiskey. Right there at the Rhythm Club, Cuban would pick up his horn and start playing a different style. He had a more melodic style of playing for that era. In that era, we played choppy and fast, but he played beautiful arpeggios, and he had a terrific ear for modern chord structure that sort of intrigued everybody. At least the trumpet players of that era gave him a lot of credit. He was not reliable to book on a job, because maybe he would get there or maybe not. If he got there, he would be drunk before the job was over. He never had any stability; you just could not rely on him.

Jabbo Smith could blow, but it seemed that Roy, Rex, and

Johnny "Bugs" Hamilton were becoming pretty good, they were like the stars of that particular era.

I played with Mamie Smith a couple of times in the Lafayette Theatre in New York, but she never really impressed me like Bessie Smith did. Bessie used to talk to the audience. This was in the late twenties, or 1930 or 1931, something like that.

You know Bessie Smith used to carry a .45 with her, because I worked with her four or five times in the Lincoln Theatre and the Standard Theatre in Philadelphia on that T.O.B.A. circuit that we used to play in those days. She used to keep that .45 in her dressing room. Quite a few guys, musicians used to go with her. Buster Bailey was going with her at one time, and he told me about it. In those days, they used to get paid and would take the money with them to the next town. Then, when they got back down South they'd put it in a bank, so Bessie had that .45 to protect her money. She had a great sense of humor, but she was rough.

I worked at the Lafayette Theatre around the same time as Mamie with the Whitman Sisters. I used to play their act many times and Butterbeans and Susie. I also worked with Ethel Waters, she was very attractive.

I played in the early thirties in a club in Sheepshead Bay, the place used to sell seafood. I was working there with a fellow called Arthur Davey. We had a four-piece combo who played for dancing, and we also entertained. We had a little piano that we rolled out on the floor. Arthur Davey was a saxophone player and was also a very good singer. I also sang and it was a fairly good job. They also hired entertainment, a different act each week. Once, we had Johnson and Dean—by then they were quite advanced in age.

Johnson and Dean—I think the man's name was Dean—and he was like a cake-walking dancer, and his wife had a nice singing voice. While she was singing, he used to strut and dance, that was part of their act. They were big stars of the Ziegfeld shows in the early years; they went to Europe, very early too. *[In fact, Charles Johnson was the man and Dora Dean was his wife.—D.G.]*

I did some records with Jelly Roll Morton in the old Victor studios in Camden, New Jersey. I am sure this was in the very early thirties. As a matter of fact, I was working with the Luis Russell band in the Saratoga Club at the time. Jelly Roll Morton, I think, was the musical director at the Victor studios at that time, and he hired some of the men from Luis Russell's band to do several recording sessions with him over there. I think "Red" Allen was with us, but now I cannot recall who else was with us. *[To date, no trace of these particular sessions has been found in the Victor recording books, so they remain a mystery. Conversely, Bill Dillard denied his presence on the Mamie Smith recording date of February 19, 1931. He, like the other members of the Bingie Madison band, is credited with being on it, but all of those questioned deny their presence.—D.G.]*

I worked with the boxer, Jack Johnson, in a restaurant that he was running at 50th Street and Broadway in New York City, it was one flight above the street level and this was on the southwest corner. I think prior to that time, it had been a Chinese restaurant. Jack Johnson was running the place and he organized the band. We had about eight musicians there for about two or three months, possible not that long. He would be conducting the band for about an hour each evening.

In the spring of 1934, I worked with Leroy Smith in a show called *Connie's Hot Chocolates*. It was Leroy Smith's band with four or five acts including Peg Leg Bates, the Four Gobs, a dance team, Avis Andrews (who was a beautiful legitimate type singer), and Radcliffe and Rodgers, that was the show. *Hot Chocolates* was originally one of the shows that was produced for Connie's Inn in New York. After the show had played at Connie's Inn, it went on tour, and I joined it then. I did not work at Connie's Inn on that particular show, but I worked there many times with other shows.

I haven't laughed like I used to laugh in those days at the humor and comedy. People would just fall over laughing at those Black comedy sketches, and the things they used to do were so close to home that you don't find that humor around anymore.

I also used to play Irving C. Miller's *Brownskin Models* show when it came to the Lafayette and Apollo Theatres, with Drake and Walker.

The speakeasy places, you know, were not only for dancing. They also had singers who used to "work the tables" like Pearl Bailey. Pearl Bailey was an entertainer; she would walk around and sing at the tables. They had a little device, where you would take up a dollar or five dollar bill, fold it up and put it on the edge of the table. The girl would lift up her dress and ease up to this dollar and take it off with her thighs or something. That's what was meant by "working the tables."

Pearl was a tap dancer and her brother, Bill Bailey, was a very good tap dancer. He worked at the Cotton Club, Connie's Inn, and the local theatres. Pearl used to come from Philadelphia to New York at weekends when she was out of school, and she used to come into the clubs on Friday and Saturday nights and return home to Philadelphia on Sunday. She decided that she wanted to get into the theatres, as well, so she started dancing with a girl in Philadelphia; we only knew this girl as "Chocolate". They had a fairly good tap dance routine together and they were beginning to do some of the local clubs, but I think it was discovered that Pearl had heart murmurs when she was very young and she was advised to stop dancing. She decided to start singing, and she had her first training by singing in the local clubs and coalmine areas of Pennsylvania.

In 1937, I went to Europe with Teddy Hill's Orchestra, as part of the Cotton Club Revue show. I had previously been to Europe with Lucky Millinder in 1933. After we came back from Europe in 1937 *[They left Southampton on September 14, 1937, for home.—D.G.]* Teddy Hill's Orchestra opened at the Apollo Theatre. Moms Mabley happened to be on the bill that week, so on the opening show Teddy Hill introduced Moms Mabley. She came out on the stage and made a big deal out of meeting the orchestra leader and gave the audience the impression that this was her old man. Teddy replied that he had a French girlfriend now. Moms asked him, "What has she got that I haven't?"

"Well", Teddy said, "She can parlez." Then he asked Moms, "Can you parlez?" Moms replied, "I bet if I parlez, you oui oui!" At this, the house broke up, but the entire joke had been completely ad-libbed.

In the late thirties, I used to go and see Jelly Roll Morton in the Jungle Inn in Washington whenever we played there. Jelly Roll had his own style of singing. It wasn't blues, it was almost a shouting style. Jelly was a funny guy, very nice, but down on musicians in a way.

In those days, vaudeville was dying. People just do not realize how the movies killed vaudeville.

Sometime, during the late forties, I appeared in the musical version of "The Little Foxes," which ran on Broadway for several months. In the show, there was a jazz segment, and five of us were hired to play it. We had Buster Bailey, clarinet; Bernard Addison, banjo; Benny Morton, trombone; and Rudy Nicholls, drums. I was playing cornet and doing the vocals. We had a special spot during the show, where the dixieland band played outside on a verandah for the guests at a party.

In 1949, Margie Fairbanks and her son, Austin, contracted for Leadbelly *[Huddie Ledbetter]* and myself to go to Europe to do a concert tour that they had planned. I went down to Leadbelly's place on 10th Street in New York. We rehearsed five or six times until I became familiar with his material.

After I heard what he was doing, I figured out what part I would play. It was mostly muted stuff, but I used to sing a harmony part too.

At the time I met Leadbelly, he still had a little trouble with one leg, he walked with a sort of limp—arthritis or something, because by then, he was pretty old. We went over to Europe and when we got there, he couldn't even walk on to the stage, he had to be seated, he couldn't stand and was sick. We went ahead with our program, and we must have had about twenty-five numbers altogether, between them some solo pieces which he did. We did a couple of concerts, I think one was at the Cité University out in the suburbs of Paris.

Then a doctor in Paris discovered Leadbelly had multiple sclerosis. They arranged for him and I to go to a recording studio, and we must have made at least twenty-five numbers, the whole program, just the two of us.

We had flown over on TWA, and during our flight, Leadbelly wrote a song with a first line of "I went to Europe on the 25th of May on TWA." During those recordings, the control man kept hearing a little click and he couldn't discover where it came from, but finally he noticed that a ring Leadbelly was wearing was hitting a guard. At that time, he had two young people that were managing him and they advised him not to sign anything with regard to the recording, so the Fairbanks family still have those masters in Paris.

We stayed in Europe for a couple of months. I think that we came back on September 1. Then Leadbelly went into Bellevue Hospital. He did not live long after that, and he died later that same year. It was Mrs. Fairbanks's son who had the idea of my trumpet accompanying Leadbelly, as he had never worked with a trumpet. He was a sweet old guy, but I had never met him before going to Europe.

Figure 8. The author (left) and trumpeter Bill Dillard (right). Photo by Al Vollmer.

Over the last fifteen years, I have been in New York. The last big band I worked with was Louis Armstrong, but as the war was coming, I had to get a job. Incidentally, I worked with Josh White in the theatre quite a few times. He was appearing in the Apollo, or maybe the Lafayette at the time.

In the 1950s, I was just doing straight acting in the radio series *Love of Life* and in 1955, I played Joe in a summer production of *Showboat.*

Charles I. Williams

As Told By David Griffiths

[On a trip to New York City during April, 1984, I attended a Tribute to Louis Armstrong concert at Uniondale High School, Long Island, organized by bassist, Arvell Shaw, as a benefit for autistic children. The lineup of names for this concert, including Joe Newman, Doc Cheatham, Buddy Tate, Chris Woods, and Maxine Sullivan, was a real all-star one, and it turned out to be a memorable musical evening.

Opening the concert was a group, which included the very fine tenor saxophonist Turk Mauro and an alto saxophonist, by the name of Charles I. Williams. This was the first time that I had heard him play and I found him to be an exceptional musician whose forté is the blues. Not only did he knock me out with his playing, but the near capacity audience loved his work too. What follows is a brief outline of his career.]

Charles Isaac Williams was born in Halls, Tennessee, on July 18, 1932. His interest in music began when his family moved in 1940 to Alton, Illinois (situated thirteen miles from that influential jazz city—St. Louis). He feels the church choirs that he heard there influenced his interest in the music and were responsible for his getting his feeling for the blues.

His family owned a diner and service station and, while listening to the radio and the diner's juke box, Williams had the opportunity of hearing all the popular bands of those Swing Era days—Benny Goodman, Duke Ellington, Count Basie, and Harry James.

Originally he started playing music on a paper and comb and even bent a newspaper into the shape of a saxophone and started humming into it. Finally, one Christmas, his father bought him an alto saxophone, which was in such bad condition that he had to have it completely overhauled. While this was being done, he worked in a barber shop to get enough money to pay for the repairs.

Williams received his first serious musical training in the eighth grade of junior high school in 1945. At that time, although the school band was not playing jazz, the band's director, Joe Brewer, emphasized how a good full sound was basic to listening to music.

He was learning his jazz outside of school with a trumpet player and mortician named Tootie Russell and a tenor saxophonist, Robert Higgenbotham. Russell was a catalyst for those who wanted to play jazz, as he organized a band and taught everyone to read big band charts. Over the next four or five years, while in junior and senior high schools, Williams worked with both Russell and Higgenbotham throughout Illinois and in St. Louis.

Later, he attended Lincoln University in Jefferson City, Missouri, where he majored in music education and studied the various woodwind instruments under Dr. O. Anderson Fuller. Williams told me that, although he received formal training in school from both Joe Brewer and Dr. Fuller, neither of them had a great impact on his playing, but he remembers them both for their rules for good musicianship.

At home in Alton, he played with a few bands and also toured with pianist and blues singer Memphis Slim, then living in St. Louis, during summer and winter school holidays from 1952 to 1954. Although he toured with Memphis Slim, he never recorded with him.

After finishing college, he decided to stay on in St. Louis and worked there with Jester Thompson's quartet. Williams was friendly with both Chris Woods and Oliver Nelson, and whenever one of them could not make a playing engagement, he would pass it on to another. In this way, Oliver Nelson obtained Williams a job with drummer J. C. Heard. Trumpeter Irving Stokes was also in this group, and together they worked in Chicago on the Sarah Vaughan Show, in 1959.

Williams held a position in a post office in Alton for about four years, until, as he said, "One day, I decided that the post office wasn't too musical a place." In 1961, he moved to New York, where he was able to obtain a job with the Board of Education as a teacher of orchestral music in St. Albans, Queens.

He had been to New York for the first time while touring with

Memphis Slim in either 1952 or 1953 and recalled how awestruck he was on hearing the amount of musical activity on 52nd Street at the time. His first engagement in New York was with Artie Suggs's dance band, thanks to Oliver Nelson who recommended him. Concurrently with his teaching career, Williams slowly began to establish himself on the New York jazz scene by working as a professional musician on weekends. Subsequently, he built up a regular working relationship with Mercer Ellington and has also gigged with Ernie Wilkins and the Fat Back Band.

In 1978, Williams spent a six-week spell working on the continent with Clark Terry's Band and during that summer played four weeks of jazz festival dates with his good friend, Frank Foster (he has recorded several albums with Foster, including one made on a visit to Helsinki). Frank Foster says of Williams that he has an exquisite tone and plays the blues like you wouldn't believe. In 1979, he returned to Europe, this time with Clark Terry for a string of festival dates and with Frank Foster on tour.

Between 1983 and 1987, he has worked off and on with Frank Foster in his Loud Minority and Twelve Shades of Black bands and has also made a number of recordings under the leadership of Frank Foster, as well as with Ted Harris's Giants Of Jazz.

In 1994 he was a regular member of vocalist Ruth Brown's superb accompanying group, alongside of Bobby Forrester, organ and keyboards; Ed Cherry, guitar; Carline Ray, bass guitar; and Clarence "Tootsie" Bean, drums. Williams received rave reviews for his work with her.

His major influence has been Benny Carter, but he has also been influenced by Charlie Parker, Johnny Hodges, and Louis Jordan. At the same time, he assimilated musical ideas from Eddie "Cleanhead" Vinson, Art Tatum, Erroll Garner, and many other pianists. (Williams considers the piano to be a whole big band.) He maintains that the important part of playing jazz is to learn the melody first and only later to improvise upon it, and he has found the piano to be the best instrument to learn the melody.

He has recorded three albums under his own name for the Mainstream label—*Charles Williams* (MRL 312), *Trees And Grass And Things* (MRL 345), and *Stickball* (MRL 381), with tenor saxophonist David "Bubba" Brooks and organist Don Pullen featured on all three.

Charles I. Williams

Figure 9. Undated photograph of alto saxophonist Charles I. Williams.

[*Charles Williams is also an accomplished musician on the flute, piccolo, and clarinet. At present, as far as I am aware, none of these albums is available, but as the Mainstream label is now slowly beginning to rerelease its catalogue, you may come across these recordings on compact disc. All three albums give insights into the rich musical character of this excellent alto saxophonist, Charles Williams.—D.G.*]

Eddie Craig

[On the basis of my own researches following the interview, I have attempted to place all the events he mentions into correct order, but it is possible that events took place not in the same order given here.

I have not been able to trace Eddie Craig's name, which incidentally, is a stage name, in any of the jazz reference books. Walter C. Allen's biodiscography of the music of Fletcher Henderson and his musicians, Hendersonia, makes no mention of him whatsoever.

Therefore, from purely a jazz research point of view, this was the most disappointing of all the projects that I have been involved in, probably because at the outset it was likely to have become the most interesting.

This experience is unlikely to stop me continuing to interview jazz personalities, but it is a warning to check and recheck your findings if you want your life-stories to be chronologically correct.

In recent years, many veteran U.S. jazzmen have died or have left the music scene. Therefore, you can imagine my excitement on hearing that such a person was not only alive but living in Pontypool, South Wales (my own home ground). Thanks to the American graphic artist, Paul Peter Piech, who also now lives in South Wales, I had the opportunity of meeting and interviewing Eddie Craig. Subsequently, I approached a couple of musicians to supplement his life story, and I have included their comments as they are of added interest.]

I was born in Yonkers, New York, on June 3, 1912. When my real father died as a result of a train accident, my mother moved to New York, and we lived in a flat. In the flat upstairs lived two musicians, Noble Sissle and Eubie Blake. One night at Christmas, they were down in our flat decorating a Christmas tree, and I came in trying to sneak a look at what was there for me. Noble Sissle smacked me and put me back to bed. I was too young, so I never sang with any of their shows.

My stepfather was a classical violinist. He wanted me to learn the violin but insisted that I learn the piano first. Well, if I had learned to play the piano, I would have had to give up playing baseball and football, which I would not do, so I never learned to play either the piano or the violin. My musical life was singing, that's all I ever did. I sang in school. Then I went to summer school at Cornell University at Ithaca.

We lived at 43 Hancock Street. It was a luxurious area—Hancock Street and Lewis Avenue in Brooklyn. I grew up together with Lena Horne. She lived with her aunt, because her mother and father were dead, and she went to Girls' High School. My mother and her aunt were bridge partners; they played whist and bridge together. We'd go to their house and attend bridge parties and they'd come to our house for bridge parties, and that's how I knew Lena so very well.

Paul Robeson came to live with us in Brooklyn, because he was having trouble in school at Columbia University and he was short of money. Dad took him in and we took care of him.

I went down to New York, but, as I didn't know a soul, I stayed over in Brooklyn. My uncle introduced me to a musical singing instructor, and he took me along to the Kentucky Club. I cannot remember who was the leader of the band playing then.

One night, I went up to the Cotton Club and Cab Calloway's Band was playing there. The resident bandleader of the relief band, which had a bandstand away from the regular big bandstand, gave me a job, and he put a little trio behind me, drums, bass, and piano. Anyhow, I started singing there, and all these beautiful rich women were watching me, and I would sing to them.

On one occasion, the owner and the manager of the Cotton Club and also the newspaper man, Walter Winchell, and Cab Calloway were all listening to me. When I came offstage and changed my clothes, a waiter came up to me and said, "Eddie, there's a gentleman here to see you." It was Walter Winchell. He told me, "I've come to give you a little advice. Always be nice to the people you meet on your way up, because you'll never know when you'll need them on the way down." I have never forgotten that. He wanted the Cotton Club people to put me on the stage of the Strand Theatre or the Paramount Theatre with a big band, but they would not do it. I was born too soon, because the only singers who were doing stage work were the Mills Brothers and the Ink Spots.

On Sunday mornings, we used to go up to Dickie Well's Club in New York City for those jam sessions and that's where we met everybody.

After the Cotton Club, I went to Syracuse, then to Buffalo, and then down to Cleveland. When I was in Cleveland, I was working on the radio station, known as the Buckeye Network, because Ohio was known as the Buckeye State. I used to do one program a week on Tuesday, and another fellow would do one on Thursday, then on Wednesday we would both rehearse. Then we used to go for coffee and talk over what we were going to do. He never changed his name when I knew him, and they sent for him to go to the New York Office. They didn't want me, they wanted him, because we sounded very much alike. They took him down to New York and made him famous, and I was out in Ohio by myself. I've never seen him from that day to this and you know who it was—Perry Como.

I met "Chu" Berry when we worked with the Fletcher Henderson Orchestra. When I was with Fletcher, we had all these jobs around Cleveland for several weeks. I asked Fletcher, where we were going (he had a way of saying, "We're going smack into Miami, Florida"), so he said, "We're going smack into Hanover, New Hampshire and from there we're going smack into Chicago, the Grand Theatre."

So I said to Fletcher, "Well, that's all right, I'll see you in Chicago." He said, "Are you going there?", and I said "No, I'm not," so he replied, "We won't see you there at all, you're through." Because when he was finished in Chicago, I knew what he was going to do. He had told me that he was breaking up the band to go to New York and do Benny Goodman's arrangements. After leaving Fletcher, I returned to Syracuse.

I went into show business when I lived in Cortland, New York, joining a band led by Dick Meddaugh. There was another band in Cortland, led by the trombonist, Speigel Willcox. Speigel used to be with Jean Goldkette and his roommate in that band was Tommy Dorsey. When Speigel's father died, they had a big coal business in Cortland. Speigel had to come back to take care of the business. He led a big band there, nine or ten pieces, and I worked with him. If Dick Meddaugh did not have a job, I worked with Speigel Willcox quite often. Good days, good music.

I was working for a radio station, WFBL in Syracuse, New York. We used to do a show there on Sunday, a commercial program called The Boy's Gang. The last show we did, we had Peanuts Hucko. He was a Syracuse boy, and we used to work together on it. Snooky Young, Jackie Coogan, and Betty Grable were on it.

[Peanuts Hucko recalled to me that Eddie Craig was talking about a time period sometime in the late thirties. He admitted that his memory was not good but went on to say that the radio program that Eddie refers to was called Roy's Gang, sponsored by Roy's Furniture Company, and performed in the Keith Theatre with a live audience every Sunday. Betty Grable and Jackie Coogan, a Syracuse native son by the way, did appear at the Theatre but not on the program. They were there at different dates, once each, as headliners of the vaudeville portion of entertainment at Keith's, which was a motion picture theatre. Finally, Peanuts said that he knew Snooky Young quite well but did not recall doing the radio program when he may have been on it.—D.G.]

In 1943, I went into the army and entertained the troops in Buffalo for a short time. When I was in New York with the army, I went to the Apollo Theatre, and Lena Horne was there with the Deep River Boys and Duke Ellington. When I went into Duke's dressing room, Duke had just greeted his shirt maker, a Jewish man, and Duke had just said to him, as I came in the door, "I want you to make me some more underwear with more dancing space." "What do you mean more dancing space, Duke?" asked the man. Duke replied, "More ball-room, man, more ball-room!"

Then I came to Europe with the army and when I was in Antwerp, I saw an advertisement that Noble Sissle was appearing at an army base in Ghent, so I went over to see him, and we had a great time.

I came to Britain in 1944 with the army, then after my army service had ended, I settled here and have not been back to America since.

I worked in London with a band led by Leslie "Jiver" Hutchinson. I toured with him for a long time. At this stage, I was living in Pontypool and worked with his band in Newcastle. I caught a train at midnight and arrived in Newcastle at three o'clock the next afternoon, just in time to rehearse. We toured all around the North.

[Thanks to fellow jazz researcher and photographer, Val Wilmer, I was able to contact Rupert Nurse, who had played bass with Leslie Hutchinson. He recalled the period as follows: I re-established contact with Leslie "Jiver" Hutchinson, who had left Geraldo's Orchestra to form his own band. This brought on a trip to Czechoslovakia in 1947 and to Sweden in 1949. It was around this time that Leslie had some contact with Mecca Dance, and we played some gigs in London before going north on tour. This trip included Manchester, Hull, Newcastle, Aberdeen, and Perth, so that must be the trip which featured Eddie Craig. I remember him as a very good vocalist, but his association with the band was fairly short, and I don't think he did any more than this tour.—D.G.]

Speaking of London, a good friend of mine, a piano player was working at the Cafe de Paris one night and he took me down there and in the audience was this Australian fellow who I recognized. It was suggested that I sing a couple of numbers with the prospect of getting a job, and I said, "I'm only here for five minutes." The Australian, who was the comedian and entertainer Bill Kerr, told me to cut that out, as I was stealing his catch-phrase.

I met Paul Robeson again when he came to Wales, it was in Ebbw Vale and then I saw him again in Cardiff, as I was a member of a group that had brought him over. We took him to Swansea, but he did not know that I had a piece of him. My business associates had taken him on. When he sang at the Royal Albert Hall, he introduced me to the audience.

Finally, I worked the King Of Clubs nightclub in Wigan. The last I heard my picture was still in the lobby, and the last performance I did as a singer and bandleader, I had a trio at St. Mellons Country Club, near Cardiff.

Freddie Skerritt

[Freddie Skerritt was born on May 1, 1904, in Montserrat, Leeward Islands, British West Indies. He left there when he was a few months old. In 1919 he arrived in New York City, via Canada. The following piece, in his own words, gives an insight into his musical career in New York.]

I started out as a drummer with "Nappy" [Napoleon], just playing parties at weekends. The violinist, Bert Howell, was also on some of these gigs. We played at many of the wealthy houses in Harlem, and Madame Walker's place at Irvington on the Hudson in New York a few times. In 1925, I played with Alphonse Steel at the Chequer Board, then in the Village with pianist, theorist, and harmonist, "Old Man" Hall. The Village job was my second one, and Steele spoke up for me. I had a set of drums from him that I never paid for, even today!

It was at a party that I first heard Benny Carter playing the saxophone and he inspired me to take up that particular instrument. He was playing a C-Melody saxophone at that time. There were few musicians playing C-Melody saxophone then and even fewer playing alto saxophones, as these were not popular. By the time I had decided to play the alto saxophone, the musicians had just started to change over to playing altos. The bands at that period had no large reed section, just two saxophones then, alto and tenor . . . like Prince Robinson and Bob Robinson when they came to the Capitol. Duke Ellington came up, and he only had Otto Hardwick, and many more bands had only one saxophone.

Benny Carter was about my age, and I used to go to his home. I lived on 64th and Benny lived on 61st or 62nd. When I played at the Rhythm Club, Benny used to come in, just playing saxophone, no other instruments. Ward Pinkett, who was one of my

91

best friends, used to come along, and Cuban Bennett as well. We'd have little jam sessions, and no one would want to follow Cuban. Russell Procope would come, and Coleman Hawkins once in a while.

My sister had signed for me to buy an alto saxophone on the installment plan, and I took lessons from Lt. Eugene Mikell. He was my first teacher; he taught most of the reedmen. He ran a formal school in his apartment on, I believe, 53rd Street. He had a fine reputation as a teacher.

I played in Willie Gant's Band at Small's Paradise during the summer of 1926. Ward Pinkett and Rex Stewart, who was later replaced by Leroy Rutledge, were on trumpets; Happy Caldwell, Son Adams, and myself were on reeds; Joe Williams on trombone; Johnny Lee on guitar and banjo; Billy Taylor on bass; and Manzie Johnson on drums. I also worked in a small combo with Willie Gant at a downstairs room called Brittwood's on 140th and Lenox. I recall that Erskine Hawkins's wife was the checkroom girl there. I was beginning to play a lot of baritone saxophone then, because Gant liked me "bootin' out the baritone."

In 1926, as well, I did a short tour in Connecticut with Duke Ellington. Duke had just finished his job at the Kentucky Club. Happy Rhone, who was the owner of Happy Rhone's, sent the band up there. Otto Hardwick and myself were on altos; Bubber Miley and another musician, whose name I can't recall, were on trumpets; Charlie Irvis on trombone; Harvey Boone on tenor; Sonny Greer on drums; and Freddie Guy on banjo and guitar.

During the winter of 1926, I was working with Happy Caldwell again. This time we were both in Wardell "Preacher" Jones's Band at The Nest on 133rd Street. We used to start at 11 P.M. and we had Ed Cuffee on trombone and Manzie Johnson on drums. At that time I was living on St. Nicholas Avenue in Harlem.

At that period I played with many groups and also did much gigging around. I went with Cliff Jackson to Newark where we played at the Cotton Club and Keeney Hall. I played at the dancing schools, including the Tango Palace, located on 48th Street and Broadway. At first, trombonist Lew Henry was the leader of the band there, but then Bingie Madison took it over . . . that was around 1928 or 1929. We also played a short spell at the Savoy Ballroom. They always had two bands, and we played opposite Fess Williams. We had Louis Bacon and Cyril Hunt on trumpets;

Fernando Arbello on trombone . . . he was later replaced by Jimmy Archey; Henry "Moon" Jones . . . we called him that because of the shape of his face, and myself on altos; Bingie on tenor and clarinet; Gene Rodgers on piano; Goldie Lucas on banjo; and Richard "Uncle Dick" Fullbright on an Helicon tuba . . . that's the kind that comes around you with the bell facing out.

I worked in Brooklyn for a while with Dave Martin on piano, his sister and brother played violins. I rejoined Bingie in 1930 at the Broadway Danceland on 60th Street and Broadway, although this engagement did not last long. Bill Dillard and Ward Pinkett were on trumpets, Jimmy Archey on trombone, while the rest of the band were made up of the old Tango Palace band. We made some recordings in October and November of that year and in February of the following year. These were all made under Clarence Williams's name. The session we made on February 19, 1931, was made primarily for the southern market, and these sides were issued under the name of "The Memphis Hotshots." Later in April of 1931, Bingie Madison's Band did a recording session with King Oliver.

Billy Fowler, who had played on Broadway and then toured Europe, had just returned to the States and had got a band together. I joined them and we did a tour of the South, playing mainly warehouses and tobacco sheds. We didn't do very well as nobody knew the band. Danny Barker, Bingie Madison, altoist Benny Williams, and trombonist Nathaniel Story were in that band.

Around 1931, I joined Frankie Newton's group. Frankie came out of Dickie Well's place and went straight into the 101 Ranch. We had Jimmy Powell on alto, Jimmy Bell on tenor, "Dusty" Neal on drums, and either Gene Anderson or "Sharkey" on piano. There was no trombone or bass, and I played alto and baritone saxes. Frankie was terrific. He wrote beautiful arrangements for us. The three reeds played and sang at the customers' tables, everyone had a ball, and we would go back to the bandstand with our sax bells loaded with dollar bills. The three saxes would play, then sing a chorus at the tables. . . . we made good money that way. We had an offer from WOR, but it didn't come good.

I also worked with Sam Wooding after he came back from Europe at the end of November 1931. We played for a short while at the Arcadia Ballroom on 53rd and Broadway, and later we played a week, I think, at the Lafayette Theatre on 132nd Street and 7th Avenue. This was during the Depression. We played incidental music in the interval at the Lafayette. The personnel of that band was Otis Johnson, Kenneth Roane, and Clarence "Graf Zeppelin" Powell on trumpets; Benny "Ferdinand" Williams on alto; Eugene Sedric on tenor and clarinet; myself on alto and baritone; Yank Porter on drums; a string bass player whose name I can't recall and, of course, Sam on piano. Kenneth Roane taught the Wooding brass section to play ocarinas.

In 1932, I played with Nat Story, Benny "Ferdinand" Williams, Al Sears, and Danny Barker in Bud Harris's Band. We went on the road touring theatres. Later, I joined Rex Stewart's big band at the Empire Ballroom on Broadway between 56th and 57th Streets. We were at the Empire less than a year, and the personnel of that band was: George Thigpen, first trumpet; Ward Pinkett, second trumpet; and Rex, third. Rex and Ward took all the solos. I was first alto, and I'd replaced Edgar Sampson, who had left to join Chick Webb. Rudy Powell on alto and Allen Jackson and Noel Klukies on tenors completed the reed section. Roger "Ram" Ramirez was on piano and Big Sid Catlett on drums. He was later replaced by Tommy Benford. I can't recall the names of the bass player or the guitarist, but they both came from Connecticut. Sonny Woods handled the vocals.

In the late thirties, I led a small group at a place called The Palace Bar and Grill at 137th and Lenox, across from the Harlem Hospital. It was just a corner we had there, no band stand. Shirley Clay, the trumpet player, originally got the job, then the man who owned the place couldn't use the trumpet as it was too loud, so Shirley gave me the job. I had Hubert Joseph on piano and Manzie Johnson on drums. When Manzie took off, Gene Brooks, a little drummer, used to sit in. Most of the big names in jazz today would come in and jam. The owner would sometimes hire three pieces, even four, five, or six pieces—then the union stepped in and wanted to stop it because they figured he was getting more than he was paying for. . . . they considered it bad. But he actually wasn't going to hire anymore, anyway, and the musicians were having fun. Around this time I went on the road a couple of times with Fats Waller, so "Skinny" Brown on alto replaced me there.

I had known Fats from school days, and even then he was fat, I'd also seen him at parties. I toured with Fats a couple of times, once we went South, and once, that was May and June 1940, we went all the way to the West Coast. We had a ball. Fats was always pleasant, the easiest fellow to work with. He drank on the stand and didn't mind anyone else drinking. Nobody went to extremes, he'd never get angry. We played for theatres and dance dates. Don Donaldson was in charge of the band for rehearsals.

Later, after the job at the Palace had finished, I joined Machito's Orchestra. Latin music was becoming very popular in New York, so we worked often. At the end of August 1942, I joined the navy. I was in the service with a U.S. Navy band and was sent to Guantanamo Bay, Cuba, and stayed there two years. We had some fine musicians in that band . . . Willie Smith, Clark Terry, Clement Tervalon, Wallace Davenport, and many fellows from out west.

When I came out of the service in July 1945, I rejoined Machito's Afro-Cubans and stayed with him until 1956. During the time I was with him we travelled quite a bit: to California twice, to South America twice. We also did a lot of recording with various Latin singers and also under Machito's own name. Harry Belafonte made his first recording with us on the Royal Roost label while we were both playing the Royal Roost, which later changed its name to Birdland. I also played in other Latin-American outfits, including one led by Miguelito Valdez and another led by Artie Bastidas from Colombia. . . . he played Colombian and Peruvian music. My style changed when I went into the Latin bands—I never was much of a soloist.

After I left Machito in 1956, I worked in the daytime for the Chemical Bank. . . . Alphonse Steel got me the job, and I still continued to play with various bands at the weekend, mostly with Frank Anderson, and I did a little rehearsing.

I retired in 1970 from the bank. I had also stopped playing professionally, although occasionally I pick up my old alto-saxophone and practice a little. . . . I call it a "pea-shooter" because it has a small bore. On looking back over my jazz career, I got the greatest kick out of playing with Frankie Newton's group. I also enjoyed playing with Fats, but Frankie Newton's was the best and most enjoyable band that I ever worked in. . . . it was too bad they never recorded us.

Leslie Johnakins

Les Johnakins has always been the greatest baritone player around, but he was never the person to get around and prove it. One only has to work with him to learn how great he is. I put him up as the best.

—Adolphus "Doc" Cheatham, August 1976

I was born in Newport News, Virginia, on October 1, 1911. My brother and I persuaded our parents to allow us to study clarinet with a Professor Adolph Davidson, an elderly music teacher of German descent. He was very good, but after about six months his heavy schedule caused him to drop us for more profitable clients. I was about in my third year in high school and about fourteen years old at the time. We had a high school band. We were all beginners and sounded horrible. Our teacher had plenty of patience, he should have worn ear-plugs. I bought an alto saxophone in my last year in high school and with some other musicians formed a six-piece band to play at the week-ends. We had Joe Jordan, trumpet; Ernest Parham, tenor sax; Lawrence "Nooksie" Laneave, banjo; George Garden, drums; Pinkey Furbush, piano; and myself on alto sax.

I finished high school in February 1928, and Joe Jordan, Ernest Parham, and I decided to join a vaudeville show and travel. After a month of going from town to town without ever receiving a full salary, we quit in Asheville, North Carolina, to form the Sky Line Syncopators (Asheville is up in the mountains). Around July of 1928 I quit and went back home. In the meantime, George Garden, our old drummer, had been working in Baltimore and came home on a visit. He persuaded me to go to Baltimore to work in a cabaret with a three-piece band that he was in. I worked with him until November 1928, and then I switched to Bill Landon's Cabaret for more money plus very good tips. There we had "Dad" Stewart, drums, and Leonard Johnson, piano. I played alto and clarinet. It was there that I met Mary Stafford, a headline cabaret singer; she was a favorite and was always good for plenty of tips.

In September 1929, I decided to go to college. My brother was attending A. & T. College in Greensboro, North Carolina, and I registered there because of him. The first week I was there, Taylor's New York Serenaders came through town and with them two of my former pals, Ernest Parham and Joe Jordan. They were attending Johnson C. Smith University in Charlotte, North Carolina, and working with Dave Taylor. I left Greensboro with them, changed schools, and joined their orchestra. Then we had Joe Jordan and Lester Mitchell (a graduate of Smith), trumpets; Campbell "Skeets" Tolbert and myself, altos; Ernest Parham, tenor; Alton Harrington, banjo; Jimmy Gunn, piano; William "Dub" Hart, drums; and [?] Moore, tuba. Dave Taylor, the leader, was a graduate of Smith.

On my first day in Charlotte, I passed a girl on the street and looked back at her and found her looking back at me. I said to myself, "That's the kind of girl I would like to have for my wife." A few days later I was introduced to her and after four years of courtship we were married. We still are and are still happy about it.

After two years at school, I quit, but I continued to work with the New York Serenaders. During the summer of 1930, when school had closed, I went to Baltimore to replace Chauncey Haughton in Ike Dixon's Orchestra, others in that band included Wallace Jones, trumpet; Ed Whittington, trombone; Robert Hicks, alto; Howard "Church" Anderson, piano; Ed Wharton, banjo; and Gene Moore, drums. I worked with them for just over a month, and then Tab Smith took over from me. In that same summer, I also worked with Banjo Bernie in Baltimore. I went back to school in September of 1930 and rejoined Taylor's New York Serenaders.

Dave Taylor ran into bad health later on, and Jimmy Gunn, the piano player, took over, and from then on it was known as Jimmy Gunn's Dixie Serenaders. Later Jimmy Gunn stopped playing

and just became leader and Andrew "Mule" Maize took over the
piano chair. We broadcast regularly over the CBS Dixie Network
Program, which originated in Charlotte, for about three or four
years, and this gave the band a good following.

In January 1935, my father died, and I went back to Baltimore
and worked in two or three small clubs, just gigging around. I
learned that Chauncey Haughton, a good friend of mine, was
quitting Bubby Johnson's Band and going out on the road with
Blanche Calloway, so I joined Bubby Johnson in the spring of
1935. We had Wallace Jones, "Fess" Holmes, and Babe Bright,
trumpets; Eli Robinson, trombone; Bubby Johnson and myself,
altos; Gil White, tenor; Jimmy Duppins, baritone; and Clarence
Hunt, piano. I worked with Bubby for almost a year; we had a
very good band—four saxes and five brass—but we made no recordings, just played dances all over the State of Maryland, parts
of Pennsylvania, and Delaware. Then about a year later, I came
to New York City.

When I first arrived in New York City, a friend of mine was
supposed to have had a job for me that I could take as soon as I
arrived, but when I got here I found that he was a nonunion man
and that the very place he had reserved a job for me was being
picketed by the union, so I could not take the job. That left me a
stranger in town with no work. Well, my brother had a room in
an apartment that belonged to a musician, Al Washington. Al, at
that time, was on the road with Fats Waller. In those days, Fats
was a big headliner attraction and would go out of town for
months touring. Al knew the problems of a strange musician. He
didn't give me any pressures so I was able to stay, and I began to
pick up gigs at the weekends from different guys. I used to hang
around the Rhythm Club in those days, that was a very popular
meeting place. Al told me, "Sooner or later, you'll get on your
feet," and gradually I did get along much better. During the summer of 1936, I went to work for Claude Hopkins. He was one of
the attractions at the Roseland Ballroom, but during the summer
months he went out on the road instead of staying in the Ballroom. I worked with him on the road for about six weeks and
then they let me go. I didn't quit, he fired me. Hilton Jefferson
was playing first alto, I was playing third, Jerry Blake played baritone, Bobby Sands played tenor. We had just four saxes, Jerry
doubled on alto and did some arrangements, but mostly he

played very good baritone. In the brass, we had Ovie Alston, Russell "Pops" Smith, Lincoln Mills, and Jabbo Smith. Jabbo had just joined the band a few weeks before I arrived, and at that time Claude didn't have any arrangements for four trumpets, but as he had hired Jabbo, the trumpets would alternate on the arrangements: some of them Lincoln would play, others Jabbo would play, but Ovie and "Pops" Smith played on all of them until eventually they could build up a book for four trumpet parts. Fred Norman, Vic Dickenson, and Floyd "Stump" Brady were the three trombonists. Fred was making arrangements besides playing. Joe Jones was the guitar player, Pete Jacobs on drums, and Abie Baker played bass—that was the band when I played with them. Just about the end of the summer, I was replaced by Buster Smith from St. Louis. He came in with the reputation of being a very good saxophone and clarinet player; even though I didn't hear him play, I had heard of him, and as far as I can say from his reputation he was good. I came back to New York and just played gigs here and there.

The night after the first of the year [1937] a guy came by my house and told me that Blanche Calloway needed a saxophone player and that they were having a rehearsal that particular day. I went to the rehearsal and got the job, and I worked with her from then up to around September of that same year, during which time we toured from Maine down to Mississippi, all up and down the East Coast. In Blanche Calloway's Orchestra, we had George Thigpen, Mack Maddox, and Joe Keyes, trumpets. Maceo Bryant and Hooks Miller replaced Keyes and Maddox at the end of an engagement in Boston, Massachusetts. Andy Gibson travelled with us as arranger and part-time trumpet. He was tops as an arranger. In the reed section, there was Scoville Brown and myself on altos, Floyd Blakemore played tenor, Tapley Lewis played alto and baritone, Earl Baker (Abie's brother) was playing guitar, the piano player was a young kid from Baltimore, I can't remember his name, he and the drummer, "Red" Dibble, used to hang out together. I nicknamed the band The Globetrotters. Everybody laughed, because it really suited what we were doing, going from place to place. Once we made a twenty-four hour jump from New York City to Bay City, Michigan; the next night we had to get from there down to Indiana, which was another 500-mile or more jump. Leaving there, we went all the way down to Louisiana, that was a jump. We had a day off in between, that's how far apart some of the dates were.

There were two things I remember about that trip. In Shreveport, Louisiana, the man at the end of the night handed me fifty cents, and I asked him "What am I going to do with this?" Then there was the day in Yazoo City, Mississippi, that Blanche Calloway got locked up. I was sitting in the bus supposed to be asleep—I had my eyes closed and saw everything with my eyes closed—I was so scared. It was just about daybreak in the summer, we stopped at a filling station to get gas for the bus. While we were there everyone, naturally as we had been on the road all night, wanted to use the restroom. There were two ladies in our outfit, Blanche and Earl Baker's wife, and they both wanted to go to the ladies room. They didn't have a ladies room for colored people. They only had a toilet for use by White people, and they were told they couldn't use it. There was no other place they could go, so they went in, while they were inside the guy called the police and before they were out of that toilet, the cops had arrived, Blanche and the manager both went to jail. That was the conditions in those days.

When we got back to New York City, we played a week at the Apollo Theatre, and, while playing at that theatre, a guy told me that "Hot Lips" Page was getting a band together to go into "Small's Paradise," so I went to his rehearsal and got the job. "Hot Lips" had formerly been with the Count Basie Orchestra, and he was contracted to Joe Glaser. We stayed at "Small's" until May of the following year. Now in that band, we had Lonnie Simmons and Jimmy Wright, tenors; and Ronald Haynes and myself, altos. Ronald was a fussy type of guy who couldn't get along with people; he was later replaced by Ben Smith. In the brass section, we had Wardell "Preacher" Jones and Bob Shoffner. Jimmy Reynolds played piano and Yank Porter was on drums. We developed into a good band, because we worked every night, and staying on a job like that is different from working just one or two nights a week. Working together every night, we got to the stage where we really could play. "Lips" had a whole lot of good arrangements, and, as he was fresh out of the Basie Band and he and the Count were still on friendly terms, he was able to get a few arrangements out of their book, especially some of the numbers he used to be featured on with the Basie Band. I never recorded with "Lips," but during the time that I was working with him, I made a recording with Jabbo Smith. Jabbo was in town, gigging around here and there, no important jobs, just getting work. He came to "Small's" one night, because Ben Smith was working with us at the time and Jabbo wanted Ben to make some arrangements for him for a recording date. He told Ben what the instrumentation would be and said, "Get the men for me," and Ben got most of the guys right out of the band. They only used three saxes, they didn't use the full brass. Jabbo just played and sang.

Ed Small of "Small's Paradise" was quite a character. There were times in the latter part of the night, especially on Tuesday or Wednesday, when we would be there sitting and blowing some "head" numbers instead of playing something out of the book. When we did this—maybe I'd be taking a solo, the rest of the guys would be there sitting doing nothing, no background—I'd play two or three choruses, then the trumpet player. One night, Mr. Small came up to the bandstand, and he just stood there—a guy was playing a solo, the rest of us were sitting there resting—so he said, "Hey Lips, what are all these boys doing over here, ain't they getting paid too?" We'd say, "We're not playing one of these arrangements out of the book, Mr. Small. We're playing a "head" number, we don't have that written down. We're just playing what comes into our mind." So Mr. Small said, "Don't be playing none of that BRAIN music in my place, get me some BIG music" (he meant by that, musical arrangements, where everybody played). He didn't want to see five or six guys just sitting there doing nothing and at the same time getting paid.

We spent almost a year at Small's and, when "Lips's" time came up, they gave him two week's notice as naturally another band was coming in. This was a smaller band than "Lips's" and it was led by Billy Hicks, so as soon as I found that I was going to have to find another job, I started looking around for one. At the same time, "Lips," being contracted to Glaser, didn't have anything to worry about, because sooner or later, he'd be working again, but for me the question was how long and how soon, I didn't know. We'd been on that job practically a year, but we didn't get much publicity. No matter how long you stay on a job, if there's no broadcasting and no records, what kind of name can you spread around? That's why I figured that the possibilities of

Figure 10. Baritone saxophonist Leslie Johnakins in July 1947.

the band continuing to work were poor, so I'd better look for work myself.

Billy Hicks, the trumpet player, was coming in right behind "Lips" and he needed a saxophone player. He asked me if I'd care to stay in there and work with him, so I started to rehearse with the band that was coming in, while I was still playing with the band that was going out. Billy Hicks didn't stay too long though. Previously he'd been working at the Savoy Ballroom with a small band—his Sizzling Sixes they were called—and he had worked there for quite a while, but after he came out he had nothing to do, so he had to look around and fight for gigs. During that time he got the Small's Paradise job, then he had to get a band together. He was on trumpet, with Dave Paige, trumpet; myself on alto; Lester Boone, alto; Jimmy Wright, tenor; Jimmy Phipps, piano; we also had a trombonist, bass player, and drummer, but I can't recall their names. One thing I remember about that band, and it is another joke concerning Mr. Small. Billy Hicks didn't have many arrangements, so we played mostly "stocks," but Hicks wanted to be real smooth and sweet—not loud, raucous, and rumpus. We were playing one "stock" one night; it was a popular tune, and Mr. Small came up to the bandstand (he used to call your name backwards as quick as he called it forwards), and he said to Hicks, "Hey Hicks Billy, listen here, I don't want no Guy Lombardo band in my place, I want you to swing in here and make me some swing music." You see Small's was known for years as a swinging place, and here was Hicks playing some sweet commercial music. Ed Small was not a hard man to work for; he attended to business and naturally the place was doing good business, and there was no hassle about money. Many guys would go to him in the middle of the week and borrow money, he was an "all right" guy. It was just sometimes, when he showed up, he'd be in such a funny way because he'd speak his mind naturally, but the way he talked . . .

I always liked working at Small's, even though it was a hard job during the first years. We worked two shows a night and on weekends, three. On Sunday night, our last show would finish about four o'clock in the morning, and, right after that finale, you didn't get off the stand; you'd start right off again into the Breakfast Dance. What would gripe me was Small's would be loaded with people—singers, dancers, musicians, and entertainers from all over the city—all the other places were closed so they knew this place was open, it was a meeting place for all of them. The place would be full of smoke, everyone had a glass in their hand, some people were dancing, some were not, but there was you trying to play and at the same time shaking hands with a guy you hadn't seen in years. Someone would say, "If these fellows go home, we could go home," but they were going to stay there as long as they could just so they could hear the music. During those days, Thomas E. Dewey became Special Prosecutor for New York, he was instrumental in getting a law passed that the bars should have a definite time to close up. Until then they had no definite closing time, we just worked until the last customer left. So after the law was passed, the bars had to have a special closing hour. It was set at four o'clock in the morning. They couldn't sell any more whiskey and, as they were not making any more business, it made no sense to stay open, burning up lights, paying salaries for waiters, bartenders and musicians. That's one thing I was thankful to Dewey for—he made it possible for us to have a special closing hour.

Billy Hicks was only in Small's for about six weeks. I don't remember who came in behind him. After that I played gigs here and there. Later I went up to Saratoga with Ben Smith, that was later in the same summer. We worked what they called the "racing season." It lasts about six weeks in Saratoga, and a lot of the nightclubs there would have bands and a show catering to the people who came to play the races. They'd do a lot of good business, because whoever won at the races that day would be at the nightclubs that night. Those who did not win wouldn't be there, but there was always enough winning and each of the little clubs was vying for business, and each of them used to get some of it.

At the beginning of the following year [1939], I went to work with Edgar Hayes; he needed an alto player, so I joined him on first alto. The personnel used to change quite a bit. Lem Johnson was his favorite tenor player at that time. Also, Al Gibson—a little short guy—the last big band I think he played in was Cab Calloway's, he was a very nice tenor player. I can't remember who the other alto player was; I think it was Tapley Lewis. Clyde Bernhardt was on trombone, and Joe Keyes was one of the trumpets. That was when I found out how good a trumpet player Joe Keyes was. He was such a powerful guy, he used to stick a mute in his trumpet and play louder than the guys who were playing open bell, if he wanted to. He had technique, he really had command of his instrument; you'd never figure it when you saw the guy and got to know him. He'd come to work with a bottle, it was for his own personal use. You or I would go to the bar for a drink, but that bottle was for him. That's why I couldn't figure out how much trumpet is this guy going to play. He was on the spot, just like that, for anything that came up in the show. He didn't miss any cues. If there was a rehearsal, the brass wasn't held up on his account. He used to play his part and look around and say, "O.K. kids, let's get with it," and anytime there was something wrong, it wasn't him, he was making it. I was only with Edgar Hayes a couple of months.

Eddie Barefield was getting a band together to go into the Savoy (the Savoy was one of the jobs you figured if you could make a hit, you stayed; if you were just so-so, you stayed a little while and they'd get somebody else). I figured Eddie was going to have a pretty good band, and I considered that a better prospect than a spasmodic weekend gig with Edgar Hayes. Edgar didn't have a steady job, just the occasional one-night stand at the Savoy. Edgar had a big band, but it was more suitable for going out on the road. I worked with Eddie Barefield for over six weeks. We had Freddie Williams playing tenor, Larry Belton and I were on altos. Eddie being the leader played with the section and also took the solos. On some numbers, though, he didn't play; he just waited for his solos to come up. While working at the Savoy, I went into the recording studios again [March 1941] to make a session with Billie Holiday. Originally Eddie Barefield, Lester Young, and Benny Carter were supposed to have been the saxophones on that date, but due to a disagreement Benny Carter cancelled his part of the date. Well, Eddie, being on the date, needed another alto right away, and, as I was working every night with him, he switched me into Benny's place. I didn't have any solos. I was playing third alto, and Eddie played the first parts. I was with Eddie at the Savoy from March 11, 1941, until April 12, 1941.

From May until July of 1941, I worked with Chris Columbus at the Elks Rendezvous; then I spent nearly the whole of August at the Speedway Gardens with Ollie Shepard. Later in the same year, I also started to make several recording sessions with Buddy Johnson; on some of them I played alto, some of them I played baritone, and one or two I made the arrangements for. The arrangement of "Toodle-Oodle-OO" [Decca 8599] is mine, and I also take the alto solo on "My Lonely Cabin" [Decca 8640]. We had different guys playing on these sessions; Tab Smith played alto on some of the dates, Billy Bowen (he started singing with the Ink Spots) played alto. Bowen used to do a lot of work with Buddy, because Buddy didn't have a large band then, he often used to play jobs as a single or just with a rhythm section. Then he would get some men together for a recording date, that was how he used me. I never worked with him on any other jobs, only those few recordings.

After working up at the Savoy with Eddie Barefield, he didn't have any other work, so we all scattered. Just before Christmas, I went into Small's again, this time with Earl Bostic, who had already been playing there a long time. One of his saxophone players left or had got into an argument, had been fired, and I replaced him. Earl had some arrangements where in the ensemble to get a heavier ensemble it was more profitable to switch to a baritone and get a heavier chord, according to the way you voice it. Earl was a good arranger, so he would voice it so that I could play the alto when three saxophones were playing, then during the introductions or interludes where you want to be heavy, then he had me switch to baritone. I was lousy as a baritone player *then*, because I had a Martin baritone, but I had a beat up mouthpiece that I never could get any sense out of. When we came out of there, Earl Bostic was trying to get work, but he didn't have anything definite. Later he cut down to a small band and recorded and made it really big. He played so marvellous, he was fabulous.

Lester Boone had a job out at Flushing. He was getting ready to leave it to go into another job, and he asked me if I wanted it. I had more work from saxophone players than I did from anybody. I could always get work with saxophone players or they'd call me if they had more than one job. Frank Powell, for instance, used to give me a whole lot of gigs. Anyway, I went out to Flushing in place of Lester Boone; it was just a small three-piece job, piano, drums and sax, just a short time, but then it was going into the war years.

Lots of the bands were being broken up by the military—the army wants you, so you go. It was during my spell with Earl Bostic at Small's that I started thinking and talking to other guys about night school, where you could go and learn a trade besides just playing music. They needed so many people in those factories, ammunition plants, shipyards and mechanical places, because their own employees were being drafted as well, so they would pay you to learn even if you didn't know the trade. Providing you were willing to start at the bottom and work your way up, they'd take you on. So I went to night school, two or three nights a week. I was still playing at Small's (it was a couple of blocks away from the school), and the teacher used to laugh at me and say, "Mr. Johnakins, you come in here, a mechanic's shop with a tuxedo, what's the idea?," because I'd go straight from school to Small's. After finishing night school, I decided to go and look for a job, and I started work in a shipyard on defense work. I worked three years on this job, sometimes in cold and miserable conditions; I didn't have to go into the service. During those days, I played weekend gigs with bass player Cass Carr. Walter Johnson, the drummer, was also in that band, as was Johnny Russell, who used to play tenor with Willie Bryant, and Jacques Butler. We had a pretty nice band. At least, it let me see my horn once or twice a week.

When the war was over, I was way behind musically. I needed a whole lot of practice. Everyone was offering me jobs, but they wanted me to go out of town on various U.S. touring service camp trips all over the world, but I stayed home so that I could practice and get back to my instrument. I started to work with some of the Latin bands. Mario Bauza, who had played trumpet with Chick Webb, and his brother-in-law, Machito, had a band, and right after the war they had to make some replacements. They were getting ready to go to Miami, but their regular baritone player couldn't make it, so they tried out a couple of saxophone players including myself, and they settled on me to join them. Then, I had an alto and a baritone sax, and Freddie Skerritt, who had come back from the service, was also playing alto and baritone with the band. We had an arrangement whereby I would play baritone, and he would play third alto parts, or, if he was playing baritone, I'd be playing third alto parts. After a while they switched all the baritone parts into my book and gave Freddie Skerritt all the alto parts. Since then I've played baritone exclusively, and very seldom have I touched any other instrument. I have used different mouthpieces, and now I have one that gives me good results and all I do is play baritone. Freddie Skerritt and I worked together with Machito for about fifteen years, before Freddie finally quit. I'm still working with Machito, and last November, 1975, I completed thirty years with the same band. I would imagine if there were no bandstands or bands, I wouldn't be here today.

Leslie Johnakins is a good musician. Anytime a musician played in the bands that he has played in, he has to be a good musician. And he acts like a gentleman, on and off the jobs that he plays on. When any musician played in the Edgar Hayes Orchestra, he had to be a good reading and playing musician, because that band had the hardest book that I have ever played. None of the bands that I have played in have had the hard music to play like Edgar Hayes had in his band. So when you read about any musician playing in the Edgar Hayes Orchestra you can bet your last dollar, that the musician is a good reading and playing musician. I will tell you now and forever that Leslie Johnakins is a good musician. He has played with some of the best in New York City.

—Clyde Bernhardt, August 1976

I never played in any jazz bands with Leslie Johnakins, but we worked together for years with Machito. Les is a good soloist, many times when we were playing clubs, if the customers wanted a little change, they would call on him to play a few pop tunes, and he would always be ready.

—Freddie Skerritt, August 1976

Roger Boyd

My name is Roger Boyd and I was born in Frederick, Maryland, just outside Washington, on August 29, 1903. Around the age of fifteen, a gentleman by the name of George Bell, who owned a small tailor's shop took about fifteen or twenty of us boys off the street and took us to his house. There he taught us to read notes on the blackboard, and soon we were reading music pretty good. One day, he picked up a newspaper and saw that a Catholic priest had about thirty horns to sell, so he wrote to the priest and made a deal with him. We begged for money on the street and eventually collected enough together. The priest shipped the horns to us intact, every instrument was in first-class condition. After just about three months, we hit the street with our first march. We also formed a small band and played for picnics and dances.

Around 1922, I moved to Washington and lived with my elder sister and her brother-in-law, Arthur Stewart. He worked for the Commerce Department of the government during the day but was a drummer in the theater at night. He arranged for me to attend a private music teacher for the saxophone, and it was then that I advanced fast. Later I took a correspondence course for modern harmony which trained my ear; I couldn't get a teacher to show me the correct way, so that was how I learned the major and minor chords.

There was an old man, who played violin and used to get quite a few society gigs, whom I joined. Sometimes we were just violin and alto saxophone, other times we would add a piano. I played the saxophone and would transpose the violin part. I would take the lead, and he would play the second part. He used to cry if he couldn't get me.

By the middle of 1924, I was going to Howard University in

Washington and was studying clarinet. My teacher's name was
Bert Maurice; he was a second clarinet in the United States Marine Band. I had been playing the soprano saxophone and the
clarinet, but when I was playing the clarinet I was making it
sound like a soprano saxophone. When my teacher heard me, he
almost jumped out of the window; you see, I didn't know the
real clarinet tone. I was mostly using the B-flat soprano saxophone, and he told me that I should leave the soprano at home
and play nothing but the whole tone on the clarinet until I had
that clarinet tone. It worked, and eventually I got the tone and
became fairly good.

While I was at Howard University, I also played at night in a
Chinese restaurant called Hong Kong Lo; it was frequented
mostly by sailors and soldiers. We were just a three-piece outfit.
I played the saxophones, Fred Slade was on piano, and Lawrence
Taylor was on drums. During the day, Lawrence Taylor worked
at the Capitol as a barber—all the barbers there were Black. We
played at the restaurant for three hours a night from nine o'clock
to twelve o'clock, every night of the week. Altogether, I played
there for three years. While I lived in Washington, I also had nine
music students of my own.

Around 1928, I went out to St. Joseph, Missouri, with a drummer by the name of Junior Powell. He was originally from Kansas
City, and he had been in contact with Jesse Stone. Jesse said that
he had a good writer, and he invited us out to join him. We paid
our own fares, but we found that just before we had arrived Jesse
Stone's band had been involved in an automobile accident. The
car in which they had been riding and the band's instruments
were smashed, and some of the band were hurt. We were stranded with them there.

It was a bad time as I had spent all of my money. At one stage,
I was standing on a corner completely broke; I had a gold pocket-
watch, clarinet, soprano, baritone, and alto saxophones, but I was
too proud to go into the pawn shop on Board Street to ask the
man to give me five dollars. Then along came this trombonist,
Eddie Durham. He had come into town with the Blue Devils from
Oklahoma, and he bought me a dinner. He really broke my fast
in Kansas City.

Jesse Stone's band had no booking agent, so we just fooled
around in St. Joseph and Kansas City. I played first saxophone in

that band, Booker Pittman played third sax and was featured soloist, Budd Johnson was on tenor, and Keg Johnson on trombone. Keg and Budd had only just come up from Texas, and I used to room with Keg. Eventually, I left Jesse Stone in Kansas City. Later, I had a job outside the city limits, just a three-piece group playing a club. I stayed there about five months and after that I went back to Washington.

Back in Washington I was just gigging around. Then one day, "Doc" Perry, who knew me, invited me to join a pit band under his leadership for a five-week tour with Duke Ellington's big show. We, in the pit band, played just the first half of the show, and Duke led his orchestra for the second half of the show. We played the Pearl Theater in Philadelphia and the Howard Theater in Washington.

Sometime after this show, I went along to the Howard Theater to hear Blanche Calloway's Orchestra. In the orchestra, I recognized Booker Pittman. He told me that their first alto player, Leroy Hardy, was leaving, and I was invited to join them. Ben Webster was there; later he left and was replaced by, I think, Charlie Frazier. Booker Pittman left and went to South America; he was replaced by Ernest Purce.

As time went by, I had a little act on stage with Blanche. It was called "How Am I Doing? Hey! Hey!" Blanche would sing eight bars, then I repeated what she had sung. It was very popular.

The first time I played at the Apollo Theater with Blanche, it was the first time that I had been backstage mixing with all the chorus girls and everything. They all knew I was green. Somebody asked me to go over to the Alhambra Theater and ask the stage manager to give me the curtain key. Well, when I got there and found the stage manager and asked him for it, he directed me to go to another theater. It was only when I was outside that it hit me that somebody was having a big laugh at my expense; I woke up then. They must have had a good laugh, I did later. The "curtain key" is one of the biggest backstage jokes that they can play on you.

I was with Blanche's band for three-and-a-half years and during that time we went out on the road with Jack Dempsey. Now that was a band where you begged for a layoff; we played theaters, dance halls, and tobacco warehouses. The small dance halls were just not big enough to hold the number of people that used to want to see us—our box office was pretty close to Cab Callo-way's outfit in popularity—so they would put us on in those to-bacco warehouses. Those floors in there were so smooth, and they could hold large crowds of people. While I was with Blanche, we played the whole RKO Circuit three times.

After I left her, Joe Garland and a couple of other guys were going around and forming the Edgar Hayes Orchestra, and I was invited to join them. Clarinet, alto, and baritone saxophones were my set-up in the Hayes Orchestra. I had lost my soprano saxo-phone somewhere along the way. I went on Edgar's European tour and, you know, if that band had been able to find a good manager, we would have gone far. A small clique in the band caused trouble, but it didn't break up the band. I left Edgar Hayes in 1939.

Following this, I spent a short period as first sax for Hazel Scott's Orchestra. We were about ten pieces, including Bernard Flood on trumpet. Hazel had come up as a soloist and was well-known as an entertaining piano player. She was just a kid, while we were pretty seasoned musicians.

During 1941 I played for USO shows with Eubie Blake. Later I returned to Washington and played at the Crystal Cavern for three-and-a-half years with Leven "Pops" Hill, bass and leader. I handled the band and paid them off.

I came back to New York City and used to gig around. I worked with Charlie Skeets at the Majestic Ballroom on the corner of 50th and Broadway; this was a dime-a-dance hall. I was on Skeet's payroll for six months and, when he left, I took over leadership of the band. I was there for about eleven months. I also later played with Cass Carr.

Eventually, in the early fifties, I had to give up playing due to ill health. I was never much of what you'd call a blues type of saxophonist, I just played straight, although I liked making varia-tions. I always played first alto.

Harvey Davis

My name is Harvard "Harvey" Davis, I was born in New York City on July 3, 1917. All of my schooling—elementary, junior high, and high school, and a year-and-a-half at Juilliard—was spent in New York City. I studied with Professor Harry Prampin, and in my classes there was a little trumpet player, Bobby Moore. He was very much ahead of me and very advanced. I started late on trumpet, and Bobby had been playing drums and trumpet and already he was almost like a professional then. He later joined up with Count Basie's Band.

After Professor Prampin, I went to the Martin-Smith Conservatory of Music in New York and studied for a while until I could get myself together and be good enough on the trumpet to have an audition for Professor Hulbert Finlay. He was in charge of a military band, and I rehearsed with them and went to conventions with them as well. Altogether I studied under Professor Finlay for a few years and, during that time, I made friends with Jasper Vaz, another of his students.

I went on to Commerce, which on the surface would seem an unlikely place to go, but they, at that time, had the best music course of any high school in New York City. Sonny White and myself went there together. Throughout my career, some names will crop up quite often, and Sonny White is one of those; we were raised together. Sonny was very far advanced; he was writing and arranging when he was in elementary school.

My first professional job was in the summer of 1935, Sonny White was on piano, myself on trumpet, and Vernon Arab was the leader; he was a guitar player when I worked with him, but he later switched to string bass. We only had a trio. We were playing in an exclusive place in West Hampton. After this, I stayed with Vernon until the following summer. During that summer of 1936, we worked at Lake Huntington, we had "Peck" Austin on alto, Sonny White on piano, a fellow called "Frisco" on drums, Vernon on guitar, and myself on trumpet.

Between those summer jobs, Vernon would have a big band. We had a group of fellows that had just graduated from Borden-town Prep School in Bordentown, New Jersey; they included Charlie Shavers, Carl "Bama" Warwick, Al Cobbs, Sandy Watson, Red Callender, and "Happy" Mitchner. We worked for a little while—club-dating. It was a very nice association, and we had a ball.

When I came from Lake Huntington, I was offered a job right across from the Savoy Ballroom at a big place, the World Chop Suey; it was famous all over New York. People would go to the Savoy and the "Renny" [Renaissance] and would come there to eat. I stayed there for six months to earn my money to join the union.

I joined the union in March of 1937, and I was only in the union about two days when I had a phone call from Bobby Neal. I didn't know him, but I had been recommended. He had a twelve- or thirteen-piece band and needed a trumpet player. I went to the Lafayette rehearsal studios and auditioned for him, and he took me on. In a few days we were booked into the Gloria Palais on 86th Street on the East Side in Yorktown. It was a very big place. The band was very nice. In the brass section was a Buddy Lowe and one heck of a trumpet player, Johnny "Buggs" [Hamilton], we were three in that section. I don't know what went wrong, but after the first week, the union delegate came along there asking questions. After our second week, they pulled us out; it seemed that someone in the band had gone to the union to tell them that we were not getting scale. You can see how I felt, having just joined the union and looking in now for a world of trouble. Well, we went down to the union, and they did have a case. It seemed that Bobby Neal had taken the job under scale. Bobby was a very small short person and played sousaphone, part of his act was to actually go through the sousaphone, coils and all, he was that small. I didn't know it, but he was famous for not paying what you were supposed to get. Well, I could not get far enough away from him; that was the end of me and Bobby Neal.

My luck seemed to be pretty fair. I was around the Rhythm Club, where we made contacts for gigs and could get phone calls. A friend of mine told me that Lips Page had formed a band and was looking for a trumpet player, so why didn't I go by and introduce myself and have a talk with him. The Rhythm Club was on 132nd Street, and Lips was rehearsing on 131st Street at the Lafayette Hall, so I went on around and had a talk with him. He told me to get my horn and come back the following day and give it a little try.

Well, I came back the next day, sat in, and walked into a hornet's nest. They had a hell of a trumpet player, Bob Shoffner, and Happy Caldwell was in the band as well. I didn't know any of the fellows then; I was only nineteen. Anyway, this proved to be one terrific association. Lips liked me, and I stayed with him and the work went down very nice. Lips never kept his band together all the time because he was often blowing with someone else. Either before or after Artie Shaw, he was always coming and going. Lips had key men, and, as it turned out, I became one of them. Anytime he had any work, he formed his band and I would be one of its members. Shoffner and Wheeler were members of the band that first time, but, when next Lips called me, neither one was there, but I met another man who was just too terrific, Joe Keyes, and another fellow who had been with Count Basie, Carl "Tatti" Smith, so that made up the brass section. Donald Coles was on trombone and, if I am not mistaken, Vic Dickenson was there. He was in and out, he was one of the regulars. Floyd "Horsecollar" Williams and Joe Evans on altos were there throughout the years, Ike Quebec on tenor, Jack "The Bear" Parker and "Jumpin' " George on drums (they called him "Jumpin' " George because he would actually jump up and down while he was playing, but he kept beautiful time; he later worked with Arnett Cobb and Billy Hicks—a very good drummer). Dan Minor and Mike Hedley were other regulars in Lips's band. These were the guys who would end up playing the engagements. A lot of times, he would get anyone from the Rhythm Club for a rehearsal, but, when the work came in, his key men were always there.

Over the years, Lips and I became very good friends. After the first few times, he'd call me Buddy. Our families became fairly close; it was a good association. I recall on one of Lips's engagements at the Apollo Theater; we were booked in with Miss Avis

Andrews [November 1942], and I used to conduct the show before Lips would come on for his main numbers. I don't know what happened to Miss Andrews's conductor, but he was not there and Lips asked me to conduct for her. It was a really beautiful experience; she was more or less a semiclassical singer and had very intricate music which had to be directed. It went down very nice.

Back, near the end of 1938, I had a phone call from Wheeler, the trumpet player who I had worked first with in Lips's Band. He asked me to come by the Apollo rehearsal studio, he wanted to introduce me to a gentleman by the name of Jack Carter, who had been in Japan for some years and was back in New York, had just formed a band, and needed a trumpet player. Well, this band was something, they were more or less semiclassic with three violins. Wheeler, "Ham" Davis, and myself were in the trumpet section, Manzie Johnson on drums. Now Bill Robinson really was not known for using Black musicians or bands, but he was going to give this one a try, and it was a terrific band. We went on a tour of the RKO circuit. Bill had a show which included the Three Peppers, Conway and Parkes, Irene Court, and Mabel Scott. This tour was something; we were playing very big RKO theatres and, with the small show that we had, even the band members had dressing rooms to themselves. Playing Bill Robinson's music was really a treat, because you were under quite a bit of pressure. He was very hard to please. The trumpets played with cup-mutes jammed into their bells all of the time. Everything would go down good, we thought it was really beautiful. But Bill was going to find some faults somewhere, and usually it was the violin players, who were old professionals. He was making $500 per night, and he would go out to the box office every night and collect his money. That is how he wanted it. He loved to gamble, so he needed that money. Funny thing, he was playing against fellows in the band who didn't have much money. He had all the money to lose, so he was a good set up for us.

After the tour was over, Jack Carter disbanded the band and went into the bar and restaurant business with two of his brothers. I stayed in contact with him for years after that, and I used to stop by his place and talk with him.

During the spring of 1939, I started club-dating and gigging around the city, just so that I could stay in town for a while. On one of my gigs, I met a bass player named Lee Norman. He seemed to like my blowing and said that he was in the process of forming a band. He had a very good and friendly connection with Charlie Buchanan (the man who used to run the Savoy Ballroom). Lee Norman had been a former member of Willie Bryant's Band, and they had also been very good friends. In fact when Willie left for the coast, he left his music with Lee. Well, true to his word, after about a week or two, I received a call to come up to the Savoy, where they were rehearsing. Lee had an eight piece band and they had something in mind for him. They were getting ready to open the Savoy out at the 1939 World's Fair that summer, and it looked like Lee had an inside on getting the job there. We rehearsed, and we had some beautiful fellows in that band. Jasper Vaz and myself were the two trumpets, Jimmy Johnson and Frank Powell on altos, Sidney Grant on tenor, Lee was on bass, Herbert "Syrup" Goodwin (we called him "Syr") was the piano player, and Joe Johnson was our drummer. As luck would have it, we did get the job at that 1939 World's Fair.

We used to do twenty shows a day, and then another band led by Fess Williams would come on and relieve us on the night shift, and they also would do around twenty shows. After each show they would empty the place and a whole new group of patrons would come in. Sometimes we would do more than twenty shows, it would depend on how large the crowds were. Up at the Savoy, there was a fellow, "Whitey" [Herbert White] he had the "Lindyhoppers," they were the ones who were supposed to have invented the dance. Those dancers were very popular up there and had a great deal to do with the popularity of the Savoy. Well, the show was made up of Whitey's dancers, who demonstrated the evolution of dance: starting in Africa playing drums, they worked up through ragtime, the cakewalk, the black bottom, any kind of dance you could think of. But coming nearly to the end of their dance was the Mutiny Swing, and those kids really did some lindyhopping, throwing and sliding those girls and fellows like I had never seen in all of my life. We had a stage built so that when the fellows threw out those girls, it looked as if they were really coming into the audience; it was really thrilling, fast and furious. What we did, that was Jasper and myself, I would set those rhythms using the derby. Then the reeds would take the middle of each chorus, and we would never let down. We really worked, but we were young and didn't pay it any attention; it worked out nice.

After the summer, when we finished, they booked us into the Savoy on Lenox Avenue. We added a trumpet player, Nelson Bryant. He had very good chops and a heck of a range. A big hefty cat, he was a very good friend of mine and lived in my block. While we were up there, we played Willie Bryant's book, which was written for four trumpets, three trombones, and five saxes, but we played it. We played against Chick Webb's Band, Erskine Hawkins, Earl Hines, any of the bands that were booked, we did the same job that the Savoy Sultans did some years before us. We worked there and during that fall, we had a chance of making a movie with Henry Armstrong, the fighter (at the time he was holding three titles). He used to like to sing, and he was a musician to a certain degree in that he liked to write songs. Working with him, "Syrup" Goodwin and myself arranged most of the music. The movie was called "Keep Punching" and it was very good; it had a story line and everything. They used our band to play the background music for all of the picture in fact, and we were seen in the night-club scenes. Edna Mae Harris, Willie Bryant, and Buddy Bowser also appeared in those scenes. A nine-piece band is not that easy to book. After the picture we made a few club dates, but nothing really happened, so it looked like I was on the prowl again.

Lips Page called me and said that he had some dates in the New England territory starting in Boston at the Tic Toc for a week. He had most of the fellows he had used previously, plus he had Rudy Traylor, a beautiful drummer and a heck of an arranger, and Earl Hardy on trombone. We made that tour, came back to the Apollo, then went to the Pearl in Philadelphia, the Royal in Baltimore, and the Howard in Washington. Usually from there you used to jump off on a series of one-nighters in the South, but we finished off in Washington and that was it. That took me just about going into 1940.

The next association I made was very nice, and it had a great deal to do in determining which way and what I was going to do with my musical career. A gentleman who lived directly opposite me, Leon "Bossman" Gross, the saxophone player, had a houseband down at a place called the Danceland on 125th Street. They catered for big social clubs, organizations, and fraternities who would book the place on a one-night basis to give their dances. The people who ran the place used to give "Bossman" his dates for the whole month; he would get between twenty-two and twenty-six days out of thirty days. In those days, you didn't just play club dates on weekends, that place was booked almost every night in the week. Those who booked in the first part of the week had a little break on the price and as we were the house-band, we could afford to work these dates we were given for a dollar or two less than them bringing in a band for a one-shot deal.

"Bossman" had a fine band. He had Clarence Grimes on alto and clarinet, "Bossman" played alto, "Son" Fredericks on tenor (a beautiful tone, could play anything, he had a beautiful ear), George Foster (who later was with Jonah Jones) was on drums, Arthur Bowie on piano, and myself on trumpet. I had to pay some dues because "Bossman" liked to read a lot, and he made it his business to buy every number that came out. I think that we were about the first band that was playing "Holiday for Strings" and "Boy Meets Horn." He had me back there playing all this stuff by myself. Well, I was in the groove, I was sharp and up to it.

I worked with "Bossman" throughout 1940. During the summer, the Danceland closed down and so we worked at Jackie's Cotton Club in Asbury Park. We came right back into the Danceland in September and worked through again to the following summer when we again returned to Jackie's Cotton Club. In September of 1941, when we came back, the Danceland was under new management and was on another policy; they didn't require a house-band, because they were not getting the bookings for the first part of the week like they used to get. They knew that they could not hold a good band, and the clubs would book the hall and bring their own music in.

In October 1941, I recorded with the pianist and vocalist Harold Boyce. I played muted trumpet, Sidney Grant was on tenor, Gladstone Thomas on bass, and I think Joe Johnson was on drums. All of the titles we recorded were written by Harold Boyce.

I stayed in touch with "Bossman," he got quite a few club dates. When the fellows in Duke's and Cab's bands, like Cootie Williams, Rex Stewart, and Johnny Hodges were on the road, they would send "Bossman" a card telling him that they would be in town shortly and to get them some gigs. He loved to have the big shots on a gig with him.

At the time, "Bossman" lived across from me on 139th Street.

It was better known as Strivers' Row, and today it is on the land-mark status. They called it Strivers' Row because the properties were all brownstones owned by professional people, like doctors and lawyers, people who could afford them. They had a lot of people who roomed in those houses. My parents lived in 223. We were strictly family; I had the top floor, and my brother and grandmother also lived in the house. We usually had one or two rooms that we would rent out: Ted Giles, the bass player, stayed with us for a while; Tommy Lindsay, the trumpet player and his wife, and Vernon Arab stayed with us for a while as well. Eddie Williams, a beautiful clarinetist and saxophonist, he and his wife stayed with us, and his daughter was raised there. Directly across from there, "Bossman" lived, that house (228) was owned by Fletcher and Lee Henderson, next door (226) lived Chick Webb, Taft Jordan, and Bob Carroll, the tenor saxophonist. Up from them, Dizzy Gillespie and his wife lived. Down the block was where trumpet player Nelson Bryant lived, and a little further down was Al Casey. Sammy Lowe was a couple of doors down, and little Freddie Webster was down there too—that finished that side of the street. Crossing over and coming up, you had Arthur Bowie, then in between was myself, then Doc Lee and Les Carr and Garvin Bushell lived next door to them. In the mornings when we awoke around eleven or twelve o'clock, we would all be getting up and going over to the Rhythm Club, the whole gang. Around the corner lived Tommy Stevenson, while down the block was Paul Webster. Billy Hicks was also in that block, as was Henry Hicks of the MBRB. All in between lived those doctors and owners of those homes. It was a beautiful block.

At the Rhythm Club, one day, I was introduced to Clyde Bern-hardt, the trombonist, and it would seem after that he was asking questions about me. Eventually, I had a phone call from him and he asked me if I could make a rehearsal at the YMCA on 135th Street, as he would like me to meet Edgar Hayes. I went around and sat in at the rehearsal. At that time, E.V. Perry, Tommy Lind-say, and Bobby Williams were playing trumpets. R.H. Horton and Clyde Bernhardt were there, but I didn't know any of the other fellows. Anyway, everything seemed to work out all right with Edgar, and we made some nice dates up in the New England territory. Maxine Sullivan was going with us. Later on, there were changes made in the band, but I was still sitting there. Joe Keyes came in on trumpet, and different other guys came in and out.

After club-dating and making some trips, Edgar was staying close to New York. We played the Apollo and also hit the Savoy for a little time, we were making theater dates, and at that time Don Byas was playing tenor with us. Edgar Hayes was known for his playing on "Stardust," but he started to relinquish some of it to Don Byas, who would come out on stage and play so much "Stardust" that Edgar Hayes had to give it to him. I remember us being on the same bill as Stuff Smith, Jonah Jones, Clyde Hart, and that bunch; they were one of the featured attractions, and Savannah Churchill was also on the bill.

I will tell you a funny thing that happened when we played the Howard Theater in Washington. Tommy Lindsay and myself had this private house, where we had rented rooms right across the street from the Howard. In some kind of way, we started gambling with some fellows as we didn't start in the Howard until the next day. When we walked in there, we were busted, and we had to work all that week. We drew some money, but it was a mess, I'm telling you.

When we came back into New York from Washington, Edgar Hayes received some beautiful news. The people from Roseland Ballroom—it was located on Broadway then just about 50th and 51st—called him down. They made arrangements for him to be the house band there for a while. When we went in there, we had a singer who I had not heard of before. Her name was Pearl Bailey and she could sing then—a beautiful voice. She only worked with us for one or two nights as she had other work pending, but everybody was asking about her, that was the impression she had made. I think that they were just getting ready to hit on her for some good things, but we were to stay down there for months. We played mostly dance music and hardly ever went into our regular arrangements. We played opposite Johnny Long, Harry James, all of the big bands. We had to make the matinees and play those rhumbas and tangos, but it was a darn good job. Tommy Lindsay, Bobby Williams, and myself were on trumpets, Clyde Bernhardt on trombone, Lem Johnson on tenor saxophone, and Arthur Herbert was on drums; he was the fellow that really started that shuffle rhythm on drums.

Just as we were about to finish our engagement at the Roseland Ballroom, Edgar Hayes was given a nice proposition by Don Redman. At that particular time, Don didn't have his big band, but he had an office on Broadway, where he concentrated more on writing and arranging. He had been approached by his managers to get a band together, so what he did, he took Edgar Hayes's Band and fronted it himself. We went down to West Virginia, all around those Blue Ridge Mountains. We were double-dating with Louis Armstrong and his Big Band and Velma Middleton. We had our own big bus, and Louis and his band had their bus. We were playing all those big tobacco warehouses, big crowds everywhere. Now, there was some beautiful music, for one thing we were playing two books, Don Redman's and Edgar Hayes's, so it was really interesting. Louis had his band and everyone was wailing. That was one of the last long tours that I did. We were out for quite a few months; we hardly ever checked into a hotel; we jumped as these were strictly one-nighters.

After coming off the road, I had been back in the city a while (this would have been in the early part of 1942 I think). Ella Fitzgerald was trying to keep the Chick Webb Band together. Eddie Barefield was the musical director and sometime before this I had rehearsed with Eddie in a seven- or eight-piece band that he was trying to get together, but it never really got off the ground, but it introduced me to Eddie. Anyway, I had a call from Eddie, and he wanted me to join Ella's band, I cannot remember now whose place I took, but in the brass section was Francis Williams, Joe Jordon, Taft Jordan, and myself. We made some college dates up around New England, but Moe Gale and others had been putting pressure on Ella to give the band up, and eventually she could not hold out any longer. She disbanded and gave us all our notices. It was a lovely experience. The lady liked to sing, she'd play a little piano "comping," I just got in on the tail-end, too bad that it did not last long.

Around this time, Pete Brown, the alto saxophonist, called me, I didn't know him, but somebody had told him about me. He had a job down in the Village on the West Side around Sheridan Square at a club called "The Place." It was near Cafe Society, and it was a jumping place. I was in for a surprise, as I had never heard Pete Brown play and here was this heavy set fellow who always stood up, threw one foot out and blew. We had "Pazuza" Simon on tenor saxophone, Marlowe Morris on piano, a very nice bass player, John Drummond, and Joe Johnson on drums. The band swung. We did so well down there, worked about eight or ten weeks, then we were booked into the Onyx Club on 52nd Street and we took the same band up there. Leo Watson, the scat singer, was on the same bill.

When I had finished there, I had a call from Benny Carter, who was working at Kelly's Stable. Benny had approached me before for his big band, but at that time I was always working with Edgar Hayes and, as Edgar and I had a good understanding, I didn't want to leave. I made one or two rehearsals up at the Savoy with Benny, but then Benny was not getting much work. Anyway I went in with Benny Carter and replaced Dizzy Gillespie. Benny and I got along beautifully; we knew each other, and he had been wanting me to play with him. I played my horn, and he played his trumpet and alto saxophone, but he concentrated more on his saxophone and let me blow. It went down nice and our relief at Kelly's Stable was Nat "King" Cole and his Trio—Joe Comfort on bass and Oscar Moore on guitar—at that particular time Nat was doing very little singing.

After the Kelly's Stable engagement had finished, I received a call from Buddy Johnson. He was going into The Place and needed a trumpet player, and the management had recommended me to him. That was the first time I had any dealings with him, later I was to play in his big band at the Apollo, and we became pretty good friends. You knew the man had some talent because he was writing good songs, and most of the things we were playing were his originals. At The Place, we had five pieces, he did some singing, and we went over nice.

It seemed as though I had made a hit with the management down there, because shortly after we left, I had a call from a guy called "Teacho" who was going into "The Place" with a five-piece group. There seemed to have been some dissatisfaction in the band, and the management had told him to get in touch with me. At the time he was changing the men in his band, so I recommended Mike Hedley, who came in on tenor saxophone, I was on trumpet, Franklin Skeete on bass, Alfred Taylor on drums, and "Teacho" was on piano. We had a ball down there and stayed about four or five months. (Normally, they were used to changing every two or three weeks.) "Teacho" was a very good arranger and writer and also sang very nice.

At this particular time, my career took quite a decided change, as Leon "Bossman" Gross mentioned to me that Murrain's Club on Seventh Avenue and 132nd Street needed a band for one week. In those days, you would work six weeks, and the regular band would get a week off with pay. At that period, Taft Jordan and Dick Vance had a seven-piece band there, so we went in and played the odd week and they liked us. In the meantime "Boss-man" had a call from Small's Paradise who were looking for a band for the one week that their own band had off (I cannot remember who was playing there at the time). Well, we made the week at Small's. Murrain's were making a change in their band, and I was invited to bring my band in on a steady engagement. While we were down at Murrain's, Ed Small wanted us to come into his place.

Small's was jumping. It was a beautiful place and was a little more prestigious than Murrain's, so we put in our notice and went into Small's. In my band, at that time, Cliff Bryant and I were playing trumpets, Curby Alexander was on alto saxophone, Butch Robinson on tenor saxophone, Clarence "Friday" Williams on piano (later on he was known as C.C. Williams and played organ), Harry Prather on bass, and Denzil Best on drums. Curby Alexander was a beautiful saxophonist; he had a great big tone, could read anything and was one hell of a musician. He was from Oklahoma; he stayed around New York and played with different bands. We became friends and worked together for a long time. This, by the way, was Denzil Best's first experience on playing drums, because at first he was a really nice trumpet player. He had a bout of ill-health and, after he recovered, we were able to get him some gigs on piano, then he switched to drums. The man was a natural musician, and what I am so sorry about is that people never really heard him blow trumpet. He could blow and sing.

Everyone was pleased with the band at Small's. We made the first six weeks, and then we had the week off with the relief band coming in for us (I think it was led by George Treadwell, who was later to be Sarah Vaughan's manager and husband). Upon my return, my tenor saxophone player had left, and I went over to the East Side and met Eddie Davis, he came in with us on Labor Day, 1943, and you knew the guy had something going for him. He later became Eddie "Lockjaw" Davis, but at that time we had a ball, because we were all friends.

It was coming towards the end of 1943, and I tried my best to get my band some bookings and steady jobs after I left Small's because they wanted me to cut the band down to five pieces. We were a seven-piece band, and I didn't want to let anyone go, but it was tough trying to get bookings for seven pieces. At that time, I could have had work for four or five pieces, and in fact I had a better chance with an eleven- or twelve-piece band. There was just nothing happening, so we decided just to ease off, but stay in contact in case I could get something.

Around this period, I played with Flo Petty's Orchestra making "soundies," we did about fifty-five recordings in three days, and George Wilson on trombone and Lester Fauntleroy on piano were with me doing them.

The Apollo Theatre was jumping then, and I started to get calls from the Apollo. I worked with Buddy Johnson's Big Band, started rehearsals with Al Sears, and we had a week there. Edgar Hayes went in there, and Lips Page called me and we went in there. Curby Alexander and I made about seven or eight of those weeks; most of them we made together, but I did about ten or twelve weeks in there altogether, spaced out, that run me into 1944. Out-of-town bands who needed a trumpet player would use me for the week. Both Curby and I were on a list at the Apollo, if anyone needed a trumpet or saxophone player, they would call on us. Sometimes, I would be sitting and playing one show and have to go downstairs to the Apollo rehearsal hall to rehearse for the next week.

While making my rounds and trying to get some engagements for my seven-piece band, I had left my name and address with a number of booking agents in the Roseland Building. One day, I had a call from one of these agents asking if I could cut down to five pieces as there was a place out in Brooklyn, the Jink's Club, where he could get me booked in. By that time, the fellows from my Small's Paradise band had been dispersing anyway, so Curby Alexander, a fellow who was introduced to me, Duke Parham on piano, Gladstone Thomas on bass, and Herman Bradley on drums went into Jink's Club and stayed there a while. Gladstone Thomas told me when he came in that he would only be temporary, as he worked with calypso bands and did a lot of calypso recordings. He was a very good bass player. Herman Bradley was a hell of a drummer and singer, a good professional man.

In the meantime, the same agent who had obtained us this job at Jink's contacted me again and told me that a place in the Village wanted me, and it would be double the salary we were making at Jink's. They didn't need five pieces, they only wanted four. If we wanted to bring in five pieces, we would just have to spread the money, but our money would look good with four pieces. Our bass player was hooked up into so many different things that he was glad to split. That then was the beginning in 1944, going to the Cinderella Club with Herman Bradley, Duke Parham, Curby Alexander, and myself. A job that was to last for me for more than ten years. It turned out to be one heck of a deal.

We went into a more or less regular routine; we had a show to play and had different acts coming in. We would have strippers down there, Radio City acts, they had the people they wanted for headliners, but we would have acts that would finish it. We would have to play their music; they were just in-between jobs. After we had been down there a couple of years, they wanted to put air-conditioning in, and I was told that they wanted us to lay off for a little while. They were going to put the air-conditioning in during the summer, as they could not keep operating without it in that place.

I had a call, they wanted me to work in the Swing Rendezvous, right down in the Village and I went along and worked there. While I was there, Ernie's, a very nice place about two doors away from the Cinderella Club, wanted me, so I decided to work there instead, as there was more money and a little more prestige. Ernie's was across the street from Eddie Condon's when Eddie had his place in the Village. We worked there for weeks through that summer, then all of a sudden, one Saturday night, one of the bosses from the Cinderella Club came in and invited me to have a drink. At the end of that night, I had my notice from Ernie's. When I asked Ernie if he didn't like the band, he just told me that I should not ask any questions; he didn't want any trouble. As I was leaving, I had to pass by the Cinderella Club in order to catch the subway to get home, and the other boss was out there, and he said "Hey, Harvey, we'll be in touch with you."

While we were working out our two week's notice at Ernie's, the grand opening notices were put up at the Cinderella and I saw Harvey Davis's Band on it. They hadn't asked me if I was coming back or not, I guess it was just understood that I was supposed to be in their band. When I passed by, they told me that they expected me to be in to rehearse the show, so they were not going to keep me at Ernie's; like the man said, he didn't want any trouble.

During our two week's notice work, Curby Alexander decided to accept an offer to go on a USO tour. He wanted to take advantage of it, as he wanted to travel and had been down at the Cinderella for a number of years. While looking around for a replacement, I found that Sonny White was available. He was working with Ben Webster, doing a couple of weeks here and there and then laying off. He and his wife talked it over, I had told them he had a job which would run into a year or maybe two, so he came in. I was also able to get Al Taylor, who I had known for years. We had worked two or three jobs in the Village together. He was a heck of a drummer. He played the drums, not loud, you just felt him. He, Denzil Best, and Harold Austin, they all played in that same way. Finally, I approached Mike Hedley, who was managing Sugar Ray Robinson's Bar on Seventh Avenue. He started with us but warned me to be on the lookout for a saxophonist, because he would not be able to work with us at night and manage Ray's place during the day.

Anyway we went back into the Cinderella Club. It started off nice and, as we had been there so long before, it was just as if we had never left the place. Sylvia Sims was one of the headliners down there at the time. Money seemed to be no object to the people who run the place; anyone who was available, they would get in.

John Hammond and his family used to stop by, once or twice a month. Joe Bushkin was related to him, I think, by marriage, and he would come down and play when John would come in. The first time I met Maynard Ferguson was when John brought him in to hear the band. He was a very gracious fine cat. We didn't know who he was as John had just brought him from Canada. He liked the band, but he didn't blow that night.

Most of the fellows used to come down and blow—Joe Keyes, Irving "Mouse" Randolph, Taft Jordan—they knew they could play. First time I met Don Goldie, he was a youngster and he started coming down there. He knew it was somewhere he could blow and I didn't mind him blowing. In fact, we would exchange eight-bar choruses and everything else, and Don became a regular down there.

Figure 11. Trumpeter Harvey Davis, 1947.

After we had been down there a while, I had to find a replacement for Mike Hedley, and I was introduced to Herbie Hall, who
had been recommended to me. I didn't know him, so I hired him
for one night and the fellows liked him. He was fine on clarinet,
alto, and tenor, that worked out good because a lot of the music
we had in there, if I had the first trumpet part and we had an alto,

well, we could play the music. Then when I had lead-sheets and all, Herbie would pick his tenor up and go on the second parts, so it worked out beautifully. He loved the band and the fellows liked him, so there was no problem at all.

Things were going down well, a very routine fashion, coming in and having a ball playing. Everything was working out good with the management, and the fellows were all pleased, with no changes in the band or anything. Well, in 1952, I had the urge just to get out and try a few more things. I didn't want to pull the band out, not from a job. These fellows had only been there a few years, but I had been there going on ten years, so I left the band with Herbie Hall in charge, left my music, left everything down there. I told the fellows to decide on who they wanted to get to replace me, and they settled on Bobby Johnson. After a while, I think, he made a change and went to the Savannah Club, and he was replaced by Bob Williams and different trumpet players. They worked about a year or so before the Cinderella Club started a change in their policy.

While making my rounds and trying to get some of my connections back, I run into an old friend of mine, Buddy Walker. Now Buddy had been a terrific basketball player in the New York college system. I had met him years ago, as a youngster, he was teaching music at the YMCA in Harlem. He taught little "Flip" Tate on trumpet, George Duvivier was playing violin then, as was Cal Manning, who later became a terrific tenor saxophonist, and quite a few other musicians.

Well, Buddy had a lot of fraternity work, and I started to work with him, club-dating and getting gigs. In fact, he would have two or three different groups working each weekend, and we worked the big places. I would always be with his big band, and if he had something small, I wound up being his main trumpet man. When he needed a big band, he would have Benny Harris, Archie Johnson, Al Killian, Nelson Bryant, just all the trumpet players around; he loved trumpets. He started using Taft Jordan, Bob Williams, and Buck Clayton. We had a little job at the Royal Manor, where he was the house band, so we played the club dates up there. Luther Henderson played piano with him for a while, and at one time Sonny White had played piano with him. On some dates he would have two saxophones, himself and Jackie Fields, and he would have four trumpets up there, Taft Jordan,

Bob Williams, Jimmie Harris, and myself—no trombones, he just liked trumpets. He did a lot for young musicians coming up in New York; he was a very nice person.

In the 1960s, it seemed just like the bottom fell out of the music scene in New York. If there were any club dates or gigs they were strictly on a Friday or Saturday. By then the Savoy had closed and the Apollo was featuring singing groups, although they had a very good house band led by Reuben Phillips, but there was no local big band. All the fellows who had been working together and forming the nucleus of Black New York musicians started to go on day jobs, so I saw my chance when I was approached about a job. A friend of mine recommended me to a fellow by the name of Fred Carrington. I was reluctant to take the job, but he told me to try it for a while. It was with the Equity Corporation, and I was hired as a floor receptionist. I ended up staying fifteen years, and I retired from there when they relocated in Hampton, New Hampshire. By then I had worked up to assistant traffic manager with Fred Carrington, and when he retired I became traffic manager.

During my years on that job, I continued club-dating, mainly with Happy Caldwell. Happy had just about all of the good work; we played all the good hotels, including the Waldorf Astoria. He used all the good fellows, including Manzie Johnson on drums, Bobby Cheeks and Bernard Flood on trumpets, Irving Taylor on alto, Mike Hedley on tenor, "Shorty" Haughton on trombone, Gene Moore on drums. He had good musicians and kept good bands.

I had a good connection out in Bayshore by the name of Ed Cornelious. He just about had Long Island sewn up. He had so much work that he was recruiting musicians from Manhattan like mad. He had around four or five jobs at the weekends out on the Island; he would appoint one of the fellows in the band to be leader. He had received his deposit for the band so when the leader was paid the fee, he would pay the other fellows off. Johnny Russell, the tenor player, was one of his main men out there, and Johnny and I would drive out together.

At the same time, I was keeping a list of between ten to eighteen musicians that I would use on jobs that I had. I was getting different gigs and going out of town to places like Philadelphia, Baltimore, and Washington with my own band. These were one-nighters that would pay very good. I kept good musicians with me; these included Robert Ashton, Conrad Fredericks, Harry Prather, and Al Casey.

I also worked a long time with Milt Larkins at the Celebrity Club, he had the house band there. He used some very good musicians. I worked with him as a single trumpet player, but Johnny Grimes, Eddie Preston, and Buck Clayton would work with him, as would Fletcher Smith on piano and Bill Graham on alto.

Actually, I was never out of work, and I have never really ever let my band go. I have my music, and periodically I keep writing and updating the music in order to keep it modern, so things musically have gone along very nicely for me.

Currently, I am supposed to be retired from my job, but I think I am working harder now than I have ever worked while I was playing music and holding down a day job. I am Secretary of the Friendly Fifty Club; Louis Armstrong was honorary member of the Club, he loved that Club. In fact, he came out of the hospital the August before he died. He said that he had to see his men, so Jack Bradley and an attendant from the hospital brought him to the Friendly Fifty picnic.

I am also Secretary of the Blue Notes. That is a small group of fellows from the Friendly Fifty. We have about fourteen members. We just got the club together following a benefit for Son Fredericks and decided to keep it going, and once a year we give a dance in June.

Now, I am still very much on the scene, as the spring and summer come in, I am starting to rehearse a six-piece band with myself and Mike Hedley on horns, Irving Taylor on alto, Jimmy Phipps on piano, Al Matthews on bass, and "Rip" Harewood on drums. We will start with six pieces and start working it up and see what I can add. I have a good idea of what I want to do. I have been doing some writing and I'm going to get Howard Johnson and Al Cobbs to do a little writing for me as well.

I think I have helped a lot of musicians during my musical career, and I have been very sincere in what I have done and am doing now.

Walter Bishop Sr.

The records will show that I was born Cyril George Bishop on January 9, 1905, at 6 Gold Street, Kingston, Jamaica, West Indies. My mother's name was Margie Anna Bishop (formerly Burke) and my father's name was Edward Bishop, and his occupation was an ice cream vendor.

When I went to public school, I took to drawing, like most kids, also writing poetry all the way up to the seventh grade. Towards the end of my public school days, my drawings and paintings were an extra source of income for me when my teacher, Mrs. Nora Morris, became my sponsor and had my paintings framed, and she personally sold them to every doctor and dentist around the city. The Inspector of Schools saw one of my paintings and was told that I had done it. He thought I showed a great deal of promise and suggested to my father that I should be sent to England to study further, but my father would not let me go as already my older brother, Harry, had been sent to New York, and he needed me to help with his accounts and could not afford to let me go.

My earliest musical experience was my father's brother, Uncle Ernest, a big game hunter who kept a violin in a cloth bag and hung it up out of reach by a peg in the wall. I used to stand up on a chair and could pick the strings through the cloth bag, for which I was reprimanded. Later, one day I popped out of my gate at home having heard the sound of a kid playing a tin penny whistle. I asked him to let me try it and after trying it, I offered my B.B. gun in exchange for his penny whistle, and he was agreeable. From then on I took to playing little tunes on my penny whistle and I was delighted with my trade. One day, my father heard me playing the penny whistle and bought me a wooden fife. And whenever company came to the house, I was called in to entertain them by playing my fife.

My older sister married and went to live and work with her husband in Cuba. About a year later, they both returned, and she found me playing a home-made violin, constructed from a cigar box made by a local kid with heavy threads for strings and lighter threads for a bow. She was so delighted that she took me to the local music store, Winkler's, on King Street and bought me a brand new violin. I was twelve years old at the time, and I fiddled away without the benefit of any lessons. Just around that time, during the summer holidays, I went to spend some time with my grandmother who lived in Old Harbor in the country. My cousin, Elisser Blair, was the organist in the local church and was rehearsing to play a concert there. I joined her at rehearsals with my violin, and she decided that I was good enough to accompany her for the actual concert. Everyone was talking about Walter, the twelve-year-old, playing at the concert.

I told you at the outset that I was christened Cyril George, that's true. However my grandmother did not like the name Cyril and changed it by calling me Walter Francis after the name of Elisser's brother, Walter Blair, who my grandmother said was very smart, and she wanted me to be very smart as well.

When I was aged between thirteen and fourteen, I had another opportunity to visit England. This time it arose through my being picked to represent my local Boy Scout troop at the Annual Boy Scouts' Jamboree held in England. Again, my father would not allow me to go, so I was denied a trip to England for the second time.

When I was between fourteen and sixteen years of age, I used to love to entertain in school plays and at little gatherings. I used to sing the popular songs of the day, mostly comedy ones. The famous comedian in Kingston was named Teddy, and they used to call me "Baby Teddy." Some of the songs I used to sing included "Take Me to the Land of Jazz," "Yellow Dog Blues," "St. Louis Blues," "Memphis Blues," and Irving Berlin's "My Wife Went to the Country." At the Wesley School, where I went, they had an organ, and, during the lunch hour or before classes started, some of the children would pass by and try to play a few notes on it. One morning, I heard a little boy who was about seven years old playing a tune entitled "I Love Coffee, I Love

Tea" on it. I was already fourteen years of age, and I was fascinated to see this kid play and I could not. Anyway I asked him
to show me how he did it, so this seven-year-old boy—his name
was Michael Campbell—showed me, and from that moment I
took off. After learning that one tune, I also started to try other
little tunes. Then another one of the kids, who lived a few blocks
away from the school, had a piano and was taking piano lessons,
so I followed him home during his lunchtime, and while he was
eating I found myself picking out my first pop tune on the piano,
"There Are Smiles That Make Us Happy." I started to buy sheet
music, mostly the things that W.C. Handy had written, and still
not being able to play a note, I took them to a young lady, Miss
Puller, who was a very good pianist, and she taught me how to
play "Beale Street Blues," "Loveless Love," "Joe Turner" and
others.

My sister and her husband returned to Cuba. My father, who
was very sick and felt that he was about to die, called me and my
brother, Bertie, to his bedside and asked us where we wanted to
go and live if he passed away. Did we want to go to our sister,
Florence, in Cuba or did we want to go to New York to our elder
brother, Harry. Bertie and I said that we would rather go to New
York. (If we had not done so, we would have been up to our necks
in speaking Spanish now.) Our father passed away in 1921; I was
then aged sixteen and my brother, Bertie, was fourteen. After two
years of waiting due to the immigration quota, Bertie and I finally
took off for New York, and, after about seven days on a banana
boat, the "Baracoa," we arrived in New York in May 1923.

We were met at the point of disembarkation by my older
brother, Harry, and we sped by taxi under what I thought was
the longest bridge in the world; it turned out to be under the
Ninth Avenue elevated railway, which ran all the way from the
Battery (lowest tip of Manhattan) to the Bronx. We arrived at 212
West 143rd Street, where we took up residence with the Hinds
family (friends of my brother). Glester Hinds, the son of Mrs.
Hinds, is well known at the YMCA and throughout the whole
Harlem political community for so many years. It was through
Glester Hinds that I heard and learned about the great piano
players of Harlem. He would talk about James P. Johnson, Fats
Waller, and "Nappy," and I met quite a few of them at several
parties which were held at the Hinds family residence. Mrs.

Hinds had a Pease player-piano, and top pianists liked to drop by and tickle those keys. I was amazed to hear Donald Kirkpatrick whipping those keys with consecutive and continuous tenths in the left hand, especially on a tune entitled "Laughin' Cryin' Blues," written by Bob Ricketts and Porter Grainger and published by Rainbow Music Co., a company that was set up by Irving Berlin strictly for the music of the team of Ricketts and Grainger. I idolized all piano players and still do; each has his or her own unique style.

The song-writing bug really bit me when I read in a local magazine: "Send your lyrics off and for a specified fee, we will write appropriate music and exploit your songs." Of course, those were the song sharks of that era. However I fell for the come-on twice, the first time was with "Oh Henry," a lyric I wrote after tasting the heavenly taste of a five-cent candy bar by that name. The second, "Sweet Darling You," after being attracted to a most gorgeous creature named Enid Julien. As far as the songs were concerned, nothing happened, but after a three-year courtship, I married the girl, Enid Julien, and she is still as gorgeous as ever after fifty-three years. She is the mother of Walter Bishop Jr. (jazz pianist), Beverly Bishop Freeman (a school teacher), and Marion Bishop Jefferis (an executive secretary).

Anyway, after those two songs, I decided and believed that I could write much better tunes than the ones I had paid for to be added to my lyrics. A couple of years had passed, and I had moved from the Hinds's residence and had gone to live with Felix Bell, who had worked for my father years before in Kingston. I bought a spanking new piano after Felix had given me permission to move it into his apartment on West 149th Street, next to the park. There, I attempted to write music on paper, without the benefit of measures (bars, that is). I spent more time at the piano, after finishing my day job as an errand boy, than my landlord cared for. He was an aspiring prizefighter and wanted to talk about fights, but I had no time to listen, so eventually he bought himself a player piano. Imagine that, two player pianos in the same small living room. Finally the way out was that I had to remove mine from the premises. I had it in storage for a few months, but in the end I sent it back to the factory whence it came.

Just around that time I was disgusted and disillusioned about my songwriting activities and decided that I was writing my very last song. It was going to be a goodbye to the music business; my effort was titled "Poor Bad Lucky Boy," as I was feeling sorry for myself. However, I took the manuscript to The Melody Music Store on West 135th Street and asked Bud Allen, the owner of the store, to make some additional copies by hand for me (this was long before mimeograph was on the scene). Bud asked me what I planned to do with them, and, when I told him that I was mailing them to the music publishers, he said that they would only mail them back. He suggested that he would get Fats Waller to have a look at the song, as Fats, who was playing organ at the Lincoln Theatre on West 135th Street, usually dropped by his place on his lunch break every day. The following evening, I popped in at the store and was told by Bud that Fats liked the tune. It was a good idea but needed fixing up in spots. After the changes, Fats recorded the song on Columbia Records through the efforts of Bud Allen, and that was the very first time I had a song recorded and put out on record.

I remember buying a briefcase, putting the record in it and walking the streets of Harlem and telling anyone who I thought would listen that I was a songwriter. Then I whipped out the record from my case to show the title of the song, "One O'Clock Blues," that was the new title given to the song, with the names Fats Waller, Bud Allen, and Walter Bishop, and proudly proclaiming, "Walter Bishop, that's me, that's me."

Bud Allen was the man who took me downtown and invited me to meet the real bona fide songwriters, and that is where I came into contact with Clarence Williams, Spencer Williams, Perry Bradford, W.C. Handy, Porter Grainger, Sydney Easton, Arthur Gibbs, Joe Gray, Tim Brymn, J.C. Johnson, James P. Johnson, Andy Razaf, and others too numerous to mention. Most of these writers worked out of the Gaiety Theater Building at 46th and Broadway. It was called "Uncle Tom's Cabin" (affectionately, that is), because that was where all the Black writers congregated, and it also housed all the Black music publishers who were Clarence Williams, Perry Bradford, and W.C. Handy.

I was in awe of everyone when I thought of the great songs that they had written, and here was I a fledgling hurled into the midst of all these great writers. However I learned a great deal being in the company of those magnificent guys. Clarence Williams was the very first person to accept one of my songs for publication. Now I was seeing one of my published songs on sale for the first time. The tune was entitled "Dispossessin' Me," with lyrics by Al Schiller with music by yours truly.

I met Al Schiller when I went to work at Movietone News as a porter. Just before the Depression hit, I was employed as a stock clerk in a hat concern in what was then the hat district in New York at Astor Place and Broadway. I lost the job because people started going around bareheaded. I was hanging around the Gaiety Theater Building after searching but not finding any job. Then word seeped around that the Fox Film Company was on the verge of making an all-Negro film in sound, titled *Hearts In Dixie*. I asked some of the fellows where I could find Fox Film, as I wanted to apply for a job as an extra with them. They said to me that I was no actor, but I remembered how well paid the extras were when Fox had made one of their very first feature films, *Daughter of the Gods*, starring Annette Kellerman, in my home in Kingston, Jamaica. I found my way to the Fox Film studio, which was situated at 54th Street and 10th Avenue, but the jobs for film extras had already been filled, so it was then that I spoke with Al Schiller. He was kind enough to direct me to the home office, where I was taken on as a porter. I had a chance to meet and talk with the Movietone News personalities like Truman Talley, who was the boss, Lawrence Stallings, who was a commentator, Ed Thorgerson, and later on Lowell Thomas.

Al Schiller worked in the requisition at Fox, and he also wrote good lyrics. The very first one he showed me impressed me very much that I wrote the music to it, and this was how we came to write "Dispossessin' Me." The Boswell Sisters were the first to do it on their radio show over WEAF, which was an NBC station. Al and I wrote several songs after that, we were able to place a few but nothing really happened. Another man I met at Movietone was their resident comic commentator, Lew Lehr. I wrote with him "Monkies Is the Qwaziest People" (this became his own theme song) and "Penthouse in the Basement," which was recorded by Louis Jordan on Decca Records.

In the meantime at Clarence Williams's office, I had met Willie "The Lion" Smith. He refused to recognize me at first, calling me a little punk, until I wrote some lyrics for Lewis Raymond, a junior organist at the New York Paramount Theater. "Beer Garden

Blues" was written with Raymond and Clarence Williams, being requested by the new jukebox people at the end of Prohibition; it did well on the jukeboxes at that time and was later rewritten under the title of "Swing, Brother, Swing" and recorded by Billie Holiday. It was then that the Lion decided to write with me. We did quite a few songs together like "Harlem Joys," "Got to Think It Over," "That Streamline Gal of Mine," "The Stuff Is Here and It's Mellow" (with Clarence Williams as collaborator). All these songs were recorded by Willie "The Lion," and I was in the recording studios at Decca when they were made. Some other tunes, I wrote with the Lion were: "The Old Stampin' Ground," "Ain't Gonna Swing No More," and "Feelin' Low," the last named in collaboration with Mitchell Parish of "Star Dust" fame.

I was hanging out with Fats Waller in the early thirties and going with him several times to the CBS Saturday Night Swing Sessions. After that he suggested that we go up to Tillie's Night-Spot (really a restaurant) situated on Lenox Avenue near 116th Street, and listen to Bob Howard, who was playing there and raking in lots of dollar bills with his singing and playing. Fats was intrigued by Bob's singing, as it was the singing which was drawing the bucks stacked on the piano like fallen leaves. That is what really urged Fats to start singing professionally. The very first number he recorded vocally was "I'm Crazy 'Bout My Baby," and he never stopped singing after that.

Once, while I was at Clarence Williams's office one day, I heard what I thought was four hands playing some of the fastest piano that I had ever heard. In fact what I thought was four hands turned out to be just the two hands of Herman Chittison, who came in from Kentucky. I started hanging out with him after I found out that he was staying at Reuben Harris's place on West 130th Street. It was while raving about Chittison that Harris told me about Art Tatum from Toledo, who did with his left hand what Chittison did with his right. I did not believe it until I heard Art, one night at Reuben's place, doing "Tiger Rag." His playing virtually lifted me off the ground; it was the most amazing listening experience that I ever had. I told Mr. Ed Cashman at CBS about Art Tatum and asked if he could put him on his CBS Saturday Night Swing Session. When he asked me if I could get him, I immediately flashed the news to Art, and he was on before you could say "Jack Robinson." So, as a matter of fact, I was the first one to get Art Tatum on the CBS Swing Session. That would have been in the early thirties.

Around 1938, I wrote a ballad with Erskine Butterfield, Percy Post, and E.P. La Freniers entitled "We Can't Go on This Way," one of Ella Fitzgerald's early recordings with the Savoy Eight. Most of the songs mentioned earlier were written in the early thirties, but in 1939, I wrote "Is It Love or Conscription?" with Lou Singer, and it was the very first song by Vaughn Monroe for Bluebird Records. When they told me it would be recorded by Vaughn Monroe, I wanted to know who he was, as I had wanted Glenn Miller to record it. At that time Vaughn was a new bandleader from Boston, and Victor was interested in building him up.

I had applied for membership in ASCAP in 1936 and was enrolled as a nonparticipating member. It was not until 1940 that I received my active membership status. Those were the days when a writer had to have ten published songs by bona fide ASCAP publishers. I wound up with six published by Clarence Williams, two by Mills Music, and two by Roy Music. Even with those, it was really tough to get accepted; however, it did happen in time.

I would like to tell you about the time that I met the famous pianist, Hazel Scott. I had been up and down 52nd Street trying to get someone to play one of my tunes and was having no luck. On talking to the doorman at Mammy's Chicken Farm (a night spot owned by Harry Richman's brother), he suggested that I give a copy to Hazel Scott, who was playing there. When I replied that I did not know her, he said that he would introduce me to her when she came off the stand. He did so, and at the start of the next set, she invited me into the club, took my music, sat me down near the piano, and began to play my songs. I was completely flabbergasted, as no other musician ever treated me or my songs that way before, without any fuss or fanfare. Out of sheer appreciation, I decided that I should do something in return for her. A couple of days later I collaborated with her on a song titled, "Home Cookin' Mamma with the Fryin' Pan." It was a good piece of material which I considered suitable for a possible recording. Therefore, I made an appointment with the recording manager at Decca for him to hear Hazel Scott and the song in the hope that he would record her singing and playing the song. Decca listened and said they liked the song but not the singer. At this news, Hazel cried and I remember telling her that those people were not gods and that they did not rule her destiny. Some several months after that, Hazel Scott was a big success at Cafe Society Downtown, the spot which was run by Barney Josephson. Eventually Decca sent for Hazel to make her first recordings for them, and the manager admitted to her that he had made a mistake the first time around. Hazel took off like a bat out of hell, she made motion pictures for Universal Pictures, Columbia, and the big one when she played the part of Josephine Baker in *The George Gershwin Story* for MGM. A few years later, Hazel was to be the very first person to record vocally the lyrics to the song "Anthropology," which I wrote for the Charlie Parker/Dizzy Gillespie progressive bop tune. At that time she was the only Black person to have her own television show on Dumont Television.

The first real money I made from songs came when I took the royalties from "Is It Love or Conscription?" and invested it in publishing "The Devil Sat Down and Cried," after trying for three years to get somebody interested in accepting or publishing it. One of the first people I gave a copy to was Harry James. I sent it to him through the mail at the suggestion of a friend, Micky Addy. Addy had told me that Harry James had just formed a new band after leaving Tommy Dorsey and was looking for material. What prompted me to send Harry James a copy was hearing him play "A Sinner Kissed an Angel" over the radio. I mailed him a copy and had completely forgot about it, until one night when I was checking with Nat "King" Cole at Kelly's Stable (his first job in New York City) about the reaction he was getting from a copy of a song I had left with him. He happened to mention that some chick had asked him where he had got the number, "The Devil Sat Down and Cried." He had told her from the composer, and she had replied that Harry James had an arrangement of the song. Nat did not know who the chick was, but the following week when I went to see him, he said that same chick had been in again and had told him that Harry James had recorded that number on Columbia Records. The chick turned out to be Helen Forrest, and she along with Dick Haymes and Harry James had done the vocal honors on the Columbia Records of my number. Royalties started pouring in as I was writer, composer, and publisher. I was still swinging the mop at Movietone and joyfully listening to my songs being played over the airwaves. Everyone wanted to know what I was going to do with all that money. I think they expected me to drive up to work in a Cadillac. I followed up with other songs like "Shh, It's a Military Secret" (written with Alan Courtney and Earl Allvine), recorded by Glenn Miller, and "Surprise Party" (written with Bob Hilliard), recorded by Johnny Mercer on Capitol.

In the meantime, having been transferred from Movietone to 20th Century Fox payroll and promoted to security guard and working nights, I took a course in musical composition at N.Y.U., the Schillenger Method. Two of my teachers there were Vic Mizzy and Rudy Schramm. Among the students in my class were Eubie Blake, Mercer Ellington, and Roger "Ram" Ramirez. I also went with Ram to WPA Music School before that. Ram was always considered to be a wizard at the piano, and even in his youth, he was the nearest thing we had to Art Tatum. Ram and I wrote several songs together, "Mad About You"; "It's Better to Wait for Love," recorded by Louis Jordan with a big orchestra for Decca; "I Just Refuse to Sing the Blues," and "Why Complain?" Billie Holiday was supposed to have recorded two numbers for Decca at the time—"Loverman" and "Mad About You"—but she said

Figure 12. Walter Bishop Sr. entertaining at a 20th Century Fox family club affair in 1943.

that she would not record two numbers of Ram's as otherwise he would make too much money. Consequently, she only recorded "Loverman," and that made musical history.

During the middle and late fifties, I wrote and collaborated on many songs which were recorded and featured by leading jazz musicians and vocalists, including "All This Could Lead to Love" (Carmen McRae), "Movin' Out" (Al Sears), "Every Thing That's Made of Wood," (Louis Jordan), "Not Now John, Not Now!" (Pearl Bailey), and "South Of The Blues" (Herman Chittison).

Addison "Addy" Amor, with whom I have written a few songs, was responsible for Peter York and his London Strings recording two of our compositions entitled "What More Could I Ask of Love" and "I'm in The Middle of the Blues." They were released on an album called *A Pair of Naturals* with Peter York's Orchestra and my son, Walter Bishop Jr., leading his own trio on the other side.

If you remember the fabulous composer Harry Revel, who worked with Mack Gordon on songs, well he has a nephew, Billy Revel, who, I am sure, will follow in his uncle's footsteps. We have written a couple of things together "How Ya Gonna Stop the Music," a real rocker, and "Let's Live and Love and Laugh." Watch out for his name; he is only twenty-seven years old.

During my leisure time, I studied for three years at Art Students' League and, if you should happen to be in New York and be visiting the Songwriter's Hall Of Fame, you will see some of my paintings of Eubie Blake, Johnny Mercer, and also an English landscape.

I have only recorded twice in my lifetime as, not being a practicing musician, I stuck more closely to my songwriting.

The first time was when the recording manager at Bandwagon Records asked me if I could find him a blues singer for an immediate recording. The chap I wanted to get him was in Chicago, and I tried but could not reach him, so I said jokingly to the recording manager, "How about me doing the recording?" and he took me up on it. It was supposed to be a cover recording for the song "Baseball Boogie," a story about Jackie Robinson at the bat. On the other side was a tune of mine entitled "Quick Watson, the Rhythm." I recorded under the name Jackie Walters, and to my surprise the record was outselling the original, but nobody knew it was me.

Another time, I recorded a 45 on WEB Records, doing "Dapper Dan" and an original, "Gonna Climb to the Top of a Mountain," written with Leonard Whitcup. I did this just with my voice, piano, and bongo. The first, "Dapper Dan," was one of those songs that I used to sing when I was a kid in the West Indies.

Today, it is so easy to become an ASCAP member, as a copyright certificate gives a writer nonparticipating status until his or her performances start coming through radio or television. I am a member of the ASCAP Writers' Advisory Council and have been for quite a few years. I am on the nominating committee of the American Guild of Authors and Composers: for several years I was their vice-president. Also I am a Board member of the Songwriters' Hall of Fame and currently also a member of the Veterans' Hospital Radio and Television Guild. The Guild is thirty-two years old, and I joined them when they were only one year old. I still make my weekly trips to the Veterans' Hospitals and work musically with the patients there. I enjoy every minute of it, as I have enjoyed ever minute of my song-writing career.

Bobby Booker

As told to David Griffiths and Frank Driggs

My name is Bobby Lee Booker, and I was born on August 22, 1907, in Jacksonville, Florida. At about ten years of age, I joined the Eagle Cadet Corps and was made a bugler. I learned to play the bugle calls, especially taps, which I did very well. A few years later I acquired a trumpet and was taught the fingering and scales by a great trombone player named Amos Gilliard. He was from the Jenkins's Orphanage Home and had travelled to my hometown. However he did not stay there long enough to really teach me; he left town too soon.

I did no professional playing down in Jacksonville. (Once when I went back to my mother's funeral—about 1928?—then I played a couple of engagements with Eagle Eye Shields's Band. We went to Savannah and played for a school dance there. Cootie Williams had been there at one time, but Charlie Frazier and Max Miller—he was the guitar player, he's from Jacksonville—were in the band when we went to Savannah.) During the early twenties, all the young boys in our set were leaving Jacksonville to get better jobs and to make a career for themselves, and the way out was to take one of the ships like I did. I got a job on the Clyde Line and came up North and I've been here ever since.

When I arrived in New York City, I worked as a waiter and did many other odd jobs. I studied a little music with a Professor Watkins, who lived at 129th Street and 7th Avenue. He would teach us how to carry a melody, the rudiments he never taught us, just the fingering and how to play a melody. He wanted us to learn many numbers so that he could take us to various places and collect money, which he would keep, while we were playing. Other fellows who had been to him found out that he was not

---

very good, so they switched to Professor Mikell. After a while, I left him and started to play with various bands that were just starting out. When I first arrived (about 1922–3), Jack Hatton was playing at a place called the Garden of Joy, which was on 7th Avenue and 140th Street. He was a kind of trumpet player who liked all types of gimmicks. He had a hat and a derby, different kind of mutes; he was quite an entertainer. He was in the category of Johnny Dunn, but Johnny Dunn was internationally known, and he had, well, a different kind of air about him. They both played about the same kind of horn. Johnny Dunn was a sporting kind of guy, wore gloves and carried a cane as he walked down 7th Avenue. He was very good for those times, and he wasn't an ordinary acting kind of fellow. You knew he felt he was a great trumpet player, he had class.

Charlie Irvis and his brother, Gibby, were playing at a nightclub on 135th Street called Fritz. Joe Smith was on drums. This was before Charlie went with Duke Ellington. Gibby was a nice piano player, he liked his whiskey. He was mostly an entertainer's piano player; he played mostly cabarets and after-hours places. He was good at following singers. I never knew him to be with any bands, and he never came downtown. Fritz's place was between 5th and Lenox on 135th Street. They kept busy in that neighborhood three or four years before it went down. I was with them off and on most of that time. Later, I used to see Charlie Irvis with Duke Ellington's Kentuckians—I think they were called that then—doing little stints at the Lincoln Theater at 135th Street. There was another place on 135th Street called Connors; that's where Willie "The Lion" Smith was playing. They had five entertainers; they had drums, piano and myself, that was right along in there. There was also a place at 129th Street and 7th Avenue where all the dancing school musicians would gather after two in the morning and play until daylight. I can't remember a time when they didn't have jam sessions. Even the parlor socials, where there was nothing but a piano, musicians would come by; these were guys like Fats Waller, James P. Johnson, Lippy, Seminole, they'd play by themselves, then a horn would come by. For a while then, I was just gigging around, playing short engagements here and there as there was not much work to be had. There would be parlor socials on Saturday, and you would make probably five or six dollars, and that would pay your rent, if you were not living with your relatives.

There was lots of fun around the Rhythm Club in the early
and middle twenties, and that was where Seminole came around
looking for some musicians to go to Atlantic City and work at the
Blue Kitten. [Paul] Seminole was a great piano and banjo player,
but he was a heavy drinker. New York was his headquarters; he
used to do a lot of Saturday night gigs, parlor socials, but I can't
recall any steady jobs he did. When we arrived at the Blue Kitten
nightclub, we started to rehearse with the three or four entertainers. There was one entertainer and "her" name was Mother Cushionberry. After we finished rehearsals, "she" invited me back to
"her" room. I noticed the other fellows laughing about something, but I went to visit this "lady." On reaching "her" room, I
realized that I had left my trumpet behind, so I went back to get
it. When I collected my trumpet, the fellows who were still there,
asked me if I was having a lot of fun with that fellow. Mother
Cushionberry turned out to be a famous female impersonator,
and I knew then that I would not be going back to that room. We
had a great deal of fun there in Atlantic City, just four pieces, but
unfortunately I cannot remember any of their names. However in
New York City, Seminole was one of the great stride piano players. He had a marvellous left hand and was part Seminole Indian.

On my return to New York, I joined a few of the T.O.B.A. shows
which were playing in the South. On one of these shows, I went
out to Wilson, North Carolina, and it was there that I met Tab
Smith and he asked me to organize a band. I asked him if he
would play with me, and we engaged some other men and called
ourselves The Carolina Stompers. We played together for more
than a year, and our band became famous throughout the state.
This was a very clever band because Tab Smith was able to take
off the records, and we copied McKinney's Cotton Pickers' style.
We did "Four or Five Times," "Cherry," and all of their numbers.
Walter Blunt was on tenor (his home was Wilson, North Carolina); on alto was Sonny Leavy (he also came from North Carolina); James Westley on trumpet and Joseph Smith on trumpet (he
came out of Clarence Turner's Band, out of Norfolk, where I had
lived for a short time before coming to New York); Laddie Springs
was on piano; Walter Miller, a very good sousaphone player;
Johnny Reid on drums; and a banjo player (I cannot recall his
name). In Greensboro, North Carolina, we joined the Miller and
Slater Show and that took us to Philadelphia, where we went into

the Standard Theater. We had the full Carolina Stompers band, but we stayed there so long that when the winter came in, the boys who had never been up North before found that they could not stand the cold weather, so each day a few of them would sneak away back home to Wilson. Finally, when we arrived in New York City to play the Lafayette Theater, we only had Tab Smith (alto sax), Walter Blunt (tenor sax), Sonny Leavy (third sax), Laddie Springs (piano), and "Smitty" [Joseph Smith] (trumpet), we had to hire New York City men to supplement the ones who had left us. We played just the week in Miller and Slater's Revue at the Lafayette. On the show with us were Margaret Sims, a singer and dancer, and Derby Wilson, a tap dancer. After that the band broke up. I know that Tab Smith obtained a job right away with, I think, Charlie Skeets in a taxi-dancehall.

During this period [the late twenties] I worked a short spell with Dave Nelson at the Savoy Ballroom and on some dancing gigs for a couple of months. Dave Nelson broke up the band to go with the WPA. Also, around this period, I made a recording session with Willie "The Lion" Smith at the Brunswick Recording Studios at 57th Street. Before the recording, Willie had come into the Rhythm Club and picked up some fellows. We rehearsed uptown for a couple of days, and then he arranged to meet us at the recording studio. We went into the studio and played a few numbers; they were head arrangements. Whatever became of them, I do not know, but we never did get paid, and there were about seven or eight of us there. I also worked and rehearsed with Canada Lee, he was an ex-prizefighter. He was sort of in between doing a little bit of both acting and boxing, mostly acting. We rehearsed, did a couple of gigs, and also played a week at the Lafayette.

At about this time [ca. 1930], I had begun to lead my own small band, and we went up to Newburgh, New York, for about a year and played at the Roxy Club, for dancing and dining only. Newburgh is about ten miles from West Point and fifteen miles from Poughkeepsie. I had Don Frye on piano; he started the engagement right along with me. These people wanted an out-of-town band, and I was recommended to them by someone who was up in that territory. It was a steady six-nights-a-week job. Roy Bumford was on tenor, Eddie Hart (they called him "Tonics" Hart) was on alto saxophone, and Gus Robinson (Banjo Bernie's brother) was on drums. There was another nightclub there called the Dixie, and Sylvia Sims was working there (I ran into her again about ten years ago and she still remembered me), and she would call me up and ask me to play the blues behind her. Eventually the Roxy Club closed down and a fellow wrote to us saying that we should go up to Albany as there was a great deal of work to be had there. Charlie Miller was like a booking agency in Albany, and he obtained some jobs for us. All of the fellows in the band made their home in Albany, and this would have still been around 1930 because I had bought my first automobile, a 1929 Essex (it was about a year old when I purchased it). The band broke up, and I was gigging around Albany; many bands from the territories broke up and stranded many great musicians there. We had many small cabarets and places to work and one morning after work I remember there was a jam session at the Rabbit's Joint on Division Street, and a real cutting contest took place with Jonah Jones, Frankie Newton, Emmett Berry, and many others taking part. They were all trying to cut one another—what a blast and lots of fun.

Alphonse Trent's band from Texas were playing around Albany and were headed for the New England states. Trent was being managed by Earl Roberts, who had the Showboat out of Pittsfield, Massachusetts—that's my old home, boy! Trent was playing piano himself, Gene Crooke was there on guitar, Eppi Jackson on bass. They were glad when I came along because they were short of transportation then. I had a car, and they needed another car to bring along the instruments and some of the fellows. They didn't have a bus then. They had a big old President 8 Studebaker. Nobody but me and George Hudson on trumpets and Leo Moseley on trombone. Peanuts Holland was in Buffalo, and Chester Clark came back in the band just as I was leaving. A.G. Godley came back too. I think it was Alvin Burroughs on drums. Trent was playing nothing but one-nighters, all of them amusement parks in New England—Maine, New Hampshire, you name it—all of those New England states. The money was not too good, and it was hard for me working in that band, because they had memorized most of their arrangements, and the few parts they could find they gave to me, so I had to scuffle to keep up with them. I don't think I ever knew any big band that was so well organized. It wasn't too long afterwards that Trent's band came into the Savoy and did a weekend there. This was after I had left them. Unfortunately, they didn't make the hit they would have made if they had come in when they had Peanuts and they were really going over big. They had novelties like Jimmie Lunceford did, and it was claimed they were an even better band for entertaining, but they had fallen far below that standard when they came to the Savoy. They didn't have that much work when I was with them, and they were going back South down to Texas, which was out of my territory and I didn't want to go. We came back around Albany, and I left them there.

I returned to New York City from Albany and worked with Danny Smalls, although I cannot recall too much about the gig. *[Bertrand Demeusy brought to our attention the following news cutting that appeared in the* Chicago Defender *on February 27, 1932: "Danny Smalls, RKO favorite, has taken over the New Saratoga Club at 139th Street and Lenox Avenue. His new show opened last Sunday. The band, Danny Small's Orchestra, features Bobby Booker (cnt) along with Ken Rhone (cl), formerly with Cab Calloway, furnish the music. Danny conducts it and always has a great chorus to sing and a few steps to dance. There is a string trio in the band. Also Harry Coles (third sax) whose work pleased so many when he was with Alex Ross' Band and Earle Howard's Cincinnatians." According to Bobby, Danny Smalls took over as master of ceremonies, not as owner of the Saratoga Club—D.G.]*

Around this time, I went out on an upstate tour with Jelly Roll Morton's Band for two weeks. The band was made up of guys from the Rhythm Club. Walter Dennis was on alto saxophone, there were three saxophones, and Big Joe Watts was on bass. The tour was all in New England. It was a burlesque show. They played the first half of the bill, and we did the second half. I remember we played two different theaters, but it didn't last too long. There was Jelly Roll's band, a chorus line of ten girls, a comedian, and I think a dance team. I can remember very well that we played Jelly Roll's own music; it was not popular at all, just mostly blues that he wrote but nobody knew.

I worked in a nightclub over in Hempstead, Long Island, called the Broad Channel. *[This has to be 1933—F.D.]* The leader of the band was Marion Hardy. He was the originator of the Alabamians. His big band had disbanded, and then he picked up this five-piece band. Bobby Henderson was our piano player; our drummer was Sonny Woodley—he was lame and wore braces on his

legs. We used to commute back and forth from Harlem to Hempstead, and the job itself lasted about eight weeks. I then started
working in the dance halls. I joined Ferman Tapps's band at the
Blue Bird Dance Hall at 47th Street and 7th Avenue: Leslie Carr
was on alto, Morris O'Bryan on tenor, Vernon Batson on piano,
Chick Landers on drums, plus some others. Later, I joined Charlie Skeet's band at the Circle Dance Hall at, I think, 66th and
Broadway. I was on trumpet, Al Robinson on alto, Charlie on
piano, and Puss Johnson and Freddie Moore played drums with
us at various times. The job lasted four or five months, but after
a while you would get tired of those kind of jobs and get another
one.

   Jack Bradley (the brother of Herman Bradley) and I led a band
at a taxi dance hall, the Broadway Danceland, around 63rd or
64th Street. Jack Bradley played tenor, Ben Smith was on first alto,
Craig Watson on third alto, Dolly Armenra and myself on trumpets, and Cripple Joe Smith was on drums. Around this time, I
joined the band led by Goldie Lucas, who played at the Cosmopolitan Ballroom at 48th Street and Broadway. We also worked at
a nightclub across the street, the Monte Carlo; it was owned by
the same people. We had Goldie on banjo (he recently passed
away, he was an old cat, though, and he was a good pool player);
Ted Colon, who came from Chicago (after the engagement he returned to Chicago) and myself were on trumpets. Ted Colon had
worked at the Renaissance Casino with Vernon Andrade before
he joined Goldie Lucas. Leonard Fields was on alto; I never heard
anybody play like him, he was really fast and used to do double
and triple tongue work on the saxophone, Son Fredericks was on
tenor, [?] Jones on bass, Vernon Batson on piano, and Cripple Joe
Smith on drums. The Cosmopolitan had two bands, and we
played opposite Fess Williams's big band. We had about eight
pieces, but Fess had around eleven pieces in his outfit.

   Later, Fess Williams, who had heard me playing with Goldie's
Band, asked Clarence Wheeler to pick me up for his band. I made
the third trumpet, although Fess Williams was on the downgrade
then and he was glad to get anybody, just like Trent. He still
made two or three broadcasts a week for Columbia Broadcasting
from a park over in Jersey City. He still had a few good jobs left,
but the band was changing like mad at that time and always
going downhill. Garvin Bushell and Wheeler were his main men

then. Wheeler came up to the Rhythm Club and asked me to join; I got the third book, because he knew that I was a slow reader. I could play the hell out of the hot stuff, they couldn't touch me with that. Old Wheeler would go over all these numbers with me, and Fess would be telling him, "Wheeler, work him, work him." He had a big old thick book of arrangements. They sounded like the rest of the bands at that time, but they sounded good if they were hitting. Fess was a terrific MC and frontman himself. He was always nice to me, and in later years I always used to run into him at the race track. We both liked horses; he'd be there every day, I'd lend him money, he'd lend me money.

I worked up in Glens Falls at the Royal Pines with R.Q. Dickerson and Ray Cully, also a local piano player named Tucker Smitty [Jimmy Smith] and the bass player from the Missourians. I used to stick my horn out the window and blow at the cars passing along the highway. The only thing R.Q. lost when he went upstate was power and endurance, he got sick from something [c. 1933–4].

In the summer of 1934, I played in Atlantic City with the Israel Thompson Band at the Belmont Night Club, a famous place for breakfast dances. Israel Thompson was a piano player out of Philadelphia. Frankie Newton and myself were on trumpets; there were a couple of saxophones; piano, bass and drums (mainly Philadelphia boys). Frankie Newton had been with Cecil Scott, he made sure that I joined the band because he had laid out a whole lot of nights to go fishing, so he made them hire me so that they wouldn't be stuck for a trumpet player. He had a hell of a style; he liked women and liked to fight them; he was a strange kind of guy. When he moved to the Village in later years, I lost all contact with him. Now at that time Billie Holiday was working at a real jumpy place called The Old Barn, around the railroad tracks in Atlantic City. I used to go by there and bring her to our breakfast dance. She'd break it up every time because she was better than the girls who worked at the Belmont; she used to come along and sing and leave the place in an uproar.

Later in 1934, I went to Philadelphia, and while I was gigging around I met Al Hall, the bass player. Al knew of a man who wanted a band to play in the West Philadelphia area where he lived, so we put together a great band, and we played at the Lenox Club throughout that winter. While we were playing there we met a manager named Charlie Johnson and, when the summer of 1935 came in, he asked us to go to Atlantic City and play at the Club Harlem for that summer and winter (we opened in May through to November). The band played downstairs for the cabaret in the club, while upstairs was the ballroom which featured all the name bands, including Duke Ellington. We were featured and played a big show with Detroit Red (she died in May 1981, and had a big funeral with all the entertainers there), the Helen Penn Dancers, and many others. On our breakfast dance mornings, Tiny Bradshaw and Chris Columbus would come along and sit in. Subsequently, I returned to North Philadelphia to the Parrish Club.

During the latter part of 1935, I had my own eight-piece band with Slim Gaillard on guitar, Bill Johnson on alto, Herman "Humpy" Flintall on third alto, and Al Hall on bass. "Humpy" was the one who put me on to Bill Johnson, because they had both worked in the same band together. He was a wonderful third alto player and arranger. We had a local drummer from Philadelphia, and Israel Thompson was on piano. Reese Dupree, who was a very popular Philadelphia promoter, presented a band contest between Charlie Gaines's band and my own band at the Strand Ballroom. I had Slim Gaillard, who was playing swinging guitar, while Charlie Gaines had Louis Jordan, who like Slim was unknown at that time. My own band played first, and the crowd really loved our group and went wild. Charlie Gaines's band would not play, so we finished the gig alone. It was no contest. We were paid all of the money because they did not play.

In 1936, I organized a new group here in New York to play at Cuba's Spanish Tavern in Asbury Park during that summer. Vernon Batson was on piano, Casey Shorts was our drummer, I can't recall the name of our alto player, but the tenor player, we always called him "Egypt" because he had a beard and everything, but nobody ever knew his real name. The alto player was a little old whiskey-drinking cat.

I went to Saratoga Springs with Leon Gross and his band shortly after that [ca. 1937]. We played at the Club Harlem, and I remember one man in that band—Stafford "Pazuza" Simon—a very good tenor sax man. [*Arthur Bowie, piano, stated that he also played in that band.*] Later, I was recommended by some performers who had been in Montreal, I think it was maybe Buddy

Bowser, and I went up alone to Montreal and joined Mynie [Myron] Sutton's Band. It was six pieces and we worked at the Club Standard for quite a while. They were all Canadian boys except myself.

Later I returned to New York and joined Connie McLean who was working at the Kit Kat Club downtown. I knew him, but had never worked with him before I joined him in the spring of 1938. Connie was from Panama originally, and three or four of the boys in that band were also from there: Ray Parker, the piano player; Tapley Lewis, alto sax; Ludwick Brown on guitar; and Luther Brown, trombone. The only job I recall them being on was that Kit Kat job, and it ran quite a spell too; it wasn't one of those quickie deals. I worked with them for a while when they came back to New York on the road. Slim and Slam joined the show then and the Clarence Williams' chorus girls.

We went on tour to South America with the Cotton Club Show. The same producer who had staged the Cotton Club Show in New York was in charge of the show. They had built a nightclub, which they called the "Cotton Club of Buenos Aires." That was our home base, but altogether we played in Santiago, Chile; Lima, Peru; Guayaquil and Quito in Ecuador. Quito was the capital of Ecuador, and in order to get there we had to ride up the mountain all day and, when we got up there, we could hardly breathe, the altitude was so high, but we got used to it the next day. We played a week in each of the places that we played; we stayed two weeks in Montevideo and then went back to Buenos Aires and did some more time. In Buenos Aires, Paul Wyer, who was a violinist, came to see the Cotton Club Show and afterwards he invited us back to his beautiful home and to the place where he was working. He was very popular and had a very good tango and foxtrot group. There were about thirty people, including Velma Middleton, who worked in the Cotton Club Show, which was very good and very popular. Ray Parker did most of the arrangements for the band.

On our return to the United States, we worked a few more months with the show. Johnny Hudgins was the star of the show, and I had to learn his act. I had to play a wah-wah pantomime kind of thing behind him, and Johnny was crazy about my playing. He asked me, "Where was you when I was on the big time?" and then I told him that I had auditioned for him three years

before and he didn't want me. That audition had come about
through Louis Metcalfe, who was associated with Johnny Hudgins. He was giving him a whole lot of money and then Louis
quit him. Somebody had told me to go upstairs to the Lafayette
Hall and make the audition. Johnny didn't like me so I never got
the job.

Soon after leaving the show and having gigged around, I organized a band with Tadd Dameron on piano, Stanley Payne on
tenor sax, Ray Culley on drums, and the famous Baby Lawrence
singing and dancing. We worked at Dorsey's Rhythm Club in
Albany and then went to Keansburg, New Jersey, to another club.
They had a big show there, and Tadd left me because he said that
he didn't want to play for any show. He had told me that he had
written for a couple of bands, but he didn't do any writing for
me on our job. I brought in Willie Martinau on piano to replace
him. From Keansburg, we went to the Silver Ball Bar in Newark,
New Jersey [ca. 1940].

Throughout the forties, I had my own small bands and trios.
With Larry Steel's Show I opened at the Elk's Rendezvous and
from there I went to Murrain's and worked with Willie Bryant
(MC) and Doc Wheeler (MC). I was at the Elk's Rendezvous and
Murrains two different times. Earl Bostic used to put me in his
place all the time at the Elk's. [*Franz Hoffmann has brought to our
attention the fact that Bobby Booker's band played a long engagement
at Murrain's, a lounge/cabaret on 132nd Street and 7th Avenue from
September to December in 1945—D.G. and F.D.*]

In 1950, I received a nice letter from Glyn Paque, who was
working in Switzerland, asking me to come over to Europe with
the intention of joining a band that he was hoping to organize in
Switzerland. He told me that I would get the cost of my transportation back, once I got there. That sounded all right to me, and,
as I wanted to go over anyway, I went on what they called a
"Youth Argosy" (students travel that way). I bought my button
and my ticket; it was about half the regular price to France. I had
a whole lot of clothes and a bunch of American Express cheques
hanging out of my pocket. In Paris, I met Merrill "Step" Stepter,
a trumpet player. He was out of New York. He used to work
above the Saratoga Club in a chop suey place in 1938 with a violin
player. While talking with various musicians, I decided to stay on
in Paris for a while. Roy Eldridge obtained a job in North Africa

and they needed a replacement trumpet down where he was working. The woman who was running the place wanted to hear me play, so I went down there and saw James Moody. He told me how bad the pay was. I played a couple of numbers, and the woman didn't say anything about me coming back, so I didn't make that job. There was another place down there, the Vieux Colombier; I played a few nights in there and that's where I heard about work in Holland. I went through Brussels to Rotterdam, where I met an agent and a group of musicians. They had an old car and were going to Amsterdam, where we played at the American Club for a few weeks in August 1950. Although I was getting well paid, my Express cheques were going, so I decided to go back to New York and drive me some more taxicabs. They told me to go to the French Riviera, where Sidney Bechet was working, and I could get a job with him. I remembered him around New York and what he was like, so I figured I wouldn't tangle with him. They told me that if I shined a little bit more than he did, he wouldn't like it; you had to play less than him at all times, don't go over him.

During the fifties, I was "retired" from music and drove a taxicab in New York. [*Bobby Williams, the trumpet player, recalled that he rehearsed with a band that Bobby Booker planned to take to Haiti, but, due to the political unrest in that country at the time, it was finally decided not to go. According to Bobby Williams, it was a big band, and seven of the musicians in it were driving cabs at that time.—D.G.*]

In 1975, I organized the Bobby Booker Big Band, and I handle all the managerial responsibilities which go with it. We have about twenty men that we can call upon, and most of these are star musicians from some of the great bands of New York. Men like Alfred Cobbs, a former member of Duke Ellington and Jimmie Lunceford's Orchestras; Edward Burke, who worked with Walter Barnes and Earl Hines; Archie Johnson, member of Zack Whyte's Orchestra and worked with Blanche Calloway; Sandy Watson, who played with Lucky Millinder and Roy Eldridge. Charles Frazier is our assistant concertmaster and featured soloist. At present we have an eighteen-piece outfit, and Howard Johnson acts as our concertmaster and arranger. We play throughout New York City and New Jersey and have built up a strong reputation as a swinging and jumping outfit. Our current personnel is: Jesse Brown, Archie Johnson, George Hancock, Ken-

Figure 13. Bobby Booker's Big Band, with alto-saxophonist Howard Johnson taking the solo. The three musicians are (left to right) Charlie Frazier, Howard Johnson, and Bobby Booker.

neth Rickman, and myself (trumpets); Dickie Wells, Sandy Watson, Alfred Cobbs, and Edward Burke (trombones); Charles Frazier, Howard Johnson, Dennis Brooks, Marion Davis, Eddie Martin, and Max Lucas (reeds); Ray Tunia (piano); George Baker (guitar); Ivan Rolle (bass); and Wes Landers (drums). Our two vocalists are my own daughter, Alyson Williams, and Jean Pruell, who also plays the trumpet. Altogether, we have some really swinging times.

Afterthoughts

I knew King Oliver around New York, but he never had much going, and I never did think that he had what Louis had, but he brought him along there around Chicago. The best thing that he did was that break on "Snag It." Oh man, I thought that was really something.

Ray Culley was a wonderful drummer, he was a real intellectual, he played all over New York State. Ed Gregory worked with me when I worked out of Poughkeepsie at Detroit's Chicken Shack. Bobby Pratt used to work for me there, he was just a young kid. His mother and father used to bring him to work then and wait until he got through.

Louis Metcalfe was working with Duke Ellington, and he grabbed me on the corner one night. He wanted to go somewhere and wanted me to work in his place. He was a guy, a hell of a dresser, nothing excited him. He drove a yellow Cadillac convertible. He could play like a demon then, and he was exciting on his horn.

I was closer to Cuban Bennett than anybody. He had a bad time with his wife; I believe that she got him on that whiskey. I lived in a building on 129th Street and 7th Avenue. There was a dancing school in the basement, and he'd be in there all night playing and all day drinking that liquor. Guys would come in from everywhere, and he hardly had a good trumpet, it was an old raggedy horn, but he'd outplay everyone who came in there. He just knew all the chord changes. He, Louis Hunt (who used to play with Chick Webb), and Louis Metcalfe, those three fellows could run more changes than anyone else I ever heard.

I was very close to Billy Douglas, I helped him get into one of the great bands. This was the Earl Hines Band when they were playing at the Renaissance [1945]. Somebody had told me that they were short of a trumpet player and Billy Douglas played so great and had such a good personality so I told him to go up there and sit in as I thought that he could get that job, and they did hire him. I remember one time Billy and I were in this place called Club Harlem on 145th Street. Roy Eldridge was there, and Roy had never seen him and they jammed together. Roy asked me, "Where you get a guy like this, there's no guys around here like that?" I told him that I thought you both played something like one another. This guy, though, was something else. They battled like dogs, and Roy couldn't get no more of him than he could get of Roy. At that time they were just running changes, then later Roy got more range. At the same place, once, I ran into Earl Bostic

and Charlie Parker; they battled for hour after hour, I'm telling
you. I will tell you something, people don't respect Earl Bostic;
they've got to be crazy, because that man was something else.

Old Kaiser [Marshall] got some nice gigs for ten pieces. He
used to carry Max Roach around with him for five dollars, that's
all Max would get, we'd get eight or ten dollars. Kaiser would get
drunk, and then Max would come in. Max just wanted a gig,
that's all, and Kaiser had a reputation as a great drummer, and
Max just wanted to learn. Max was studying, he learned something from Kaiser, but he got way past him, because he was the
damnedest technician. I'd be sorry when Kaiser would get up
from the drums and wouldn't sit down no more because Max
played a funny kind of bass drum, and the fellows didn't like
the way he was playing. He couldn't swing that much then, you
know.

Bobby Woodlen

My name is George Robert Woodlen, and I am also known as Bobby Madera. I was born in Baltimore, Maryland, on December 4, 1913. When I was in junior high school there, I studied music with a Mr. James Young. He was a violinist and also the conductor of a small symphony orchestra. Later, when I went to Douglas High School, I studied with Mr. Llewellyn Wilson; he was a very fine music teacher and conductor. During those times, I studied piano and trombone, but later I changed to trumpet.

While in high school, I was a first trumpet player and naturally, being a young kid, I also enjoyed playing football, and so one day I would study the trumpet and attend rehearsals and then the next day I would go out and play football. You can guess what happened. I used to come in for rehearsals with a punched lip or something. One day, Mr. Wilson called me into his office and said,"I'm depending on you as my lead trumpet player; now either you make up your mind to be a trumpet player or a football player," so I chose the trumpet.

During that time, in the summer, there was a little band around town—I can't recall the name of the leader or any of the musicians—and they were going out on the road doing a few nights around West Virginia, and I decided to join them. The leader thought it would be a good idea to add a second trumpet player to the band, and there was this particular fellow who used to hang around the band every night, and we had all got to know him pretty well. Therefore, our leader decided to add him as an extra trumpet. Anyway, payday came around, and the leader had the money on the table ready to pay off all the fellows, and then this same fellow came up and pulled a gun and took every nickel and disappeared into the night.

I played with quite a few of the local bands around Baltimore,

including Ike Dixon, Percy Glascoe, Reggie Haymer, Harold Step-
toe, and Banjo Bernie. Now, it is a funny thing, but we youngsters
loved to play with Banjo Bernie. You would go out and spend a
couple of days out on the road with him, and many times he'd
never pay you. Mostly, we'd do this in the summertime, and we
just could not get the money out of him. He was a wonderful
musician. He played trumpet and banjo—of course, banjo was his
instrument. He also used to arrange things, and he was famous
for writing the melody. For instance, in the case of the trumpets,
he would put the melody in one key for one trumpet and in another for the other. Therefore, you had a very unusual sound. It
was good for those days, but I don't know how it would be for
today.

Around 1930, I left Baltimore and went to Washington, D.C.,
where I joined Elmer Calloway's band at the Club Prudhom. We
had Lester Henry, Val Valentine [*actually Raymond "Syd" Valentine—D.G.*], and myself on trumpets, Fred Norman on trombone—he also did the arranging. William Smith, Ray Forrest and
John Harris were in the reed section, Henry Bowen played the
accordion, Joe Bailey was on piano, Al Stewart on bass, Percy
Johnson on drums, and Elmer Calloway was our leader.

After leaving them, I returned to Baltimore and joined Bubby
Johnson's band. Bubby had a very good band at that time [1932].
We had Fess Holmes, Wallace Jones, and myself on trumpets;
Bubby Johnson, Jimmy Duppins, Gil White, and Chauncey
Haughton on reeds; a man we called "Trummy" on trombone;
and a rhythm section made up of Clarence Hunt on piano, Billy
Mackel on guitar, a tuba player whose name I can't recall, and
Jake [?] on drums. Chauncey Haughton, our alto sax player, was
one of the best.

Then, in 1934, I came to New York City and worked around
with Rex Stewart's band doing various club dates. From there, I
joined Earle "Nappy" Howard's Melody Lane house band, and
later we played at Remy's Ballroom. We had several fine musicians. Billy Kirkley was our drummer, Allen Jackson and Frank
Caines were both on altos, and "Brownie" on bass. I left the band
and was replaced by George Hancock.

I went on and joined Willie Bryant's band at Connie's Inn at
131st Street and Seventh Avenue, but I was only with them for
about seven or eight weeks. Dick Clarke and Jack Butler were two

of the trumpets besides myself, Johnny Russell and Glyn Paque were in the reed section, George Matthews was on trombone, Roger "Ram" Ramirez played piano, Ernest "Bass" Hill was on bass, and Manzie Johnson on drums. Cozy Cole had been the drummer but he left a few days before I joined. Ram, Glyn, Johnny, and Bass were my very good friends in the band, and they, together with Manzie Johnson, left to go to Europe. [*All five musicians were in Europe in June 1937, playing with Bobby Martin's band—D.G.*] Around that time, I left Willie Bryant to do other things. It was a very good band he had.

After that, I did several rehearsals with Jelly Roll Morton. This was a few years before he died. My brother, Haston, used to sing with him on club dates. Anyway, Jelly rehearsed a full band in a basement at Connie's Inn. I think we had two trumpets, but I can't recall the names of any of the other musicians. We were supposed to go to Russia with him, but Jelly had problems with the money—I don't think they were paying enough. We were supposed to do some things with Bessie Smith as well, but they never materialized.

Around that time, I also did lots of sessions for Decca's race records. In those days, you'd play a little background music behind various singers. A piano player would come along and offer you five dollars a side. It would be mostly blues, and you'd get paid off right away. Most of the time you never even knew who the singer was you had accompanied. In fact, I can't recall any of their names.

Then around 1938, I joined Maurice Rocco's band at the Kit Kat Club. I was on first trumpet, Clarence "Graf Zeppelin" Powell was on second. We had Arville "Bunky" Harris, a very fine clarinet player, George James on alto. "Slim" Moore was on trombone; Cliff Jackson played piano; Leroy Harris played guitar, the flute, and did the arranging; Olin Aderhold was on bass, although he was replaced by Wellman Braud, who came in for a while. Finally, Chick Morrison was on drums.

In 1939, I worked with Benny Carter's Orchestra. Now in that band we had some really fine musicians, including Joe Thomas, Jimmy Archey, and Vic Dickenson. We recorded four sides in June of 1939, and these were my first legitimate recordings. I left them later in 1939 and played in a pit band on Broadway in a show entitled *She Gave Him All She Had*. It starred Jacqueline Su-

Figure 14. A publicity shot of trumpeter Bobby Woodlen.

sann, who was later to become famous as a writer. I left the show before it closed.

During the summer of 1940, I worked at the Paradise Club in Atlantic City with Bardu Ali, and in that band we had a very fine pianist, Bill Doggett. At the end of the summer, I went to another club in Atlantic City and joined Blanche Calloway. Frank Wess was also a member of that band.

Then I came back to New York City and, after working odd club dates, I joined Eddie Barefield's band. We played at the Savoy Ballroom and Small's. I remember we had Leslie Johnakins and Freddie Williams on saxes, George Tate on trombone, and our excellent bass player was George Duvivier. We worked together for six months in and out of the Savoy.

I left Eddie Barefield and joined Machito's band in 1941 and I remained with Machito until 1955. During all those years, I recorded with practically every big Latin artist in the business. I have also recorded and played under the name of Bobby Madera. I have composed a number of tunes, including "Mambo Inn," recorded by Count Basie's Orchestra in 1956. During all my time with the Latin bands and artists, I was doing much studying as I had decided to become a music teacher. At present, I am busy teaching both trumpet and trombone in New York City.

George Hancock

My name is George Hancock and I was born in an old section of New York City called San Juan Hill on October 15, 1911. This section of New York was very rich in music, and it was not difficult for me to become interested in it. I grew up in a neighborhood with musicians such as Bobby Stark, Freddie Jenkins, Russell Procope, and Benny Carter. These giants of jazz used to play Saturday night house parties and parades in the district. I was in awe of them and I made up my mind after hearing them play many times that I, too, would become a musician.

During my formative years, I lived in New Jersey. My mother and father had separated, and my father raised me and my sister. He didn't want my sister and I to be separated, so he had us boarded out in a town called Plainville, New Jersey. There I took musical appreciation as a subject, and I won a contest in the high school on this subject. The principal of the school, a Mr. Floyd, told my father that he should bring me to New York and let me get into music, because there were no facilities in Plainville for learning to play. So that is what my father did.

My father, who was a professional fighter named Al Hancock, had other ideas for me, and convincing him that a musician's life was for me was indeed another matter. In those days, a professional fighter's fights were few and far between, and a nickel was a nickel. My father, therefore, had already decided that I was to keep my head in books, and study, so that one day I would become a lawyer.

I also had an aunt. Her name was Alice Trainor; she was my mother's sister and she played piano. She was born and lived in Nashville; she used to work in the college there during the day, but at the weekends she played all the joints around Nashville. She didn't read music, but she could play any tune that you could name. I saw her once while on a visit there in 1928. They used to say that she was a natural, that's what my uncle told me about her. I used to just sit and watch her play. That was before I played an instrument.

At first, my father was reluctant to allow me to play the trumpet because he felt that I was too frail and did not have enough stamina to be able to blow a trumpet, so he said that he would buy me a violin. That is when I rebelled. Later, as I began to put on weight, he agreed that I could have a trumpet. I will never forget the day he took me to buy it at the New York Band Instrument Company Music Store on 14th Street in New York, as a Christmas present.

After I arrived home with my horn, a funny incident took place. The valves did not work, so I took the valves out, oiled them, and put them back wrongly. I didn't even know how to put the valves in, so I went running back to the store and asked for my money back because the horn didn't play! The man looked at me and just laughed, and then explained that the valves went by numbers and switched them back correctly on my horn. That just goes to show you how much I knew about the instrument.

Around that time, I spoke with Clarence "Graf Zeppelin" Powell and I asked him if he would teach me to play the trumpet, but, unfortunately, he didn't teach, and he recommended me to go to Lt. Eugene Mikell, who had taught him. Lieutenant Mikell was a great brass man and had taught most of the fellows around there. Everyone urged me to go to him but, shortly after I did, he passed away.

I was then taught by a lady, a Miss Spiller. She had an act called The Five Musical Spillers; they were a musical family who played in vaudeville. She played the trumpet and the piano. She had come off the road and had a studio on 138th Street, where she started giving lessons. Another humorous incident in those early days was the fact that she used to say to me that I was the only trumpet player who could make the wrong fingering but make the right notes come out. I was in such a hurry to play that I was using all the short cuts. When I used to make the wrong fingering, she would crack my knuckles with a ruler.

I went to Haaren High School on 59th Street and 10th Ave' and it was there that I first heard Doc Cheatham play. He with Cab Calloway's band to play a dance, as we wou' regular Friday night dances at the school. Doc's playing impressed me very much, and he influenced me greatly in my own playing. I used to admire the way he used to sit up there and hold his horn.

I also used to go to the Alhambra Theatre where they used to have vaudeville acts. Edgar Hayes was the leader of the band there. It was seven or eight pieces, and I admired the trumpet work of Ovie Alston and how he played those shows. Every chance I would get, I spent it watching the shows, and my ambition was to play like those fellows.

One of my first musical jobs came when I was living down in the sixties in New York and a chap came through whose band had deserted him. He needed some fellows to play a circus, but as none of the fellows down there knew him, they were a little wary of taking the job and going with him. At that time, I was a very adventurous person and, never having played a circus, I agreed to go with him.

He was a drummer named [?] Curtis, and he came from Ohio. I quickly got my bag packed and my father, who was not at home, did not even know I had gone. Curtis drove me by car to a place called Nyack, New York, where the circus had only just arrived in town. Now, what he didn't tell me when he offered me the job was that we had to do all this ballyhoo by playing through the streets. I thought that we would just be playing in the circus.

We played at Nyack for three or four nights, but what made the job hard was the fact that we were only five pieces: a trumpet, saxophone, piano, banjo, and drums. We left Nyack without incident and moved on to a town called Pearl River, New York. We had to sleep in tents, and that particular night it began to rain. It rained all night and all the next morning so, eventually, when I came to put my feet out of bed, I discovered that the water was quite high in the tent. Immediately, I was ready to go home, as were the other fellows. We called the manager, but he managed to persuade us to stick it out for a while, which we did. Finally, after a couple more days, we told him that we were going to quit. None of us had experienced that type of life before, and so he paid us off and drove us back to New York.

My father was furious with me and said he hoped that would teach me a lesson. You see that was around 1931 and I was still in school and my father was afraid I wouldn't finish school. That was my first really steady professional job.

At that time, I used to play what they called Saturday night parlor-socials: they had these house-warming parties and Jimmy Phipps, who was a good piano player, would get these jobs. Jimmy Phipps was the man who gave me my first job playing jazz. At the time, I wasn't interested in playing jazz, I wanted to play "legitimate" music; but he changed my ideas, and from then on I wanted to play jazz. He exposed me to all those great jazz players. I used to go up to Reubens and hear Art Tatum, Clarence Profit, Ram Ramirez, and others. Reubens and the 101 Ranch were the places that I was able to get my experience. Rudy Williams and all those musicians from the Savoy Ballroom would jam at the 101. I used to jam with them until the early hours of each morning. The opportunity to play with them all gave me a wealth of ideas.

One of my first jobs with Jimmy Phipps was when we played a show called *Miranda*. We rehearsed for that show for two or three months and the show didn't even last a week. We opened at the Harlem Opera House in the Bronx, and we had Irving Taylor, saxophone, and his brother Al on drums. They were, like me, just starting out, and all their relatives came along to see the show. In fact, the only people who saw the show were relatives of the people who were in the show. It was a flop.

I remember that Marlowe Morris, at that time, was a dancer in the show. He didn't play piano then, but he used to watch Jimmy Phipps play, and Marlowe had such a terrific ear that he started playing piano backstage for the dancers.

After I joined Local 802 Musicians' Union, pianist and leader Earle Howard gave me my first job. He needed a trumpet player, and Bobby Woodlen recommended me. This was in the summer of 1935 and we played in a ten-cents-a-dance hall called Remy's.

Bobby Woodlen and I used to get up early in the morning and go down to the beach on that job. Naturally, by the evening we were both pretty tired, and sleep would start to come down on you when you were playing at the dance hall. That work was so monotonous that what the fellows used to do to combat it was to put on their dark glasses and go to sleep. Earle Howard caught us out a couple of times sleeping, so then, in order to keep us awake, he would call out numbers for us to play. We had about five hundred numbers in the repertoire and we would read awhile and then do a lot of "blue-booking," playing without music; you would have played the numbers so often that you knew them off by heart.

Bobby Woodlen eventually left that job to go and work for Maurice Rocco at the Kit Kat Club. I was afraid to go with him as I did not think the job would last very long. In fact, he stayed there almost a year and made good money and met many celebrities. I stayed on with Earle Howard at Remy's until the job closed.

After leaving Earle Howard, I joined Tommy Stevenson's band. The personnel of that band was Tommy Stevenson, Forest Morgan, Courtney Williams, and myself on trumpets; Sandy Watson, George Robinson, and Weldon Hurd on trombones; Ulysses—we called him "U.S." for short—Scott on first alto; Irving Taylor on third alto; and Clarence "Sonny" Fredericks—he is dead now—on tenor; Frank Powell on baritone; George Mordaunt on piano; Herbie Thomas on guitar; Ted Giles on bass; and Al Taylor on drums.

Tommy Stevenson took the band up to New Rochelle and from there we went to Boston. Our alto saxophone player, U.S. Scott, was very short and when we used to broadcast from WABB in Boston every Friday and Saturday night you just could not hear him on lead alto. Therefore, the engineer stood him on a chair, and he was head and shoulders above everyone in the band and at last could be heard. He was a real comical guy; he used to conduct the band before Tommy Stevenson came out.

Another member of the band, Herbie Thomas, now he had a habit of asking for cigarettes all the time for guys in the band. Well, this particular night, the piano player was given a cigarette and then, while we were playing, we heard this large explosion. We thought a bomb had exploded. He'd been given one of those exploding cigarettes; he had no idea who had given it to him. Everyone had a good laugh about that.

On that circuit, we followed Jimmie Lunceford around. We got the job thanks to Blanche Calloway, because she liked Tommy Stevenson. We were supposed to play for Harold Oxley and Jimmie Lunceford at their club in Larchmont, but something happened and Oxley did not take up our option. Altogether the band didn't last a year, and we folded due to a lack of work.

I then joined Baron Lee for about a year. We were doing the RKO circuit. Dick Clarke, Earle Howard, and Frank Powell were in that band, because later they made that trip to South America with Baron Lee. I regretted not having made that trip, but I was married and my children were small, so my wife didn't want to go.

During 1938, I went to work at the Kit Kat Club with Earl Durant's band. We had Cyril Newman and myself on trumpets, Irving Taylor and Walter Beezie on altos, Winston Jeffrey on tenor, Earl Durant on piano, Floyd Morris on guitar, I can't recall the name of the bass player, and Harold Austin on drums. Cyril Newman was later replaced by a very fine female trumpeter and vocalist, Dolly Armenra. We brought her into the band because she could sing and we needed a vocalist for a radio broadcast that we used to do once a week from the Kit Kat Club. I worked there for close to one year.

The war years saw me working in the Brooklyn Navy Yard as a welder. I met with an accident there when one day I didn't have my shield on while I was welding, and the next thing I knew there was some guy hitting me and putting a fire out. My arm had first-degree burns. That was around 1942 or 1943.

Then I met Bobby Hicks, the trumpet player, and he suggested that I should go and work at Todd's Ship Yard in Hobart in their electrical department. Bobby said that he could get the job for me, he tried to help the jazz musicians. They also had a band there, and one musician who played with them was drummer, Larry Hinton.

Sometime after D-Day, I quit the job and went back into music. At first, I went to work with Lester Boone at the Horseshoe Bar out in Woodside, Queens. Alan Nurse was on piano, later he went into teaching, "Frisco" De Silva was the drummer, and Ben Richardson was on tenor, doubling on clarinet. Alan Nurse wrote the book, and it was a tough one too; Ben Richardson always talks about that book.

After leaving Lester Boone, I joined Tab Smith at the Savoy Ballroom. This was about 1948. The trumpets were myself and Pat Jenkins; Tab Smith was on alto; at first Johnny Hicks from Los Angeles was on tenor but after a while he went back to the Coast; we had several players including Mike Hedley. Red Richards was on piano and Walter Johnson on drums. While I was with Tab Smith, we cut some titles for Hub Records. They were "Too Late" and "Easy Street." Deborah Murphy was the vocalist, and I may have soloed on mute behind her.

I also recorded with blues singer Dinah Washington. We made the titles at the W.R. Studios for Mercury Records. It was a lengthy recording session. Russell Royster was the other trumpet player on the session. Three titles were released from this session; they were "A Slick Chick," "Postman Blues," and "That's When a Woman Loves a Heel."

At that time, Russell Royster would take my place in the band and at other times he would take Pat Jenkins's place. That was his job, but eventually he became so busy with his arranging and copying that he would just fill in occasionally. When I left Tab Smith, my place was taken by Harold "Money" Johnson.

I worked down the Tango Palace in 1951 and stayed there for about a year and eight months. Bingie Madison was the leader, Carl Frye was on alto, Tommy Fulford on piano, and Goldie Lucas on guitar. Leonard "Ham" Davis was the man who got me the job. He was working at the Majestic on 50th Street, and he told me that there was a job going at the Tango Palace where I could stay and I wouldn't have to do any running around.

Later, I went to work in the Civil Service, but I also worked with many of the Latin bands playing Afro-Cuban jazz music. More recently, though, I have been playing with Bobby Booker's Big Band. This first started out with just a bunch of musicians playing various jazz sessions around town. Bobby Booker was the promoter of these affairs and he would hire names like Roy Eldridge, Clark Terry, Howard Johnson, and Robert Ashton. The whole thing became so successful that he started up the Bobby Booker Big Band. We have three arrangers, Howard Johnson, Al Cobbs, and Bobby Green.

Apart from playing in the Big Band, I also do much gig work and am pretty active. In fact, you might say, "Have trumpet, will travel!"

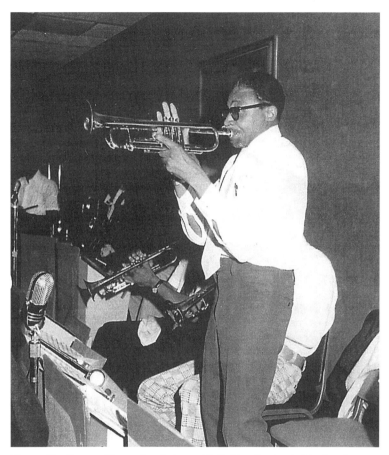

Figure 15. George Hancock soloing with Bobby Booker's Big Band. Holiday Inn, New Jersey, July 1975.

Greely Walton

I was born in Mobile, Alabama, on October 4, 1904, and my mother, who was a fine pianist (not professionally but she taught piano) was also a good seamstress. My father was a cotton sampler; he worked in a warehouse where he picked the cotton from the bales and marked down on paper what type of quality the cotton was in that bale. His father before him was also a cotton sampler. We lived beautifully because both my father and mother made plenty of money.

When we were living in Mobile, many musicians came to visit our house, including Clarence Williams, Spencer Williams, and Scott Joplin. My mother got to know Clarence Williams through his partner, Spencer Williams, as Spencer was from Mobile and he and my mother both went to the same school. Any musicians who came to Mobile, at that time (this would have been around 1909 to 1911) used to play at the Pike Theater, it used to be a theater in the colored neighborhood. Musicians like Eddie Heywood, Sr., there was one called Johnny King (he married my father's sister and they moved to New Orleans), all of them used to come to our house. Because my mother played the piano, Clarence Williams used to send her his music, the new copies that he would get when he moved to New Orleans.

My father died when I was around eight years old. He had tuberculosis and to try to help him we moved all over the country. We moved to Denver, then to Phoenix, from there to St. Louis, and then finally back to Mobile, where he passed away. His hobby was driving those horses, you know the "pacers." We had two and they were real mean, and the kids could not go near them; we used to throw bricks at them. After my father died, my grandfather, who was the County Clerk in Mobile—he had been educated in Princeton and was half Choctaw Indian and half

Irish; his name was Horace Greely—he took all the family to Pittsburgh. My brother, Alvin, and I went to school in Pittsburgh and my mother remarried. Later, we moved to St. Louis, where my step-father worked as a dining car waiter on the railroads. He made plenty of money in that work and probably had the most influence on anything I ever became.

I started studying music when we moved to St. Louis on the violin. Prior to this, my mother had tried to teach me the piano, but I didn't want to learn how to play that. She even had a French teacher come along and teach me, but the teacher gave up. She said that I could learn but wouldn't. I didn't want to learn. I just wanted to get out on the street and play, but when we moved to St. Louis, my mother asked the first violinist from the St. Louis Symphony Orchestra to come along and teach me, and I studied under him for about seven or eight years. I played in the local high school symphony and in that same symphony were Jerome Don Pasquall, George James, and Henry "Moon" Jones.

In St. Louis, they have these alleys in between the streets, and, right at the back of our house, this man who sold coal had his coalshed, and Eugene Sedric used to work for this man delivering the coal. In between doing his deliveries, Sedric used to practice his clarinet playing there, and I used to go out to hear him. He was a fine clarinet player. This would have been around when I was twelve or thirteen. In St. Louis, I heard some fine bands, there was a trumpet player who was one of the best there was—Charlie Creath, boy, he was some trumpet player. Then there was Irving "Mouse" Randolph, Leonard "Ham" Davis, and Eddie Allen. When I was about fourteen, I used to hear all those musicians playing at a cabaret called Jazzland. My parents took me on the boat to hear Fate Marable's Band and Louis Armstrong.

On Saturdays, I had to attend the concerts held at the Center in St. Louis, and it was here that I heard the St. Louis Symphony Orchestra play. My love to this day is symphonies; I have more symphony records than I have jazz records. Later when I could play jazz, I played jazz, but my love was still symphonies, and it remains the same today. I never intended to be a musician. I was very good in mathematics at school and I wanted to become a mechanical engineer. I went to the University of Pittsburgh for two years studying mechanical engineering and never had any intention of becoming a musician.

I used to go back and forth to Pittsburgh, because my grandmother lived there after my mother had moved to St. Louis. I
went to college in Pittsburgh because I could then stay with my
grandmother. While I was in Pittsburgh, my uncle who was living there was playing with a group. His name was Horace
Thomas, and he played banjo and guitar. The group he was playing with needed a tenor saxophone player at the time. They persuaded me to get a saxophone. I had never played one, nor did I
know how to play one, but as I had studied violin for so long, I
thought that it would be very easy for me. I therefore induced my
grandmother to lend me the money to go to a pawn shop and
buy a tenor. In about a month I was playing with the band. I still
continued to go to school as I didn't intend to play music as a
career, but after a while I started to make pretty good money, so
I quit school and just started playing music.

Bands that used to play in Pittsburgh in those days included
Fletcher Henderson and Lloyd Scott, that's who we used to hear.
Then there was a band that came out of Pittsburgh led by Lois
Deppe, that was some band. He had a saxophone player who
fronted the band, Vance Dixon, and Earl Hines and Louis "Bass"
Thompson, worked for him. Coleman Hawkins and Benny Carter
were early influences on my playing.

In 1925, Joe Eldridge, Jimmy Cole, two brothers by the name of
Carter Dykes (piano) and Earl Dykes (trumpet) and I—we were
all from Pittsburgh. We were six pieces and we took a job up in
the northern part of Wisconsin at a place called Chicago and
Lake. The man who had booked us would rent us out, and we
went all over that area of Wisconsin and Michigan playing at the
resorts up there. That's where I ran into Eli Rice—he had control
of all that territory up there—they were all crazy about him. We
played up there just during the summer, about six or eight weeks,
and we got $30 a week plus room and board.

Around this time, we formed this band together, called the
Elite Serenaders. At the time Benny Carter was working at a place
in Pittsburgh, and he arranged for a man to come down from
New York to hear us. I had first met Benny Carter when he had
been working down at the Paramount Inn with Earl Hines. By
the time we had formed the band, Benny had left Pittsburgh, but
when he returned the band sounded good. At that period the
attraction for us of going to New York was because of the amount

of work to be had there. The man who came to hear us booked us for this job at the Renaissance Casino in New York City.

We came to New York in 1926. We had Archie Johnson and Jimmy Cole on trumpets, we had a trombone player named Paul Butler, Joe Eldridge directed and played alto, Joe Thomas played alto, I was on tenor, Skinny Brown was on piano (he was a young boy from Pittsburgh, a fine piano player but he died very young shortly after our band broke up), [?] Waterhouse (bass), my uncle Horace Thomas played banjo and guitar, and Herman Goldstein was on drums. *[According to Archie Johnson, the band had an apartment in which they all roomed together and used to get drunk every night—D.G.]* We worked at the Renaissance for about six months, that was how long the contract lasted. While we were there, Jimmy Cole went back to Pittsburgh as his father made him go back to school, and a trumpet player from Lloyd Scott's Band replaced him *[Greely said his name was Dickerson.—D.G.]* He was later replaced by Rex Stewart, who left Fletcher Henderson and joined us at the Renaissance. Paul Butler and I had known each other since we were kids. He was a good trombone player, but he was on dope then and the other guys didn't know it. All the guys came home one afternoon and found him stretched out on the floor and they called a doctor. He was so ashamed that he left the band and went back to Pittsburgh. He was replaced by "Monkey" Joe Williams.

After we finished our contract at the Renaissance, we did some work at the Capitol Palace, it was on 139th Street and Lenox Avenue. All of the bands worked there, Lloyd Scott's Band used to come there and Johnny Hodges was playing tenor at that time when he worked with them. We worked at the Capitol Palace for a little while and then the band broke up. I stayed on in New York, as did Archie Johnson and Joe Eldridge. My Uncle Horace went back home because he obtained a job with a millionaire, the man that started Marathon Oil. Horace, who was married to my mother's sister, had been his chauffeur. Later this man created the oil company and moved to Tulsa, Oklahoma, and Horace passed away there five or six years ago.

I worked in the Lincoln Theater in early 1927 with Allie Ross's Band, the only member of that band that I can recall was Garvin Bushell. Then I went with Elmer Snowden. We had Walter Johnson (drums), Wardell "Preacher" Jones (trumpet), a pianist who later went to Europe named Charlie Lewis—he was a hell of a pianist. Charlie was a highly trained musician, he earned a degree in music at Fisk University. One night at the Nest Club where we were working in 1927, Paul Whiteman and George Gershwin came down to hear us. Whiteman came over to the piano and asked Charlie, who was at the head of everything, if we would play Rhapsody In Blue (he was going to make a fool out of us, because he thought that we were ham musicians). Charlie, who was a peculiar guy we used to call him "Mushmouth", asked Whiteman how much of it do you want. Whiteman placed two fifty dollar bills upon the piano, and Charlie said, "Oh, you want all of it!" and told Walter Johnson to put the money in the box. Charlie stood up and announced to the audience that Paul Whiteman and George Gershwin had requested "Rhapsody In Blue" and with their kind indulgence, he would play it for them. He really played it, the entire twenty-eight pages from memory. When he had finished, he received a beautiful hand, and Charlie stood up and said, "Anything else you'd like to hear, a little Bach, a little Beethoven?" It was beautiful, believe me.

Charlie Lewis left the band to go to Europe with Peter DuConge and his group. I was supposed to go as well, but I had just married and decided against it. Freddy Johnson replaced Charlie in the band. Ed Cuffee was on trombone, but he was replaced later by Henry Benny Morton. Two Black guys, by the names of Johnny Carey and Mel Frazier, ran the Nest Club. After a while, I managed to get Joe Eldridge a job with Snowden. We must have worked at the Nest for maybe five or six months. It was a pretty hard job; we worked all night. We used to make nice money. We would get about fifty dollars a week in tips, and so I used to send my mother and father my salary. They didn't need it, but I didn't know what to do with it, so I sent it to them in Chicago.

Around this time [mid-1927] I started working in the pit orchestra at the Lafayette Theater. There was a lady who had the band there. Her name was Miss Franklin; she was a young violinist. A guy who we called "Stick"—Horace Holmes—he was on trumpet, Harry Hall was on string bass, Garvin Bushell was on clarinet, and George Howell on drums. I was on tenor and clarinet. We worked in the pit, and I was doubling at the Nest. It became kind of tough for me, so eventually I quit the Nest and stayed in the pit. It was quite an experience for me. I learned a lot. I could read—after having studied violin for eight or nine years, I should have been able to—I was an excellent sight reader; if they wrote it I could read it. I enjoyed playing there and must have stayed about six months. When I was working at the Lafayette, there was an alley which we used to go down to get to the theater and on one side of the alley were some stores, including a saloon. At that time Fats Waller used to play the organ at the Lafayette, and he would accompany the pictures on the screen. I would come along and Fats would call out, "Hey, Greely, go over to Blackie's Place (the bar was called that) and get me a shortie of Scotch" (a "shortie" was a four-ounce bottle), so he would give me a dollar, and I'd go and get it for him. Then I'd sit on the stool with him, and he'd take a drink and then another drink, and then he'd say, "Hey, listen to this." Now at that moment they might have somebody crying up in the picture, and Fats is supposed to be playing this crying music, but instead of that he'd start playing some swinging music. Fats would break into these pictures and play whatever you wanted him to play. He was some fine character, a beautiful person, and could play.

When I left the Lafayette Theatre, I worked with Henri Saparro at the Bamboo Inn on Seventh Avenue, but it was only for a short time. Roy Butler, Joe Eldridge, and myself were the reeds, Manzie Johnson on drums, Ward Pinkett, Jimmy Archey, and Frank Smith (bass). I stayed there about a month because Saparro was quite a hard guy to get along with and at that time I could go anywhere and practically get a job. One night, Vernon Andrade, who used to bug me all the time, came along and offered me a job with his band at the Renaissance.

With Vernon Andrade's Band there was "Jazz" Williams; he was an old clarinet player who had been with Jim Europe's Band. The trumpet was Elmer Chambers; we also had a good solo trumpet player but I can't recall his name. The drummer was Aubrey Walks, and we had a bass player by the name of "Bass" Vernon, a big fat guy—I don't know whatever happened to him. We played at the Renaissance throughout the winter of 1927–1928. It was a good job, and we also played some club dates. You worked every night and a matinee on Sunday; the pay was good, it was much better than the Savoy. When the summer came, he didn't have much to do, so that was when I joined Willie Lynch.

I went up to the Savoy with Willie Lynch's Band, we had Joe

Steele (piano), Charlie Holmes (alto), Archie Johnson (trumpet), Willie Lynch (drums), Freddie Jenkins (trumpet), Frank Smith (bass)—he was a friend of Jimmy Archey, they were both from Norfolk. That band worked up there during the summer of 1928.

When the fall came in, I went back with Vernon Andrade. I was married in October of 1928. I used to do some work with J. Rosamund Johnson and that's how I came to record with Bessie Smith. It was just after I left the Renaissance (recording date was May 15, 1929). I did record with Elmer Snowden on Victor; I don't know the names of the tunes, but at that time we had megaphones which we used to play through. They would sit the drummer facing the wall in another place back there; they would pad his bass drum, it was a big deal.

In the summer of 1929 I joined Benny Carter at the Savoy. The band was terrific, the music was out of this world. Ted "Jobetus" McCord, Benny, and myself were on saxophones, Red Hicks and Danny Logan on trombones, Shelton "Scad" Hemphill and Wardell "Preacher" Jones on trumpets, Al Talcott was the guitar player, Bill Beason was on drums. We had a tall light-skinned piano player but I can't recall his name. We went out on the road to Pennsylvania, Ohio, and Kentucky, and the deal while we were out on the road wasn't any good at all. The guys had to pay the transportation out of their money for the guys with cars; both Jobetus and Danny Logan bought new cars. I quit Benny while we were on the road. It didn't suit me at all.

Horace Langhorne had an accident and broke his jaw, and I took his place up at the Lenox Club with Cliff Jackson for about four or five months. Rudy Powell was on alto, Ed Anderson on trumpet, Ed Cuffee on trombone, Jimmy Cannon on guitar, and a drummer from Washington who stood up while playing because if he sat down he went to sleep. *["Sleepy" Percy Johnson, according to Jack Butler—D.G.]* Andy Jackson came in replacing Cannon, and Henry Goodwin came in on trumpet. Now a funny thing that happened up there was that most of the guys chewed gum all the time, and everyone was always borrowing gum. I bought some and then mixed it with some laxatives and gave them to the guys. They had only a small men's room, and there was this queue outside with the guys trying to get in there, and I'm laughing and so Cliff thought it funny as well. We would play over at the Cotton Club from nine o'clock to eleven o'clock and then Duke would come in, and we would start at the Lenox Club at eleven o'clock.

I returned to work with Vernon Andrade at the Renaissance and then Luis Russell came after me. Luis Russell, at that time, was working at the Saratoga Club on Lenox Avenue, and he wanted me to go into his band, but I didn't go into the band straightaway. I stayed on with Andrade, but then Red Allen came after me, and I did some recordings with Red and later with Adrian Rollini and that group.

I replaced Teddy Hill in the Luis Russell Band and Red Allen, Otis Johnson, J.C. Higginbotham, Charlie Holmes, Albert Nicholas and myself, Bill Johnson, "Pops" Foster, Paul Barbarin, and Luis Russell—that was the original personnel. I worked with them and later with Louis Armstrong fronting the band until 1936, and then I was fired because I was involved in a hassle with Joe Glaser. He had taken over the band. There were quite a few changes while I was in the band. Charlie Holmes left and Henry "Moon" Jones replaced him, Red left a couple of times but he came back, Coleman Johnson [Bill Coleman] was in for quite a while at the same time as Red, Bill Dillard came into the band and stayed quite a while before he left, then there was Leonard "Ham" Davis. Luis Russell and I became pretty good friends, and I was in the know of practically everything that went on. It was some band, believe me. They had a little deal in the band where the New Orleans guys would play and the rest of the guys would rest. Just the five pieces—Red, Nick, Pops, Russell and Barbarin—and they would play, you better believe it. They would come out with their New Orleans music, and then we would come on and play our music which was quite different from theirs, because they played nothing but the New Orleans stuff and we played what we could play well. You had two small bands that were in the band, but we had J. C. Higginbotham, and we did just as well as the guys from New Orleans.

At one time, Red and Russell had a little hassle. I don't know what started it, but they were not getting along so well, so Russell sent to New Orleans to get a trumpet player to take Red's place. Russell told us all that, "You know what, you guys haven't heard a real trumpet player. I've got a trumpet player coming here tomorrow, he's coming down to the Saratoga Club, and I want you all to be there."

I replied, "So I'm working with the band, so I've got to listen." His name was Lee Collins, and he was a good enough trumpet player. And everyone is sitting there waiting for Lee Collins to knock Red out and Red blew Lee Collins right back to New Orleans. Poor Lee couldn't make it, he only stayed three nights, he was ready to go back. In passing, I would just like to say that Red Allen was one hell of a trumpet player. There are many people who didn't like him nor his playing, but I don't see how they couldn't because he could play, and he knew it and wouldn't let you know he could. He was arrogant and nasty and everything, but he could play!

Red nicknamed all the guys in the band; he nicknamed Henry Jones "Moon." There used to be a comic strip in the papers called *Moon Mullens*, and there used to be a character in the strip called Banjo Eyes and Henry Jones had kind of big eyes, so Red nicknamed him "Moon" and it stuck. Many people never knew his name was Henry. Incidentally, he was a good saxophone player; he was also a hell of a violinist too in St. Louis. He studied under the same teacher that I studied under, and "Moon" worked in the theatre playing the violin.

After Louis Armstrong joined forces with Russell, we went into the recording studios a great deal. They didn't care how the band sounded as long as Louis sounded good. I recall one occasion when we had recorded a tune a few times and Louis had fluffed up on it, and then Otis Johnson had blown the water out of his trumpet just at the end of the tune, so we had to record it again. They were mad at Otis because Louis had done a good one.

In 1936, I had this hassle with Joe Glaser, and I left Russell and Armstrong and went down to the New Gardens Taxi Dancing School on 14th Street with a good trumpet player that we called "Bindad"—we used to call him "Bindad" because any place you named he would say "I'd been there." I stayed there for about three or four months; Harry Dial and Henry "Moon" Jones were in that band. Then I went back with Vernon Andrade for about a year; we had Gene Mikell on tenor, Alan Brown on trumpet, Al Sears played alto, "Fats" Green played clarinet and saxophone. Ram Ramirez worked there for a while then Victor Sharkey replaced Ram.

Around 1940 or 1941, I worked with Horace Henderson. Franc Williams (trumpet), Skinny Brown, and Bob Dorsey were in that band *[Clyde Bernhardt recalled in November 1981 that in August/September of 1941 he did a two-week tour with Horace Henderson, when the Edgar Hayes Band was laid off. In the band at that time were Franc Williams, Shirley Clay, and Chester Boone. He recalled that they went down to Tennessee and Georgia—D.G.].* While I was with Horace, I switched from playing tenor to baritone. On leaving Horace Henderson, I went with Cootie Williams's Band in 1942 and switched exclusively to playing the baritone with Cootie. Charlie Holmes, Eddie "Cleanhead" Vinson, Lee Pope, and Sam "The Man" Taylor (saxes), E. V. Perry and Louis Bacon (trumpets), Eddie Burke and R. H. Horton (trombone) were some of the men in that band. I stayed with Cootie until 1943, and then I went with Cab Calloway. They needed a flute player, and I was one of the few flute players around. When I first joined the band, Illinois Jacquet was there. We had Hilton Jefferson, Andy "Flat" Brown, Ike Quebec, and Al Gibson on saxophones (I replaced Walter "Foots" Thomas); Jonah Jones, Shad Collins, Russell "Pops" Smith, and Lammar Wright (trumpets); Tyree Glenn and Claude Jones (trombones); and Milt Hinton was on bass.

While I was working with Cab Calloway's Band in Chicago, we were playing in the Sherman Hotel, and Fats Waller was living in the Dusable Hotel. All the guys lived there, but I lived at home with my parents. One night, we were all off on the same evening, and Fats, who was playing at the Three Deuces (Red Allen was working there, as well) had not been allowed to take his organ there. The union would not let him, so he had put his organ in the hotel suite. Above five or six guys from Cab's Band, including Milt Hinton, Jonah Jones, and myself were standing outside the hotel one evening about eight o'clock, and Fats invited us all upstairs to his suite. He called up his agent and made him bring up a "caser" of Scotch—Johnny Walker Black—that's what he would drink. He sat there all night and played for us. Fats played out of his mind. He didn't play any music that had been written; sometimes he'd play something that he had written, but that was very seldom. He was so prolific, he'd say, "Hey, listen to this, I've got an idea," and man he played some of the most beautiful things you ever listened to. He was terrific.

After leaving Cab Calloway, I became the bandmaster in charge of Eddie Vinson's Band. This was around the latter part of 1945. Eddie sent to Texas for the musicians in his band, and I had to teach them. I taught trombone, trumpet, and saxophone. While I was rehearsing the band here in New York, I made some recordings with Joe Louis's ex-wife, Marva Louis, and Coleridge Davis. They needed a baritone player, and they sent me over to the recording studios. We worked at the Rhumboogie Club in Chicago and the Zanzibar Club in New York, I worked them into a good band. I was the conductor of the show when the Inkspots took it over. I did very little playing. I finally quit the band at the Zanzibar as they were going out on the road. I then joined Claude Hopkins at the Zanzibar, Scoville Browne and John Brown (bass) were in that group. After that, I joined the Afro-Cuban bands and in 1955 I retired from playing professionally.

Figure 16. Greely Walton (left) and R. H. Horton (right). Photo by Al Vollmer.

Barclay Draper

I'm not really what you would call a jazz musician, yet I've lived a long, long time and I have been associated with jazz musicians for practically all my musical life. I didn't follow any particular line of jazz, because economically it didn't fit into my program of life.

I was born in Camden, New Jersey, on February 20, 1901, and I can remember the small yellow house where I lived when I was young. My home, as I recall, was a three-bedroomed house with two floors and no basement. It was opposite a small one-story building used as an office by the company which my father worked for. This was the office of the Smith Lime Company. It was owned by a man named Barclay S. Smith whose Christian name I inherited.

At this plant, which was located in Camden at 12th and Federal Streets, my entire family lived, a brother, two sisters, my grandmother (my father's mother), my mother, my father, and myself. The yellow house where we lived had three bedrooms, parlor, dining room, and kitchen. We had running water and a privy that was attached to the house. We bathed in washtubs; I think they were made of wood (later we may have had aluminum ones). The lamps burned kerosene and for mild heat we used kerosene stoves, but for cooking and heating, the stoves burned wood and coal. My mother baked most of the bread that we ate.

The house and office were separated by a driveway that supported a set of wooden scales that were strong enough to weigh a large wagon loaded with sea shells. The wagons were filled with oyster and clam shells which were used to make lime. The scales washed the wagons with their contents on arrival, weighed them and then when the wagon was emptied and before it left, it was weighed again to determine the weight it had held. These scales were operated and read in the office.

My father was the foreman of the plant, and a Mr. Cole was the superintendent. Our home was included in my father's wages. He was also custodian of the plant, which covered about ten acres that included a railroad which brought in the materials needed to operate the plant and from which the shipments were made. My father was also an engineer. He operated the engine that powered the machines and conveyor belts that crushed and conveyed the crushed shells (the shells themselves were crushed into different sizes to meet their particular needs). The lime, after it had been refined, would be used for many purposes, such as plaster, white-wash, fertilizer, deodorants, and various other things, even chalk and pottery, while the crushed shells were used in chicken farms, fish bowls and tanks, bird cages, and other sundry things.

On the plant itself, we also had horses. They were used to move the coal that was used to fire the boilers that furnished the steam to operate the mechanism which crushed the shells. These horses were also used to haul the finished product (the lime and shells were put into bags that were then sewn at the top by hand) to the railroad sidings to be shipped to their destinations. One horse was used to pull a rope attached to a pulley which hoisted the shells to the top of the kilns that burned them into lime. A large wooden bucket would be loaded with several hundred pounds of shells and hoisted to a platform about fifty feet high, where the shells would be deposited and then dumped into the kilns. I would sometimes help to feed and water these horses.

I began my schooling in Camden at an all-Negro school. My father was an ordained minister and had a small church in Camden. When I was a boy, all the families had a piano in the house; it was a sort of "must." My brother, who was five years older than myself, and my sister, who was two years older, both of them had a piano teacher, but my mother felt that I was too young to learn the piano. But I could play the lessons better than they could. At that time, I was only seven or eight years old.

Sometime, in the year of 1909, we moved along with the Lime Plant Company from Camden to Philadelphia, which was just across the river. It was a much larger plant, and most of the men that were working with my father went along to Philadelphia and continued to work at the plant. Mr. Cole, the superintendent, died shortly after we moved to Philadelphia, and my father was made superintendent. After we moved to Philadelphia, we no longer lived on the plant's property. My mother would assist with some of the work on the plant. She would sew the bags up before they were shipped; it was piece-work, and she was paid a certain amount for each bag.

At the plant in Philadelphia, a steam boiler was added to hoist the shells to the kiln platforms. These shells were loaded into a steel bucket and hoisted up. In my days away from school, it became my job to attend the guy line that was wrapped around a large steel spoke attached to the engine. This rope, by loosening and tightening, helped guide the bucket to the platform. My father trained me to do this and I was paid a dollar a day.

By now, music had engaged my attention, and I would attend the theaters and movies. At the theater, there would always be songs with melodies that I liked and I would remember them; it was the same at the movies, the pianist would always play a song that would stick in my memory. We always had a piano, my grandmother had one, also my aunt (my father's sister), whom I adored. Pianos in those days were a part of the parlor furniture.

Around 1911, my mother and father separated, and I moved from Philadelphia to Bridgeton, New Jersey. My mother's parents lived there, as did most of my father's relatives. My brother remained with my father, while my younger sister and I went with my mother. I think we at first lived with my aunt (my father's sister). We had an infant baby, who was the last of my father's children; his name was Herbert, but he died soon after we moved to Bridgeton. My father attended the funeral, but I don't ever remember seeing him after that. My father was quite a competent person; he was an engineer, quite good at figures and able to handle most of the bills of lading and the necessary office work. He also knew how to handle men; he would train the men to do their jobs by showing them how it was to be done. He would work with them personally and sometimes, when it became necessary, they would engage in what was called the manly art of self-defense, and after the fight they would return to work without malice. He was admired by all who worked with him and he even learned how to drive a motor truck, just in order to be prepared when the truck would replace the horses and wagons.

Life changed for me, at that time, as I was the sole male with
my mother and sister. I attended school in Bridgeton, after receiving a transfer from George Sharswood Public School in Philadelphia. I believe I attended Sharswood School for about two years,
prior to moving to Bridgeton. Bridgeton was a small town with
approximately 12,000 inhabitants. The principal industries were
glass manufacturing, farming, and canning. The farm products
for future storage were sold at the local stores and stores in other
cities. They would can or jar the vegetables and fruits for the en-
suing winters. A vast number of men were employed in the glass
houses during the winter months, as the heat in the glass houses
was too severe for summer work.

I did my share of farm work in the harvest season when school
was closed. I would top onions, pick potatoes, strawberries,
beans, and tomatoes. In rural districts they closed school earlier
than in the city, in order that the children could be used to help
the parents with their chores. The local farms would hire school
children to help with the work as it was necessary to harvest
crops when they were ripe or mature. I can remember walking
about five miles to reach a farm to be employed to pick beets or
pull them from the ground at five cents a row. We would arrive
at seven in the morning and worked until noon. We had an hour
for lunch and then started over again at one o'clock and finished
at six o'clock. Those of us who did the job well would be hired
for the next day, but those of us who had left some of the beets
still in the ground were not permitted to return. We also picked
potatoes for eighty-five cents a day plus lunch. Even though our
homes were miles away, we made it on time. In less than two
weeks I had purchased a second-hand bike which enabled me to
ride to work. We also picked strawberries, but I was so slow at
picking these that after half a day I gave it up and went back into
town. I also sold newspapers in town. I would buy them two for
a penny and sell them for a penny a piece. My mother did not
have to give me any money as I earned enough to take care of
most of the things I needed.

Outside of this work, I still had plenty of time for recreation. I
played baseball, football, basketball (which I did not like) and
shinny, which was a form of ground-hockey. We learned to swim
in the creek that flowed near the house where we lived. We also
caught fish and crabs there. It was called the Cohansey River, but

to us it was the creek. We used to cross over it as it was a short cut to the racetrack and farms that we wanted to get to. Crossing that creek saved us some two miles of walking. We would bundle our clothes on our heads and use boards or logs to kick our way across, whenever we couldn't get a rowing boat.

I used to go to the theater a lot, one theater that showed vaude-ville charged a nickel for two tickets which were good only for the peanut gallery at the very top of the building. The shows usu-ally changed once a week, whereas the movies generally changed shows twice a week. I went to the theater so often that I learned the lyrics to most of the tunes.

In 1914, after school closed in the summer months, I went to Newark to visit my older brother. He had moved to Newark after my father had died, and he had a flat on Earle Street, near Fre-linghuysen Avenue. He worked in a plant there, and his flat was part of that plant. I stayed with him throughout the summer, and it was a pleasant stay in Newark. I was able to visit New York and, more importantly, Coney Island, where I was able to enjoy the amusements while sampling the hot dogs, hamburgers, clams, and corn on the cob.

I returned to Camden in 1915 and went to school again, this time at the John G. Whitten School, for a year and a half. While attending that school I joined the Boy Scout troop that was in some way connected with the church of which my mother was a member. I also sang in the junior choir and belonged to the senior class in Sunday school. We formed a bugle corps while in the Boy Scouts; most of the members of the corps belonged to the church but they were all Boy Scouts. I was a patrol leader and also was the temporary assistant scoutmaster. We only made one camping trip to Burling Island which happened to be across the Delaware River near a town called Bristol, Pennsylvania. Some hoodlums from Bristol decided that they did not want us on the New Jersey Island and crossed the river to chase us off. Fortune was on our side, as some company mechanics belonging to the U.S. Army were also camped on Burling Island at the same time, and these hoodlums from Bristol were easily disposed of and sent scurrying back to their hometown.

There was very little difference between North and South at that time. Most places of amusement were segregated, and Cam-den had two segregated schools. The city had only one high school. Therefore it was integrated, but you were taught your place. In high school, we were told by our home room teacher that we were no longer children, but were young ladies and young gentlemen and were going to be treated as such. Quote— "I am going to seat you by the first letter in your last name," and alphabetically by having the name of Draper, the letter "D" came very quickly. But when I arose at the sound of the letter "D," Miss German, my teacher, promptly told me, "I don't mean you Mr. Draper"—unquote. Five of us, who were considered Negroes were seated in the same row, now we were in our proper place, but we were still called "Mr." and "Miss."

We had a good music teacher who conducted singing classes in the auditorium. She divided us into groups of sopranos, altos, tenors and basses. My voice was too low for tenor but not low enough for bass, so I sang tenor anyway.

Around this time, a man by the name of Richard "Dick" Little, who was a trombone player, organized a brass band. Most of the members were recruited from the Boy Scout Bugle Corps of which I was a member. We had developed a very good bugle corps, and he gathered a group of us together and started the band. He lived next door to my church, and we used to meet at his house and rehearse. I wanted to play the trombone, but as I didn't have the instrument, Mr. Little gave me a trumpet. He taught me the scales on the trumpet and when we had rehearsals I learned more and more about it. Already I had a fairly good musical background from public school. He bought books for beginner bands, and we practiced regularly until we could play some of the tunes very well. Some of the boys had more experience than others, as there had been another man who had the band before Mr. Little. There were also one or two adult bands in our town and Mr. Little had created an incentive in us that our boy's band would be better than the adult band, and soon we were playing better than the men through diligent rehearsing. It wasn't long before we were ready to present our band in front of the public. We were quite ambitious in our endeavors, and we would play for any affair, just for the sake of playing and getting the exposure. Soon we were being proffered the opportunities to play for lodges, sermons, funerals and the like. We began to compete with the lodge bands, and we reached our mecca when we finally landed the Veterans' Parade on May 30, Memorial Day, honoring the Civil War and Spanish-American war veterans. When World War I came along, some of our key players were inducted and that just about ended our band, but during this time, some of us thought that we'd like to play dance music, so we organized ourselves into a small dance group.

During the First World War years, we played one night a week in Roebling, New Jersey, at Roebling Steel Company's center there. We entertained their Black workers. We also had one night in Penns Grove, New Jersey (the Dupont Powder Company was located there). We had five pieces, Tom Johnson (trombone), Sammy Watkins (saxophone), Herb Williams (drums), Maurice Vaugh (piano), and myself on trumpet. Occasionally, we would change our piano player. We called our group the Blue Band Syncopators.

We even financed some of our own dances, we would rent a hall and have placards and handbills printed and do all the presentation ourselves. Most of our affairs were successful, and the exposure helped a lot, as a number of clubs hired us to play for them.

During those years, I was given my first professional gig by a lady that lived in my town. She hired me together with a drummer and a piano player to play a dance at a small town called Salem about forty five miles from Camden in southwest New Jersey. Walter Briscoe was the drummer on that gig; he was one year older than I, but I was ahead of him at school. We left our hometown at about 5:30 P.M., as the dance was due to start at 8:00 P.M. and travelled there by train. The dance did not end until midnight and when we arrived back at the railroad station, we discovered that we had to wait for the milk train. It did not leave until 5:30 A.M. and stopped at every station. We did not arrive back in Camden until 8:30 A.M., and for that gig we were paid $2. Walter Briscoe's mother complained about his long absence from home and the small amount of pay to the lady. She agreed to pay us $4 for any other engagements in the future, but she refused to use Briscoe again.

We youngsters used to go to dances and hear bands like Madame Keene's in Philadelphia. We would go over there and hear her band, as one night a week she had a dixieland combination, consisting of Doc Hyder on clarinet, Napoleon Bizell on trumpet, Bernard Archer on trombone, Bass Edwards on Tuba, Ned [?] on drums, and Madame Keene on piano. Now they played dixieland music better than the Original Dixieland Jazz Band. Napoleon Bizell was a good trumpet player, but when he was about 25 or 30 years old, something went wrong with his mind. But he could play; he was extremely talented. After he left Madame Keene, he went to play at the Standard Theater in Philadelphia. Bob Ricketts, who was an exceptionally good piano player, was the leader there.

The first time I ever heard Gus Aitken was at the Standard Theater, he played with Gonzelle White. She had quite an act. Gus Aitken would stand on one side of the stage playing trumpet and another fellow—I don't know his name, but he played good trumpet—was on the other side of the stage. In those days, everything that had to do with the trumpet, I can remember. There was another act called "The Musical Sheiks," where the trumpet player fingered the trombone and the trombone player fingered the trumpet—it was a unique thing at the time. Another guy, Jap Foster, played the piano with one hand and the trumpet with the other at the same time.

Our own dance group, by now, had gained most of the dances that had been previously played by musicians from Philadelphia. We would charge the union scale, which was comparable to the Negro Union in Philadelphia. We did very well for quite some time. I wasn't taking it too seriously, but then an old schoolmate of mine, by the name of James Kennerman, returned from his army service and his return heralded the start of my serious professional musical career.

James Kennerman had served in the army during World War I. He was a tuba player when he left Camden, but when he returned from the army he was playing the tenor saxophone. Anyway, he came to me one day and said that he was working in Atlantic City at a cabaret called The New World. It was owned by Mike Keeley, I think. They needed a trumpet player and James Kennerman talked me into going down there and applying for the job. I was a little shaky about doing this as I had no experience of this sort of job. By now, I was married and we had a six-weeks-old baby girl. Well, eventually I decided to go to Atlantic City, and I was given the job at The New World. This was around 1921. The host and M.C. at this cabaret was an old time trouper named [?] Ramsey, whom I had seen with S. H. Dudley's "Smart Set" (it was one of the top Negro shows at that time). They gave me $30 per week plus tips. I don't know what the opening hours were exactly, but the closing hours were when people stopped spending their money.

We had six girls who entertained with songs and dances. The host, Ramsey, also sang some songs, mostly these were request numbers. In the early evening when we opened we would play a dance tune, and then we would play a song for each of the girl entertainers. When they had finished the chorus of their song, they would dance. After that most of the songs or dances would be "by request," which usually meant a tip for us. There were four of us in that band, a very good drummer by the name of "Juice" Miller ("Juice" because he did a lot of drinking), an excellent pianist [?] Williams, James Kennerman on tenor saxophone, and myself on trumpet. Now the girls would go to each one of the tables and sing and people would give them tips. One of the girls came out of the Tennessee Ten, and she danced at a tempo that was almost too fast for me to play, but I learned. The tune she danced to was called "I Left My Door Wide Open and My Daddy Walked Out." Whatever money was given to the girls or the band as tips was put into a box, and at the end of the night we would split it up between us. My share on that first night was about $20, and I would say that in a week we averaged between $65 and $70 without salary. My stepfather was working for $15 a week and supporting a family, so that gives you some idea of how big the money was there. I was not playing for the love of music; I was playing for the love of money, and at that time I couldn't see a more lucrative job than the one I was in. I could read the music better than I could play it, but most of the songs we played were played by ear or they needed to be transposed to fit the voices of the singers. I don't remember just how long I remained there, but when I returned to Camden I was much more experienced than when I had left.

Atlantic City seemed to be the place for bands in those days. Ethel Waters, Ethel Williams, and Snow Fisher were the entertainers at the Philadelphia House, and Sam Wooding led the band there. What impressed me more than the "Two Ethels," though, were two of the musicians in Sam's band. He had a trumpet player named Jack Hatton and also Big Charlie Green on trombone. Jack Hatton was a little different from other trumpet play-

ers. He made different sounds and he had different gadgets—
they didn't call them mutes then—different tin cans and
plungers. Big Green also had these gadgets and between them
they had a vast array of different things that they put over the
bells of their instruments making odd and unusual sounds. Jack
Hatton used to flutter tongue on the trumpet and make sounds
that came out like a laugh. Later I tried to copy this, and I had
some success with it. At that time, Jack Hatton was considered
one of the greater exponents of what jazz was at that time. In that
same band, they had a West Indian by the name of Edwards who
played clarinet, and I think "Diamond" was the drummer at that
time. The man I admired, though, was Jack Hatton, and so I copied his growling and flutter-tonguing, and James Kennerman
said to me, "When you learn to play like Jack Hatton, you'll be
just like him."

When I returned from Atlantic City to Camden, I regrouped
the outfit that I was working with prior to going to Atlantic City.
We did quite well as we were booked into Clementon Park, New
Jersey, for three nights a week. The dance hall was situated in the
park, and it was strictly for Whites. We were paid $8 a night. We
also played local dances for both Black and White customers, and
things were quite good.

Around this time, a very talented clarinetist named Joe Joiner
had a band that played mostly in the Philadelphia area. He had
some difficulties with his own group, so he approached us with
a proposition that we should go and work with him. He was one
of the best clarinet players that I had ever heard, and, since he
was organized already, we joined him. He was terrific and he had
a lot of bookings, so we were quite happy to work for him. This
was during the early twenties. We played a movie theatre on
South Street in Philadelphia; there we played the score for *The
Sheik* starring Rudolph Valentino. We were also hired to play at
the leading dance hall in Philadelphia on Market Street, opposite
Charlie Kerr, who was the leader of the biggest name White band
in Philadelphia. Kerr had about ten pieces, but we only had
around six pieces. We worked with Joe Joiner as our leader for
several seasons. We even returned to Atlantic City with him, but
the cabaret that had booked us decided to open before Easter.
The owner thought that he would have a head start over the other
cabarets. Unfortunately our location was bad; we were too far

from uptown and by Decoration Day, we were ready to close, while most of the other cabarets were opening. Undaunted, we decided to return to Camden, and we began working there again.

We were engaged to play in Wilmington, Delaware, for three nights a week and also one night in New Castle, Delaware. Some weeks we would manage to add another night to the week. We picked up a local piano player by the name of Willard Chippy—he was a genius—we also added a tuba, a fellow by the name of [?] Gordon. At that time, we had Tom Johnson on trombone, Sammy Watkins was on alto saxophone (he eventually went off with Doc Hyder as his first alto). Altogether we had seven pieces in our combination. The auditorium where we played in Wilmington was the largest one in the town, and we played the whole season there.

While we were with Joe Joiner, we had a chance to break into the Keith Vaudeville Circuit. At that time Keith Vaudeville was the Number One. The manager of the Towers Theater in Camden had Joe Joiner build up our band into a vaudeville act. The idea was, if we were successful, they were going to put us on their circuit. We broke the act in at a small town called Millville, New Jersey (some forty miles from Camden) and things went well. We played there for three days and then returned to our hometown of Camden to play the next week at the Towers Theater. If we had made good, it would have led to ten weeks' work in and around Philadelphia. Our act was next to the finale, which was good billing, but on the very last night of the week, our leader was late, and when he came on stage we had practically finished our act. Unfortunately, as a result, that was the end of our vaudeville career.

Shortly after that, we parted company from our leader, and I took over the group and managed to keep them together for some time. We were quite successful playing various dances in our hometown and in the vicinity. We would hire somebody to drive us to the surrounding towns. I think I was the only one with a family. We also worked at Vic Hamilton's Cabaret in Philadelphia; they had two cabarets, one upstairs and one downstairs. June Clark, who was quite a trumpet player, was working upstairs with a lady piano player (I think her name was Minnie Timber), but the place just couldn't support the two acts, so we lost the job.

I then tried to book our group into the Paradise Cabaret in uptown Philadelphia. The manager would not hire my group, but he offered me a job with the band that was playing there. I took the job, because as I said before, by then I was married and had a child to take care of. I stayed at the Paradise awhile, but the job didn't turn out the way I had expected it would and I learned from the other fellows that sometimes you had problems getting paid. In the meantime I had talked with someone who knew a man by the name of Bill Leonard. He had a cabaret down on Lombard Street, and I made secret arrangements to leave the Paradise and go and work for him, but I really didn't know how to get out of it and get my money at the same time. They had a rule at the Paradise that the band was not allowed to leave the building during performances. When I found out about this, I told the fellow I had to go out to get some cigarettes. He told me that I couldn't go, so I just walked out anyway. He fired me, but he gave me my money. The next night I went to work at Bill Leonard's and worked there for almost a year.

In the fall of 1923, I was approached by a trombone player named Ford, who had contracted a job in Atlantic City (now the fall is when the season is over as far as Atlantic City is concerned). He had made a connection to play at the Bellman's Home, a Black cabaret that was owned and operated by a Negro named Sam Daniels, who kept the place open the year round. He had asked Ford to make arrangements for a band to play there. We had five pieces: Joe Johnson on alto saxophone; a good cabaret piano player by the name of Kessler Cherry from Norfolk, Virginia; George Richardson from Philadelphia was on drums; Ford, the trombone player, was from Kentucky, and I was on trumpet. Ford made us into a very good band. He taught me how to transpose the third alto part for trumpet by changing to the bass clef and altering the key signatures, and we played most any orchestrations. I played the third alto part on trumpet, Ford played the tenor saxophone part, and Joe played the first alto part, so we had three-part harmony. We were quite successful, and the job paid well. By that time, I had a second child, and it became necessary for me to keep sending home regular money to my family. We worked together for several months, but, as the season came near to closing, the owner decided to let our trombone player go, as he considered him to be the least important musician in the band.

In fact, he let us all go, under the pretext of alterations, but then the owner re-hired us all again, minus the trombonist. Our piano player was put in charge, but it was not long before they let the pianist go, and we had several piano players after that.

During the spring of 1924, I was offered a job at the Blue Kitten. Cliff Jackson was the very good pianist there. We had six pieces in the group, and each musician was hired individually. This was a cabaret and most of the cabarets at that time operated in a similar fashion. The girls would sing their songs to the customers at the tables and then return to the floor to do their dance. We had a female impersonator who was actually the star of the show. Now this was around the time that I first saw trumpeter Henry Goodwin. He was with Sam Taylor in Atlantic City; they played a dance-hall on Kentucky Avenue. Sam Taylor was evidently an E-flat piano player, because the band played everything in that one key.

I left the Blue Kitten and went to work with a group at Egg Harbor. The leader of the band was a tuba player named Jim Winters and in the band with me was Jim Stewart, a trombone player. I finished out that season in Atlantic City and then returned to Philadelphia (where I was living by that time), and I started an aggregation of my own. I had that same fellow Jim Winters on tuba, plus a banjo player, piano player, and drummer. We had a job in a roadhouse on the White Horse Pike in South Jersey. It was enough to keep us together for that winter.

Later I put together a very good group for a job that I had been offered at the Pekin at 16th and South Street in Philadelphia. There, I had Irving Johns on piano; Albert Berry, an exceptional tenor saxophone player; Mike "Prince" Venable on alto saxophone. Mike had been a former leader of the Barnum and Bailey Circus Band. He was also one of the finest baritone horn players that ever lived. He was also a great trombone player; in fact he played most instruments, taught harmony and arranged. Harry Marsh on drums was one of Philadelphia's top drummers. Jim Stewart was on trombone, and I was the weakling on trumpet. That was the best band that I ever put together. We kept that band together for some time, and some of the entertainers that I remember that we accompanied were Eva Mason and Rosa Henderson (they were the partners of John Mason and Slim Henderson, both talented Black comedians of that era). Jim Stewart, my trombone player, went off to work with Bobby Lee's Band, and I replaced him with Jim Winters, the tuba player. We worked at the Pekin right through that winter.

The first time that I ever broadcast was over WLIT in Philadelphia with Bobby Lee's Band. Jim Stewart had asked me to make the session. I guess that some of the guys who worked for Bobby Lee didn't want to play without pay and they didn't come. I did it, just for the excitement of playing on the radio, and I did it for no pay. To date that broadcast, a new tune at that time was "Who?," and the first time I played it was when we were on the air.

When the summer came, I arranged to go back to Atlantic City to work a cabaret at the Pekin (by coincidence the same name as the job I had left); it was situated at North Carolina and Baltic Avenue. We changed our drummer and piano player and brought in Emory Lucas from Washington, D.C., on piano and our drummer was Harry Williams from Homestead, Pennsylvania. He was one drummer who read music; he also played clarinet but he was an excellent show drummer. I added Harry "Unk" Waters on banjo, he was Ethel Waters's uncle and we nicknamed him "Unk" (short for uncle). Billy Mitchell (his theme song was "Anybody Here Want to Buy a Little Dog?") was the producer of the cabaret show. This would have been in 1926, and we went down to Atlantic City from Philadelphia by train. We had arranged to rehearse the show with Billy Mitchell for two o'clock in the afternoon (the show was due to open the same night). Well, he brought along the music, and we ran through the entire show. By 3:30 P.M. I told him the rehearsal was over and he was very upset, but we had to find rooms and get some rest so that we could play that night. Billy Mitchell felt that we had not rehearsed long enough to be able to play the show properly. I informed him that we had gone over all the show music and that we understood what was to be done. The show opened that night at midnight. It was a one-hour show, and Mike Venable not only played the alto, but he picked up his soprano saxophone and played right along with me. When we had finished Billy Mitchell came over to me and said that we had played his show better after one rehearsal than the band at his previous engagement had played it after a week. The men I had, though, were experienced. Albert Berry, for instance, was a musician who had more than thirty pupils in Atlantic City. One incident that occurred while we were on that engagement was the night that George Gershwin came to the bandstand and asked to play the piano. He played "Rhapsody in Blue," a new tune that he was plugging.

I was offered a job in Miami for the winter, but most of the men declined. They did not want any part of the South, which was quite understandable, race relations being what they were at the time. At the end of that season we disbanded.

During the fall of 1926, I decided to come to New York and moved in with my in-laws. My uncle was quite popular. He worked for the post office, and he knew a number of musicians. He introduced me to some of them and gave me a lot of good advice. He told me that I had come from a city where you had special Sunday clothes, but in New York every day was Sunday and that was the way you had to dress: the less money you had, the brighter the shine on your shoes and the sharper the crease in your trousers. He told me that a neat appearance made it easier for people to accept you.

I don't know how long it took me to get started in New York, but it wasn't long. I was walking along 7th Avenue, near the Lafayette Theater, when I was approached by a young man. I was carrying my horn in a case, and he asked me if I was a trumpet player. He offered me a job at a salary of $40 per week with one meal. We played dance music from 7 P.M. to 1 A.M. at the Bamboo Inn, a Chinese restaurant, on Seventh Avenue and 139th Street. The leader who gave me the job was Claude Austin, a very popular and good pianist. We also played at Herman's Inn at 145th Street. Claude Austin was a composer, arranger, and a very fine person; he eventually settled in South America and married a wealthy señorita.

Later on in that same year of 1926, I worked with Willie Gant at Connor's on 135th Street, right across from the Lincoln Theater. Ward Pinkett, Happy Caldwell, Jimmy Archey, Freddie Skerritt, and Manzie Johnson were in that band. We played at Connor's for about three or four months.

Around this time I also had the opportunity to do a little sitting-in. I had a very good friend, a tuba player named Henry "Bass" Edwards who was filling in for Chink Johnson (by reputation an extremely fine tuba and trombone player). The band was the Savoy Bearcats and their leader was Leon Abbey. Freddie

White was there, Otto Mikell, Demas Dean, Gilbert Paris, James Revey, and Jejo (he was a clarinet wizard), Hernandez (who was an ordinary tenor player), and Willie Lynch was on drums. Bass Edwards introduced me as his friend, and I was invited to sit in and play a set with them at the Savoy Ballroom. I was too excited to decline, and, although I did not have my instrument, Demas Dean, who I now consider a good friend, gave me his chair and loaned me his horn. I really was unaccustomed to the baton and therefore when Leon Abbey brought his bow down or up, I was completely unprepared. I believe I joined in after the introduction, but by the time we finished the set, which was about three numbers, I was quite ready to give Dean back his chair and horn. I didn't know whether I did well or not, but they were seasoned musicians, and they made me feel quite at ease. Fess Williams was the band opposite them. They had seven pieces and George Temple, their trumpet player, offered me an opportunity to sit in, but I declined graciously; I was not ready for the exposure.

By this time, though, I had met a lot of musicians, the most important being John C. Smith, who played trumpet. Most of his work was limited to the dancehalls around Harlem. John had his own office on 135th Street, right across from the Y.M.C.A. He had a lot of dance engagements and would hire many musicians to play them. His orchestras were quite popular, and he had enough engagements to keep twenty-five to thirty musicians working four or five nights a week. I had as many as twenty-four engagements with John C. in a month. He had a rehearsal room at the Harlem Casino, located at 155th Street and 8th Avenue, about once a week in order to familiarize the musicians with his book. Sometimes there would be large numbers of musicians at rehearsals. He had enough engagements to send out several groups on the same night.

I was working with John C. Smith when Herb Branch, who was an old-time trumpet player, told me that Bobby Stark was looking for someone to take his place at a speakeasy called the Blackbottom on 56th Street. It was situated right over a garage and right across the street from it was a club called Le Perroquet where Roger Wolfe Kahn led a big time band, and was between 6th and 7th Avenue. Bobby Stark wanted to go with Chick Webb, who was opening at the Paddock Club downtown. It was an ideal job for me, as I didn't have to get to the Blackbottom until 2:30 A.M.

or 3:00 A.M. to report for work, and this allowed me to play other gigs earlier in the evening. Business started there when most of the other clubs were closing. We made good money as the tips were very good. We had a girl playing the piano by the name of Alberta Simmons; she played more piano than the average person and played as well as James P. Johnson. In fact, some people credited her with having helped James P., but whether that's true or not, I don't know.

Texas Guinan and Helen Morgan had their clubs operating then and, when they closed, they would come by the Blackbottom. Many of the big names would drop by: George Raft was a dancer at Helen Morgan's place at that time, Paul Whiteman, Vincent Lopez, and some of their musicians. Duke Ellington had his seven piece band working at Leo Bernstein's Club Kentucky, and he used to come along with some of his men. I played the whole score of *Rio Rita* before the show opened, because the fellow who wrote it brought the score along to the Blackbottom. It was the most lucrative job that I ever had, and the working hours were almost unbelievable. I used to work a lot of other gigs while I was working there.

When I left there, I became a little homesick, and I accepted a job with Cliff Edgerton's Arcadians in Philadelphia. They were the house band at the Arcadia Ballroom at Broad and Bambridge Street. Leroy Rutledge was our first trumpet player, but I can't recall the names of any of the other guys. I worked with them for several months.

Later I worked with Madame I.O. Keene for about a year. Madame Keene had the leading dance band in Philadelphia, and, on my first gig with her, she played the tune "Snag It," which was in her repertoire and which I knew from memory. I believe my playing of that tune sold me to Madame Keene, as I became her first trumpet player; whenever she had a job, I was there. Being the number one band in Philadelphia and having been working there so long, she had more gigs than anyone else. She played good piano, [?] Coleman probably was the loudest alto player that I ever played with; our drummer was Howard Whiting; I played trumpet, I can't recall if she had a trombonist. She could give us four or five nights work every week. I used to sing when I was working with her and, to give you some idea of when that was, I was doing "Ain't She Sweet" with her. Trumpeter Bill Dillard told me that he was a kid and heard me playing, but I don't remember him until I met him in New York. He turned out to be a very fine trumpet player, a much better trumpet player than I. Somehow or other, I rank most all of the trumpet players above myself, but I was able to get more work than they did. I was just lucky.

In 1927, I went to work in Newark, New Jersey, and I played at the Cotton Club for seven or eight months. I had Eddie Wells, George Cooper, Harry Schofield and Unk Waters; we had a good band there. The guy who had the place was a gangster, and at first he threatened to fire me, but instead of giving me the sack, he would call me into the bar to have a drink with him, and in the end we had no problems at all. My cousin, though, who was the drummer in the band had a habit of oversleeping and as a result of this, we eventually were fired. I was replaced there by Cliff Jackson, who brought a band in and took the job. That was the last band I ever had; those bands were too much trouble.

While working at another nightclub in Newark, I met a piano player named "Skinny" Johnson. He was an excellent pianist and he got me a job at in the Orpheum Theatre in Newark. That is where I met Jack Butler; he was just a youngster and played trumpet in that theatre. Floyd Hickman, who was the leader played violin, Joe James was the other trumpet player, [?] Singford was on trombone, [?] Smith, a man from Oklahoma, was the drummer, and on clarinet and saxophone was Clarence Adams. He was one of the finest clarinet players that I have ever heard.

Around 1929, while I was working at the Orpheum Theatre, I was asked to join the Drake & Walker Road Show. At that time, they were one of the strongest shows on the road. Later I left them, and I went to Albany to work at a nightspot with a piano player called "Nigger" Nelson. He could load a song for a singer, and we made good money there. He needed a saxophone player so I contacted Bill Alsop, who I had met in Atlantic City, and Alsop joined us there. Alsop remained on after I left.

When I returned to New York City in the early thirties, things had changed a little, but, having been around once before, I did not find it too difficult. The New Amsterdam Musical Association was still in operation (and still is). The Clef Club had sold their building but still kept a booking office. The Band Box, operated by a trumpet player named Addington Major, had closed or was failing, but a new club called The Rhythm Club had opened. Operated by Bert Hall, a musician from Chicago, it became like an exchange for musicians. Everyone went there, performers as well as musicians, big names and those who were to become big names. Bert Hall was quite influential with the Negro musicians. He was appointed as a business agent for Local 802, and the club itself became so strong that the candidates for office in the Local 802 Union would campaign there at election time. Another reason for its popularity was that they had three pool tables, and lots of musicians liked to play pool. They also had poker, and the club soon became the focal point for musicians to meet.

I gigged around with different groups on my return to New York. I met Jelly Roll Morton for the first time outside the Rhythm Club, and I played numerous dates with him, more than thirty-odd gigs, but they were always pickup groups with all different guys. At the time when I met him, he had lost a lot. He was a good talker. He claimed that "St. Louis Blues" was a blues that practically all the piano players were doing, they called it the "Jogo Blues," but it was Handy who put it down on paper. I have been credited with having made a record with Jelly Roll, but I can't recall ever having done so.

It was while on a gig that I met a drummer named "Dinah" Taylor. He introduced me to men like Wen Talbert and Freddie Tunstall. These people were showmen; they were the men that producers would get to play shows, because they knew how to direct the shows. Dinah Taylor recommended me to Freddie Tunstall, a good arranger and show business piano player, and I became his trumpet player. Whenever he had a show at the Lafayette Theater he would use me, Dinah Taylor, and Joe Britton on trombone. The three of us would play most of the shows. Wen Talbert also played the shows in the Lafayette. I worked there with Noel Klukies, Ellsworth Reynolds, and many others. Joe Britton and I worked with most of the bands that played there, until it seemed that we were working as the house brass team. They changed the format while we were working there from vaudeville to presentation. I recall we had finished a second week with Freddie Tunstall when "Hutch," the manager, asked us to work without pay for the midnight show. Bass Edwards, who was working with us, and I refused so they ousted our outfit and hired another, and I understand that after that a number of groups worked there under the scale.

Later I worked with a group led by Cliff Drake at the Alhambra Theater when it closed. Mr. Gee, the owner, said that he could not afford to play the union scale, so after about six weeks that folded.

Somewhere along the way, I worked with Fess Williams for several months, but we rehearsed more than we worked. It also paid badly, and by then I had two children to support. Fess used to keep practically the same personnel that he used at the Savoy. He had Jelly James on trombone; Perry "Stoney" Smith (everybody called him "Stoney" because of his bald head); Gregory Felix; Lloyd Phillips, an exceptional piano player; and Ray Carn was one of the trumpets. The arrangements that Fess had were tough on first trumpet; a lot of first trumpeters who played it thought that the punishment did not fit the crime. Fess, being a clarinet player had some E's and F's which he expected the trumpet players to hit.

I left Fess and went to work with Bob Fuller. The only fellow in that group that I can recall was Joe Williams, one of the best jazz trombone players that I ever knew; nobody ever speaks of him. He was a trombonist out of Jenkins's Orphanage and could play more jazz trombone than many of the other trombone players. The dancing school we played at was called the Dreamland on 125th Street between 7th Avenue and Lenox. Bob Fuller, our leader, was a very good clarinet player.

Around this time, I had a big thrill when Duke Ellington called up the Rhythm Club for a trumpet player. Arthur Whetsol had taken a night off, and Duke, who was playing at the Cotton Club on 142nd Street and Lenox, didn't like to put the show on without a full brass section. I accepted the call and went along there. I arrived about 11:30 P.M., and they briefed me as to exactly what was to be done. After I played the show, I finished the night out with them. One thing I recall—I don't think I will ever forget it—they had passed out the music for the dance, and one of the numbers they stuck in on me was an arrangement of "Twelfth Street Rag." One part of it was written in a minor key, but I was able to do it. After I finished the night, Duke came over to me and said that, if he had known who he was getting, he wouldn't have been more pleased with their work, so I must have done all right. Incidentally, Arthur Whetsol told me that he bought a Bock horn because it had a big bore and that enabled him to hold his own against that powerful Ellington brass section. He needed that tone because he wasn't that strong a fellow, but he was a hell of a nice guy. On another occasion when I went to the Cotton Club, I substituted for Cootie Williams. At that time Freddie Jenkins was the third trumpet player, but they didn't gamble on me. You see the night Whetsol took off, Cootie took over the first trumpet chair, and they put me in the second chair, and Freddie was in the third chair. Now the night Cootie took off, they gave me the second chair because Whetsol was already on first, but then when it came to the dance music they gave me the first part to play in order to find out what caliber of musician I was. I only subbed those two times for Duke.

In the early thirties, I also did a short stint in vaudeville with Allie Ross, Bubber Miley, and Zutty Singleton; it only lasted three weeks. How it happened—well, I was playing for Wen Talbert, and Allie Ross had this chance to make some extra money playing vaudeville, but Allie didn't use all the men in his band. He just used Bubber, Zutty, and the violins. We had Maude Russell, Snakehips Tucker, and two dancers from Connie's Inn. The show was called the "Connie's Inn Revue," but it wasn't really *the* Connie's Inn Revue; it was just an act that Wen Talbert and Allie Ross had put together. Wen was at the piano, and Allie directed the band. Bubber and myself were on trumpets, Joe Britton on trombone, Norman Thornton on reeds, Roy Bumford was on tenor, I believe Paul Burnett was on banjo, Bass Edwards was on tuba, and Zutty Singleton on drums. Although it only lasted three weeks we had special uniforms made for it, but the amount of work we had out of it, it really just wasn't worth the endeavor. I got paid for it and enjoyed doing it as I preferred the theater and intimate entertainment.

Later, shortly before Bubber Miley died, I did another vaudeville stint, this time with Bubber's own band. Irving Mills was the producer, and he had arranged for Bubber to have his own band. Frank Belt, an old time trumpet player that I knew, recommended me to Bubber, as Bubber was living at Frank's house. Frank called me up and I went over the parts with Bubber. Then I was invited to attend the rehearsals, but unfortunately the act only lasted about five or six weeks. I stayed with them from the beginning to the end. We had a nice act featuring Bubber and the band, comedian Tim Moore, Izzy Ringgold, and the Five Blazers. After about four weeks and while we were at the Lafayette Theater, Bubber became very ill and for the last few shows I had to do his feature, where they called on "Brother" Bubber to lead us in prayer and of course Bubber would make those sounds on the horn like he was preaching. Without Bubber we had no act, as Irving Mills had put it together especially for Bubber. There were three trumpets, Bubber, Ray Carn, and myself on second trumpet; R.H. Horton was the trombone player; Booker Pittman was one of the saxophone players; Gene Anderson was on piano; Paul Burnett on banjo; and Zutty Singleton on drums. Ralph Cooper took over that band after Bubber died and put in three new trumpet players and went abroad with them. That was one of my most pleasant experiences I had with big bands. Everyone had a great deal of respect for Bubber because he was so creative. Bubber, I feel, was responsible for the "jungle rhythm" which Duke was supposed to have created.

I worked with Bill Benford as well; now that had to be in the early thirties too. We played for six months at the Star Ballroom on 42nd Street. Buddy Murphy and I were on trumpets, Joe Williams on trombone, Norman Thornton and Roy Bumford were on reeds, Gene Rodgers on piano, Bill Benford on bass, and Steve Wright on drums.

Then, while playing at the Ridgewood Grove Dance Marathon with Marion Smith, who was our leader and pianist—Arthur Davey and Zeno Lawrence made up our quartet there—I had an offer to work for Ford Dabney, a society bandleader. Dabney, who was the composer of the tune "Shine," was responsible for a great deal of society work. I had met Alonzo "Lonnie" Williams, who was Ford's right-hand man at the time. Lonnie had been with the minstrel shows and had worked with Ford Dabney at the Ziegfeld Roof in his teens when he first came to New York (Lonnie Williams remained my best friend until he died). I accepted their offer, and I asked Gus Aitken, an established trumpet player much better than I, to take my place at the Dance Marathon for that night, and I went with Ford to Sands Point, Long Island. He had about ten musicians at that party. We played from 9 P.M. to 2 A.M., and, at the end of the gig when I asked Lonnie about my money, he told me to report to Ford's office the following afternoon and collect my check. The following day, I did as instructed and discovered to my surprise that the check was for

$27 for one night's work, whereas I had been getting between $28 and $30 a *week* at the Dance Marathon. That was the turning point in my musical career in New York.

After I had worked that night for Ford, I continued to work for him for more than twelve years. In those early days, Ford Dabney worked for the Vanderbilts and the Carlisles. Franklin D. Roosevelt was running for President, so it had to be around the year of 1932. Barbara Hutton and Mrs. Randolph Hearst were the sort of people that we played for, and we would earn more money playing for one night than many musicians earned playing for a whole week. On these dates I met Bernadine Brown, an excellent piano player; Wesley Johnson, a trumpet player; I think our trombonist was John Mayfield; Carl White was the banjo player. This same group of musicians, who were considered as entertainers, worked for different leaders such as Tom Fletcher, Hughie Woolford, Bill Conaway, Joey Coleman, Deacon Jones, and Billy Elmore. Their clients were more affluent, and they paid more money. For instance, Hughie Woolford's connection was with Franklin D. Roosevelt. Every time Roosevelt was in New York, Woolford would take a band and go up to Hyde Park and play for him. Now, Joey Coleman for some reason paid more money than anybody else; he had something about him that enabled him to demand and get more money.

I became number one choice as trumpeter, as far as these leaders were concerned. Lonnie Williams played with everyone, he

Figure 17. Hughie Woolford's orchestra in New York City during the early 1930s with trumpeter Barclay Draper (third from left in the front row).

was that popular. "Peekaboo" Jimmy used to play drums on these jobs. Sam Speed a banjo player, he'd be there too. They had a bass player who worked with most of them; his name was James Drayton. Jimmy Green, a guitar player and banjoist, worked with Ford, because he was a good entertainer. Others included Ted Brown, a violin player and saxophonist, and Elmer Howell, a good tenor player from Boston; he worked with Billy Elmore. Elmore was another of those who came out of the Clef Club and did society work. There were so many names, but, although there were different leaders overall, you were working with the same group of musicians. I was the only trumpet player, so that when they wanted another trumpet player they would ask me to get one for them. Whenever it became necessary for me to change from one leader to another, I would always call and arrange for a substitution. I always tried to find fellows who had good deportment, were dependable, and fitted with the group. If I didn't do that it might spoil the whole affair. George Winfield was a nice reliable guy; I also used Herman Autrey and Gus Aitken.

Early in the forties I went to work for the Aluminum Company, and there Jake Porter had a military band. We were led to believe that we would get preferential treatment as band members, but after we were hired, we were assigned special jobs for Negros (the term "Black" had not been adopted yet). The wages were poor and after a short stay at the plant, I went to work on the railroad as a dining car waiter.

One day, I had decided to take off a few days from the railroad in order to play a gig for Hughie Woolford. Anyway, I looked in at the Rhythm Club, and Eddie Allen approached me with an offer to fill in for him at a job in a dancing school called the Tango Palace. Eddie Allen was filling in for Lionel "Bindad" Howard at the New Gardens Ballroom, located at 116 East 14th Street. At that time nobody wanted to work at the dancing schools, and, as I was around 45 years of age, I thought that if anything is secure in music then this is it. Nobody is going to try and beat you out of the job, so I took it. Meanwhile, "Bindad" had died, so Allen stayed down at the New Gardens and I stayed at the Tango Palace for about four years. We had Sonny [?] and myself on trumpets, Henry Jameson on alto saxophone, Theodore Daley on tenor saxophone, Charlie Johnson was the piano player, and "Slim"

Mathis on drums. Later Sonny became sick, and we hired Marian Tatum. Altogether I was there for several years, but then in the late forties, I left and went back to gigging again.

Around 1951, I realized that with my family, it was necessary that I ensured their livelihood. My wife was working for a real estate broker, and I became a building superintendent. At first I had twenty apartments to supervise, then I left that for one with sixty-two apartments. When I first went to work at 50 West 106th Street, the building was occupied by all White tenants. It was considered a better building than most buildings renting apartments. Colored people, such as performers and musicians, were considered poor risks, but my position allowed me to rent to any race, so therefore Black musicians and performers were not discriminated. Some of the people who secured apartments there included Doc Cheatham, Juanita Hall, Benny Morton, Paul Gonsalves, Emmett Berry, Earle Warren, and Slim Gaillard. It was here that my early basic training was to put me in good stead. I had learned a lot about boilers and coal while helping my father when I was young, and the boiler in the building where I was superintendent was a coal-fed boiler. I knew that the most important things in the building were water and heating.

In the sixty-two apartment block, I started employing musicians to assist me. The first guy I hired was George Winfield, then the next was Henry Jameson, then came John "Jazz" Williams, a clarinet player who had played with Jim Europe (he was with Europe the night Europe was killed in Boston). Later I hired David "Jelly" James, Frank Garcia, Marian Tatum, Harry Wiggins, and Sandy Williams. Maybe they would have found themselves other jobs, maybe not. The fact that they did have that job made life a little better for them. It was an asset for me, because they all knew how to get to work on time, and they did not make unnecessary excuses for not coming to work.

I played trumpet up to around 1960, just gigging, but then I had a heart attack and my doctor didn't want me to work, so I discontinued blowing the horn. The first horn I ever had was a J.W. Pepper, then I had a Conn which I kept for many years, and finally a hand-made Parduba. When I was at school I had an almost photographic memory, and at one time I could write out every clause in the Constitution of the United States from memory. In later life this was to serve me well as the different groups

I played with used me because I had a full repertoire stored in the back of my mind.

I was never sold too much on playing jazz. I liked to play pretty, and I liked my horn to sing. That's the way I tried to play; it helped me in some ways, but not in other ways. Within big bands, maybe I didn't fit in too well with many of them, but most of those big bands didn't work a lot, they rehearsed a lot. In my musical career, once you made the connections you could do well. Your ability did mean something, but your connections actually meant more; it was not always what you knew, but who you knew.

George Winfield had this to say about his friend Barclay Draper:

> I did not do too much music with Barclay Draper, but we have been friends for a very long time. There was a piano player by the name of Ford Dabney who had quite a bit of society work, and Draper was his trumpet man. On a few occasions Ford would use two trumpets and Draper would get me for the second trumpet work, as we worked very well together. Ford Dabney had a very unique system of working. He would open the dance and play a medley of tunes. You never knew what he was going to play. Anything that came into his mind, and that meant the men had to know a vast number of tunes.
>
> Draper and I also were in the Masonic Brass Band together, under the direction of Kenneth Roane. This was during the summer of 1951. We gave a band concert at the Rockland Palace Ballroom and the band played a parade during this period. It was this association that prompted Draper to offer me the job at the apartment building after we had talked of my mechanical ability. I guess he told you that the staff were made up of musicians.
>
> Draper never went in extensively for big band work as he had good connections for high paying gigs. I always respected Draper as a good trumpet player and a very fine musician.

Sal Dentici

I was born in Allegheny County, Pittsburgh, Pennsylvania, of Italian-Sicilian parents, on December 4, 1903.

At the age of six, I began studying the violin under the tutelage of my Uncle Frank Ristiro, a talented mandolinist and guitarist, in New Castle, Pennsylvania. At the age of ten, my family moved to the East New York section of Brooklyn, New York. Here I studied under Professors Jacob DeAngelo and George DeLuca, and finally at The Gates Conservatory of Music, also in Brooklyn.

In 1917, at the age of fourteen, I played my first engagement at Jimmie Kelly's famous nightclub and restaurant, at Sullivan Street in Greenwich Village. I substituted for the regular violinist, Lew Feldman, who took off sick at least once or twice a week. George Miller, the drummer in the band, would come to my home (and with my parents' consent) pick me up, and then, after the evening's playing was over at Kelly's, would take me home in the wee hours of the next morning. This job was an "until" job, from 8 P.M. evenings until closing, which was usually in the early hours of the following morning. When I played at Kelly's I played hookey from school the next day, as I was too tired to go there. Some of the famous entertainers I played for at Jimmie Kelly's were The Happiness Boys of radio and nightclub fame; Gilda Gray, the famous shimmy dancer; and Sally Rand, the famous fan dancer.

I would play hookey from school on Monday and Thursday mornings and go to the Bushwick Theater, a B. F. Keith vaudeville theatre, and to the Halsey Theater, a vaudeville tryout house, both situated in Brooklyn. Andy Byrnes, pianist and leader of the Bushwick Theatre Orchestra, and Mike [?], violinist and leader of the Halsey Theatre Orchestra, gave me many valuable tips, which during my later years came in very handy. They were both excel-

---

lent theater orchestra pit musicians and were very respected in the theatrical field.

On a Sunday afternoon in 1918–1919 I would take the Wilson Avenue trolley car (near my home) to Canarsie, a local Brooklyn resort, and listen to a real good jazz violinist, Joe Rizzo, and his partner, Joe Buscemi, on banjo. They were playing at Bigg's Hotel, a family-style hotel. They were excellent jazz musicians, and I picked up many good tips about jazz violin playing from Joe Rizzo, who at that time I thought was the greatest.

At the age of sixteen, I joined up with The Highland Jazz Band, a local boys' band under the leadership of Benny Burkhardt. The band consisted of Benny (drums and leader), Ralph Straub (C-Melody saxophone), Al Murphy (trumpet), Archie Schwab (banjo), Andy Schaffer (piano) (sometime later Andy Schaffer went into the Navy and resigned from the band, and his place was taken by Harry Fallon), and myself on violin. We became a very popular band playing club dates, restaurants, and hotels in the New York City, Staten Island, Long Island, and Queens areas, and we were one of the first bands to broadcast "live" from stations WEAF, WABC, WCR, WHN, and WWRL in New York City.

In 1920, this band broke up and it was reorganized under the name of The Melody Six Orchestra, under the leadership of Al Murphy. The band consisted of Al Murphy (cornet), Ralph Straub (C-Melody saxophone), Archie Schwab (banjo), Harry Fallon (piano), myself (violin), and Nick Mareno (drums). Nick took the place of Benny Burkhardt, who had to quit music due to a severe illness. This band existed from 1920 through 1928, when eventually we broke up. We broadcast from many of the New York area radio stations and played many of the finest dance halls, hotels, restaurants, and club dates during our existence. I played with the band quite steady and then on and off during the latter days, due to the fact that I was becoming widely known for my jazz violin playing and was being booked with other bands around town. I also did some travelling for a while, so I was not always readily available. Harry Warren, the famous song-writer, and his brother-in-law, Jimmie "Red" Winslow, played with us occasionally. Harry and Jimmie came from the Ocean Hill section, adjacent to the East New York section of Brooklyn. I remember Harry (in between dance sets) sitting at the piano and jotting down music on pieces of manuscript paper, which in later years were to become famous. One of Harry's greatest song hits, "Rose of the Rio Grande" was to become years later our theme song when I organized the Sal Denton and His Melodians orchestra in 1929.

From 1923 to 1927, I played many broadcasts with pianist Harry Fallon as a duo; we were called The Sal Denton—Jazz Violinist and Harry Fallon—Pianist Duo. The newspapers of that era placed us in their radio columns as "One of the Ten Best Bets for an Evening's Entertainment." At radio station WHN in the Loew's State Theatre Building in New York City, we had the pleasure of having two of the greatest radio announcers in the field announce our program, namely N.T.G. Nils Grantlandt and Norman "Red" Brokenshire. In 1922, N.T.G. introduced me to Mr. Arthur Kraus; who conducted a musical talent booking office in the Knickerbocker Building at Broadway and 42nd Street. Mr. Kraus and his secretary, Miss Helen Zimmerman (who later married violinist Ernie Warren), heard me play and took a great liking to my jazz style of violin playing, and they booked me into The Captain's Flagship, a real nice restaurant, and at The Breakers Hotel, then later in some of the nightclubs in Atlantic City, New Jersey. Here I met Joe Venuti, who was playing at that time at The Steel Pier. I remember one Monday evening when Joe Venuti with two of his buddies came into the restaurant where I was playing, sat down at a table close to the band, and listened to me play. Afterwards he came over and asked my name. I told him and he complimented me on my playing and told me to keep playing the style of fiddling I was then playing. He said, "Kid, you're going places, keep it up." He never gave me his name and, to tell you the truth, I thought he was a booking agent. Later the bartender came over to me and asked me if I knew who had spoken to me. I told him no, because the man had not said who he was. Then the bartender told me it was Joe Venuti. I said to him in an offhand way, "Who the hell is Joe Venuti?" At that time Venuti was much less known, but years later he was to become one of the greatest jazz violinists in the business. He and Eddie Lang became a great team, and their recordings are now collector's items. Joe Venuti and I became great friends; he was about six or seven years older than me.

Between 1923 and 1925, I travelled through the South with some of the Kraus Office pickup bands playing one-nighters. I played two ship cruises with Mickey Sanella, saxophonist and the brother of the famous Andy Sanella of the Lucky Strike Cigarette and the Campbell Soup programs on radio. In 1924, I played at the beautiful Rosemont Ballroom, a famous place in Brooklyn owned by the same family who own the Roseland Ballroom in New York. The Rosemont Ballroom was situated at Flatbush Avenue and Fulton Street. I played there with The Melody Six Orchestra, and later at the Rosebud Ballroom in Coney Island, a resort town in Brooklyn, and a series of Sunday evening basketball and dance dates at Prospect Hall in South Brooklyn, for the famous Visitations professional basketball team. Then at Danceland in Jamaica, Long Island, with Charlie Eberhardt's Orchestra.

At the Rosemont and at the Rosebud Ballrooms there were two playing bands, one on and one off. Some of the bands we played together with were the Memphis Five—Phil Napoleon (leader/trumpet); with Jimmie Lytell, a great clarinetist; and Frankie Signorelli, a very talented pianist. The Indiana Five with Tommy Morton (Monaco) leader and drummer. The Georgia Five with the Drewes Brothers. The Way Down East Orchestra with Chauncey Gray, leader and pianist; Ralph Waders, banjo; Tony Gianelli, trumpet (a very good trumpet man); and others. We can't leave out Fess Williams and his Orchestra, Fletcher Henderson and his Band, the always genial Andy Kirk and his Orchestra, and Johnny Ringer and his Orchestra. All great bands.

Around this time, I recorded for the Columbia Velvetone studios with the University Six Orchestra, under the direction of Edward T. Kirkeby, then director of the famous California Ramblers Orchestra. The recording studios were located at 59th Street at Columbus Circle, New York. Mr. Sam Shapiro was the recording director. We recorded three or four numbers that day (Harmony Records) and the tunes we recorded, as I can remember, were "That's Just My Way of Forgetting You" and "High Upon a Hill-Top," with Gay Ellis [Annette Hanshaw] the vocalist. Some of the musicians that I vaguely remember recording these tunes were Tommy Fellini (banjo), Irving Brodsky or Jack Russin (piano), Bill Moore (trumpet), and Tony Gianelli (trumpet).

I played at the old stately Lafayette Hotel, located in Greenwich Village, for Arthur Kraus Agency with Sven Van Halberg, a terrific banjoist from Norway, who was making his home in New York for a while. Then at Barney Gallents famous nighclub at 12 Washington Square, also in the Village.

In 1926, I had the great pleasure of broadcasting from Station WMCA with Mr. Elmo Russ, who at that time was house organist and pianist for the station. Later he left WMCA and moved over to station WWRL in Woodside, New York. A great talent.

Again in 1926, the Kraus Agency booked me into Miami, Florida, for a series of dates at the Roney Plaza Hotel and at the Bernard McFaddin Deuville Club Health Spa and later at some of the nightclubs around town and at the beautiful Spanish-Moorish style restaurant, Sabastians, about a mile away from the heart of Miami, a real class restaurant. Joey Chance, at that time, was playing at the famous Everglades; he was an excellent violinist. Then at Coral Gables and then later at some of the night spots in Miami.

Some of the fine musicians I met and played with in Miami were Frank Victor (guitarist), Adrian Rollini (vibes and saxophone), Don Romeo (banjo), Harry Volpe (guitarist), Irving Weiss, a real good night-club pianist, and "Rubber-Face" Gallagher, a great comic who could stretch his face into many comical expressions and who was a great favorite in nightclubs in Florida and in New York City.

Later in 1926 I left Florida and rejoined The Melody Six Orchestra doing a one-nighter tour through New York State into Canada. We returned from the tour and were booked for a series of Sunday evening dances at Fritz's Dance Hall in Maspeth, Long Island. Here I met my future wife, Josephine, a Polish girl, who was introduced to me by her sister, Verla, and her girl friend, Margie, at one of the Sunday night dances. We kept company for about a year and then we were married on June 4, 1927. On August 8, 1928, a son was born to us and who, in later life (1953), was ordained into the Holy Priesthood. A little while later, in 1928, The Melody Six Orchestra broke up.

In 1927, just before I married, I played with a fine Southern gentleman, Charlie Bacher, and his orchestra. We played college dances, hotels, and club dates throughout the South. Charlie Bacher played tuba and string bass, and was very popular.

In 1929, I organized a group of young musicians under the band name of Sal Denton and his Melodians Orchestra. We were a very popular band and played many fine spots around the Brooklyn, Queens, Long Island, and Staten Island areas of New York. We played steady for a while at the Glenwood Manor in

Ridgewood, Queens, and occasionally at The Ridgewood Grove with the Syd Riley Orchestra, and at the beautiful Triangle Ballroom in Jamaica, Long Island. We broadcast live from Station WWRL of Woodside, Long Island, twice a week from the Glenwood Manor Ballroom. This band consisted of myself (violin and leader), Freddie Stamm (E-Flat saxophone), Jerry Izzo (banjo), Harry Rahner (trumpet), Charlie [?] (drums), and Emil [?] (piano). This band broke up in 1931.

In 1932, I played on Swing Street (the famous name for 52nd Street), New York City, for the Al Romano Musical Agency at the Three Deuces nightclub with Freddy Mace's Band and later at the Yacht Club and some other spots around town. Directly across the street from the Three Deuces was the famous Onyx Club where Stuff Smith (a great jazz violinist) and Big Sid Catlett (drummer) and Toy Wilson (not to be confused with the famous Teddy Wilson) on piano, played nightly. They were one of the finest groups of Negro musicians who were playing on the street. Swing Street, at that time, was one of the hottest jazz streets in New York City. Some of the greatest musicians and entertainers were spawned on this street. There was the great Alec Templeton (blind pianist), Art Tatum (pianist), Johnny Guandrius (a terrific pianist at The Three Deuces, 1933), Billy Daniels (the great ballad singer), and the ill-fated Billie Holiday (songstress). Who can forget Lois DeFe, the six-foot, three-inch Amazon Bouncer at the Yacht Club—she was something to behold. Some of the talented musicians I met here and played with were Gabby Budd, a talented pianist who played at Leon & Eddies Restaurant and Night Club with Willie Farmer's Orchestra; Joe Mareno, a very fine violinist, who had also played at Leon & Eddies in earlier days; Frankie Rash, a terrific tenor saxophonist; Sal Pace, a great jazz clarinetist who played at Jimmy Ryan's; and Freddie Whiteside, trombonist and string bassist; Joe Mallin and Charlie La Ruffa, good tap and rhythm guitarist; and Johnny Morris (Paraddidle Johnny), one of the great drummers and MC and singer of comedy songs, also a great imitator of Louis Armstrong. He played with the Vincent Lopez Orchestra at the Roosevelt Hotel in New York City for twelve years.

I played at The Pirate's Den in Greenwich Village with Joe Campo on drums, and at Luigi's famous Italian restaurant also in the Village. Then in 1935, I quit music as conditions were so bad around New York City and went to work for the Independent Subway System of New York (Transit), a Civil Service position. I worked for them from 1935 until August 1968, when I retired. After my retirement, I resumed playing.

In 1974–1975 I went to Honolulu, Hawaii, with my wife, Mary (Mae) with our St. Mary's Church group of Woodside, N.Y. We stayed at the famous and beautiful Hilton's Hawaiian Village Hotel on our first trip and on our second trip at the Holiday Inn. In the Rainbow Lounge at the Hawaiian Village Hotel, I played with John Norris and His New Orleans Jazz Band, a great band. I was guest violinist and was greatly received (both trips) by the guests at the Lounge. John Norris and his boys have invited me back many times, perhaps sometime soon with the good Lord's permission, I will go back because Hawaii is "Heaven on Earth" and the people are so friendly; it is beautiful and majestic. Once you go to Hawaii, you will want to go again. At the Lounge on my first Sunday afternoon jam session, I met Joe "The Fiddler" Bourque, a real talented Western hillbilly violinist, a swell guy. He was instrumental in getting me to play my jazz violin when he heard me play (on my first visit, I did not bring my own violin with me). He introduced me to John Norris, the leader of the New Orleans Jazz Band and then introduced me from the stage to the guests. The next morning at 7 A.M., Joe called me at the hotel and told us he was taking us for an automobile tour around Honolulu; it was a great seven hour ride, very picturesque. Then in the evening, I was invited with my wife to his brother's, Rene "Frenchy" Bourque's home. Frenchy's wife, Anne, a beautiful Hawaiian girl, made a wonderful juicy spaghetti and meatballs, a real Hawaiian menu. Here, at one of the class hotels, I also met, through Joe, Trummy Young, the great trombonist who had played with Jimmie Lunceford's Orchestra and Louis Armstrong. He was playing with his own band at a hotel situated on Waikiki Beach. We had many jam sessions while we stayed in Honolulu, and believe me they were great.

During the period from 1975 to 1979, I played many memorial dates for The New Amsterdam Musical Association of Harlem, New York. The president of this group is Sammy Heyward. I played a date at the Storyville Club on 54th Street, for Rudy Powell's memorial, which was sponsored by the group and the Duke Ellington Association.

In 1976, I joined the Senior Musicians Association and the Senior Musicians Concert Orchestra of Local 802 (Musicians' Union), New York City. This orchestra is composed of between sixty and seventy semiretired concert musicians between the ages of sixty-five and ninety. We give about six or eight concerts a year.

In the summer of 1977, I played a jam session with Bucky Pizzarelli, one of the great jazz guitarists in the business, and his combo at the Rockefeller Center Mall at 49th Street. Bucky told me, "You play just like Joe Venuti". That was a great compliment to me even to be classed with Joe, as in my estimation, he was the greatest.

I am still very active and going strong and hope to be around for a long time, God willing. I hope that those who read this article on my life will forgive me if I am a little hazy about dates and the names of some of the musicians and entertainers I have worked with but *Tempus Fugit* (Time Flies) and I am not getting any younger.

Earle "Nappy" Howard

[Earle "Nappy" Howard was born in Petersburg, Virginia, on June 3, 1904, and, sadly, passed away in Modena, Italy, on December 31, 1978. During the latter years of his life, besides corresponding regularly with me, he also sent me many sheets of paper on which he had written musical recollections with a view to the publication of his life story. His passing unfortunately ended our collaboration, but in May 1979 Earle's family kindly invited me to visit their home in Modena for a couple of days and allowed me to go through his two musical scrapbooks. Most of the material in these books detailed his musical career since his arrival in Europe but there were a couple of cuttings about his early bands, and details from these have been incorporated into his life story.

Both Earle's parents were musical and his own first attempts were made on the clarinet. Later, he tried the trumpet, but he finally settled on playing the piano. In an interview with Johnny Simmen, which took place at the Sans Souci Bar in Zurich in June 1953, he stated that his first teacher was a preacher, Baptist Minister B. Brown, and his early inspiration on piano was James P. Johnson. In the same interview, he named his three "top pianists" as James P., Fats Waller, and Teddy Wilson, and the musicians he most admired as Louis Armstrong, Coleman Hawkins, Benny Carter, and Dickie Wells.

Here then are "Nappy" Howard's recollections.—D.G.]

Although I was not born in New York City, I have always considered myself a New Yorker and, inasmuch as I have spent most of my days there, you can understand my pride in being a small, ever so small, part of its musical scene. Proud am I that I arrived on the scene at just about the time New York City, or rather Harlem, was stirring itself to become the Negro musical mecca. I have read and heard about Chicago, but there has been little or no mention of New York City and what was happening there, or, I

217

might add, what happened in Philadelphia, Baltimore, and Washington in the years since then. Those towns weren't exactly asleep, but that is another story. I am interested in Harlem and why it has been neglected so long, and I hope that this will inspire some writer or jazz historian to get busy and give New York City its jazz due.

At a very tender age, my family moved from Virginia to Hoboken, New Jersey, first Dad, then Mama and me. When Dad got a job in the local ferry-terminal restaurant, with a good salary, good place to work, and first-class clientele to work for, Pop seemed to have figured that this was a good place for him to settle, because thirty years later he died there from a heart attack. During many of these years he was an extra chief-waiter and was able to give his family a fairly good living, so I guess he had the right idea. Only once did he deviate from his job and that was when he tried for a job in the Williams Walker Show, where my Uncle Albert was a dancer. Mama came one day to see a rehearsal and seeing all those half-undressed women there was too much for Mama, so that was the end of Dad's show business aspirations. Me, well, I was sent to Virginia, where I became old enough for school, as New York City winters were considered too much for me, so it was winters in Virginia and summers in New York City, but no music.

Mama sang, and Pop also, he quite well. This music around the house was augmented by a piano, which Pop played by ear, and then Pop bought an Edison gramophone that played such things as "The Preacher and the Bear." Mama heard me singing snatches of this one day and that was it. Dad taught me another favorite, "Under the Yum Yum Tree," and I was on my way. I made my first musical appearance by singing "Let Me Call You Sweetheart" at a mock wedding. The locals thought I was something, the neighborhood's child singing star. Ugh! Neighbors' houses, guests in our house, church concerts, etc., I got the full treatment.

When I was about twelve, my Uncle Charles, who had been travelling in Europe for a couple of years as a valet, came home to Virginia during my school term. He stopped over in New York City to visit Mama and Pop and decided to get a gramophone for the family in Virginia. He bought a round wax record player, and that was really when I knew this music stuff was for me. Noble

Sissle and Eubie Blake had some discs, the most popular one was "Exhortation" and another disc called "Emmeline," but the records that got to me were "Memphis Blues" and "Yellow Dog Blues."

In September of 1918, when I was fourteen, my family moved to Harlem, and I was a pupil at the famous Public School 89. I started in Class 5b and then into Class 6a. Another pupil of the same class was the great Fats Waller, who quite often played the hook from school, and when he was caught and brought back to the school by the truant officer, he was made to play piano during the morning assembly as punishment. How we kids loved to have Fats punished! He rocked the joint like mad.

Public School 89 was located at 135th Street and Lenox Avenue, a few houses away from the Lincoln Theater, where Fats was just starting as a pianist. On the northwest corner was a United Cigar shop, on the northeast corner a drug store, and on the southwest corner was Public School 89, Harlem's most popular and most well-known school. We used to spend as much free time as we could ducking into the Lincoln Theater and listening to Fats, the new King of the Box Beaters.

We lived on 132nd Street, and across the road from us lived the then-young Henry "Bennie" Morton, whose step-father was a violinist. At his suggestion, Bennie, Charlie Irvis (the original Duke Ellington trombonist), his brother Gibbie, myself, and several other kids in the neighborhood started getting together at nights and having playing sessions. As time passed by, other kids from other parts of New York began to come along, and there were nights when the session had such kids as Bubber Miley; Freddie Johnson, the pianist; and Bobby Martin on trumpet—he shortly after began playing with what was later to become Sam Wooding's band. Another young man who moved into our neighborhood was Herbert Flemming, who was a great inspiration to us youngsters.

Early on, I came into contact with Noel Klukies at the Martin-Smith's Music School, which we both attended when we were young. Dave Martin's father owned the school, and Johnny Russell, Noel Klukies, Edgar Sampson, and many others all went there. It came into the musical picture as the chief music school, after the Harlem Music Settlement went out of business.

In 1920, I decided to go professional and took a job with the

J.C. Godman Concert Group that travelled through New England giving concerts and playing for dancing later in the evening. At the start, I had no experience, but for Mr. Godman I was his accountant, the second dancer, and his pianist. I did a dance solo to start them off too. We played one-night stands, giving half-night concerts and first-night shows. I was accompanist for a concert singer; she retired some years later. All that work was for thirty-five dollars a week, the pay was regular, and the company sort of decent people.

During one of these trips we were in Maine on July 4, 1922. At the end of the evening, as it was a holiday night and a big dance was the attraction in town with a band from Boston called Hicks's Negro Ensemble, I, after hanging around to be sure that we didn't have to work, started over to the dance hall. Hicks's band was quite popular in that part of the state. After walking to the other end of the town, I finally found the place. The band was jumping, and at that moment a little short guy was playing a gold soprano sax and he had all the folks cheering him on. When the dance was over I went up to the bandstand and introduced myself. He appeared to be quite young and had on knickers instead of long pants and when he told me his age I understood why. He was just sixteen. His name was Johnny Hodges! The next time we met was when Johnny Hodges was working with Chick Webb as his first sax in the original band at Club Richmond on Broadway, New York. We were good friends until he died. Some of the folks had never seen a Black man before that night in Maine!

[Dr. Albert Vollmer telephoned Charlie Holmes and he provided the following information: Harry Hicks, piano teacher, composer, and arranger; he could play several instruments, including the saxophone; older fellow (older than Jelly Roll); great musician, well-liked, popular throughout New England. Almost everyone in Boston gigged with Harry Hicks, who had lots of jobs. He was well respected and a nice man to work for, loved kids, and would help you as much as he could, was very helpful and generous to youngsters coming up, gave them pointers without charging them for it. Johnny Hodges and Charlie both gigged with him, once even together, both playing altos. Composition of the band varied with the jobs. They travelled to the jobs by car. Harry Hicks had a small music studio at the Black union and, when not teaching students or arranging for his jobs, he hung around playing cards at the *union. Hicks helped out Harry Carney, Howard Johnson, as well as Charlie and Johnny.—D.G.]*

Because I could read music and dance enough to hold a spot in the show, as well as play for the other acts, I was doing the work of two people, but after one and a half years of these one-nighters, Christmastime in the year of 1922 found me at Hartford, Connecticut, looking for work. But there was no work in the town to be found, no money in my pocket, so it looked as though I had a tough time coming up. I found work at a house, cleaning with a guy for five dollars a day on a basis of five days a week. January found me about to give up. I had no work, no jobs, nothing. There was no place where you could meet the local cats for jazz sessions, so that you were known and open for gigs. An old man named Dave Murray, he was some kind of local politician, ran a band, such as it was. Upon meeting him, he made it clear that he was the boss, so I worked for him, otherwise I had no work. Anyway, this made me decide to get a band of my own together.

On Sunday, February 1, four of us guys met at a friend's house. His name was Mr. John Pound, and he and his wife Daisy made us very welcome. He was all for us—plus the fact that he had a piano. We had Paul Wilson, drums; Mike Jackson, alto sax; Paul Burnett, banjo; and Bill Short, tenor sax. After a two-and-a-half-hour rehearsal, we decided that we had a chance and would call ourselves the Serenaders. We met every Sunday, and, after two months of these rehearsals, we began looking for a few jobs to get us started. We were also lucky in that we had an aspiring promoter, who was related to one of the members of our band; she was their aunt, her name was Lil Jenkins, and she became our first promoter.

Two months later, we, the Serenaders, made our debut at the Town Hall in Plainville, about ten miles from Hartford, Connecticut. The personnel that night was Charlie Jennings, trumpet; Mike and Allen Jackson, saxes; Paul Burnett, banjo; Paul Wilson, drums; Herb Johnson, tenor and bass saxes; and myself, piano and vocals. This first public appearance was a great success and our next big job on September 29 was also a great success. We also had a big surprise that night in four strangers from the local park theater. They liked us and gave us a job for four nights plus all holidays. We also obtained other work as a result of this job; in fact it was the job that did things for us.

Right about then, I met Bill Tasillo. He was the owner of the Cinderella Ballroom in Hartford. He offered me the number-two-band position with his ballroom, so my Whispering Serenaders opened there in 1924. By now I had increased the band to eight extra men. We had Tommy Jones, trumpet; I. Lanier or Weldon Hurd, trombone; Allen and Mike Jackson, saxes; Percy Nelson, saxophone and clarinet; Nelson Clark, banjo; Paul Wilson, drums; and Herb Johnson, tenor and bass saxophones.

Up to then, there just had not been any organized colored bands locally, and we were playing in places where colored musicians had never played before. We were really stretched to play all the spots we were booked to play, first a date in Boston, then a big place in West Springfield. Gradually, as we became known, the demand for us became greater.

During the fall of 1924, Fletcher Henderson did a one-night stand on October 12 in Hartford. That was a night never to be forgotten by the members of my band. We had been digging the Henderson band's records and their broadcasts over WHN, and we were doing our best to play like them. In fact, that night, many of the local folks, who were there in full force, remarked to us, "Man, they sound just like you guys." Allen Jackson and I were up on most of Fletcher's records. As soon as they came out, we bought them from the local record shop and used the ensemble passage arrangements, adapting them to our band's instrumentation. The loyal locals didn't pay any attention to the fact that Fletcher's band were the originators of that particular type of jazz. The locals were on our side and that was it!

Billy Butler's band came to Hartford during, I think, that fall of 1924, they opened on Saturday, November 1. They played at the Palais Royal, the best nightclub in that part of the town. They played there a month and were the first colored band to play the club. [*In an attempt to confirm this and other dates, I wrote to the Hartford Public Library. Although they checked through both local newspapers for that period, they found no mention of Billy Butler, or Earle Howard, or Fletcher Henderson. The Palais Royal, situated at 900 Wethersfield Avenue, Hartford, carried an advertisement for "Dancing and dining every night 8 P.M. to 1 A.M."—D.G.*] In spite of the weather, we went nightly to the back of the building and listened to them. When they returned in the spring, we met several of them as they happened to spot us outside of the place. Then they had Bobby Johnson as banjoist, and some of us knew him. Bobby Stark was with them, and Joe Steele was the pianist. Another two men with them were Chink Johnson, the tuba player, and a clarinetist who was a really exciting player to us at that time, by the name of Jejo. Bobby Johnson had taken Jimmy Greene's place. The great turnover in personnel was typical of those times, and between the first time the band was in Hartford and the second time, there could have been any number of changes.

[Dr. Albert Vollmer kindly spoke with Billy Butler about this event. Billy Butler did not think that the Palais Royal was the venue involved. He confirmed that the tuba player was Johnson and also recalled Carmello Jejo. He added that Joe Steele left to go with Lew Leslie, where he was featured pianist in a production of "Rhapsody in Blue."—D.G.]

After the Billy Butler band left, we had a real mickey-mouse band, lots of fiddles and stuff. They were good—if you liked mickey-mouse bands!

Many times I am sure that I was born at the wrong time—too soon—in the music business. Today, the guys get a boost from somebody and they've struck it rich. In those early days, every town of any size had a hall for its big affairs. Sometimes it was a place in the local park, a grange hall, or the town hall. Some of these places housed a popular band. For instance, Springfield had its Cook's Riverside Ballroom, while Hartford had its Cinderella Ballroom. When Bill Tasillo, the owner, first called me to open and report for the first night of work, I discovered there was no advance notice, no advertisements, no papers telling people about us. A few weeks later, though, we passed the ballroom and saw the porter changing the signs out front, so we knew we were in from that night on. From then on, we were able to get advertising by him just for the asking, and soon the newspaper was giving us mentions too. Bill was very generous about such things.

In Hartford, it was the shortage of personnel that was the reason for there being no other band in town. For a long time, there was just the Gurley Brothers to compete against, and they were just not able to come up with an organized band every time. So there was our one band in Hartford town serving the musical needs of 150,000 people. We were not long in gauging our audiences. In those days, we needed about six numbers that could be featured before the intermission and about the same number for afterwards. There was no radio to kill a tune, and as long as the public went for a tune they would accept an encore, but it really had to be an applause-getter. With the radio and electronic age, all of that has changed; now you need more than a dozen arrangements, and the entire picture has altered.

Another thing that has changed—the reason for there being no colored people in many of those towns was the economic factors. The race thing was never greatly enforced. For instance, we had a man with us, a colored man named Charles Jennings; he was light brown skin in color and a good musician. The local White musicians all tried to get him to work with them, but he liked the jobs we worked; there was so much more fun to be had. Firstly, we were the first colored group to play in the Cinderella Ballroom; secondly, we had the Carpe Diem Fraternity getting bookings for us.

In the spring of 1925, we did a two-week tour for Paul Sullivan, who was a promoter. We had a number of dates around Concord, New Hampshire, and dates from Stanford, Connecticut, to northern Maine. We met, and battled against, all comers: the Gurleys, Ernie Fields, Henry Moon, the Tinney Brothers, and George Rickson.

Among our early musical meetings was the night we were met by Mal Hallett. It was at the Monday night session at Nuttings-on-the-Charles. The open dates were Mal versus Duke Ellington's six men. Mal had a big fifteen-man-strong band that was famous all over New England. That night was special as the guitar player's young brother, Toots, was joining their band. He had refused for some time to join Mal, who had been trying to get him. Anyway, the night was going good, they were doing one of their best entertaining specialties, "Tiger Rag." In the refrain part, the singer and the speciality singer were alternating fours. The guy who was featured soloist was about to come up with a real crazy riff; he was about to wash Ollie Melsman away. He started his riff from a bent-over position and when he hit the beat he meant to end it with a flair. He never got there because the old chair on which he was playing collapsed under his weight. The chair came down with a crash and broke. It was the crash of the night and broke up everybody in the hall.

June of 1926 saw us at the Strand Danceland, Brooklyn, with Bob Labell, trumpet; Mike and Allen Jackson, saxes; Arnold Canty, banjo; Leonard Reed, drums and vocal; and myself, piano and vocals. Later, Johnny Russell, tenor sax, replaced Mike Jackson, and then we added Geechie Fields on trombone and Ben Campbell on tuba. We ended there on the last day of May 1927 and headed for a summer of one-night stands in New England.

We left the Strand Danceland on June 1, and we had booked a tour that started at a dance in Poughkeepsie, New York. That first date was a real bust! We left home base at 2 P.M. on Thursday to get there at what we figured would be around 6 P.M. One hour out of town on Avon Mountain, and we had tire trouble. While we were repairing the tire, our banjo player, Arnold, and a couple of the other guys tried to scale the hill close by where we had stopped. He had just had a new wooden leg fitted the day before to replace his left leg that had been amputated below the knee. When we had fixed the flat, we called all the cats to come back so that we could get going. Arnold started down the hill and his cane went down into the soft dirt and broke off at the handle. He sat there looking stupid. "Well, I'll be a son of a bitch," he exclaimed, and got up and threw away the handle. That was the first and last of his using a cane; he just would not be bothered with anything else that caused him to show he had anything missing and that hindered him from walking. From then on, he walked, danced, and did everything else; in fact, he outdanced us all.

A few miles on and there was another flat and then another. Finally, we arrived at the hall at 1 A.M.! Needless to say, that was the end of our first engagement on that tour. The man who hired the hall was a Mr. Winfield. He was an old friend of my father's and the uncle of Tom Winfield, a good friend of mine from my home town in Petersburg, Virginia. Tom, incidentally, was a great left-handed pianist, who played by ear. He was right in there with that needed left-handed stride feeling that was beginning to be the thing that was emerging from the ragtime style that was being played by all the up-to-date pianists of that time, circa 1917.

To get back to my story, Mr. Winfield was very angry to say the least. It was he who had to pay for the hall. However, he was able to get the owners to extend the night until 3:30 A.M., so we just about broke even, thanks to the sale of a few bottles of the local brand of spirits.

We went to Maine to play several one-night stands. We reached, I think it was Bangor, and Miss Sourrel Gerard, the owner of the taxi-dance hall in that town, had recently become a widow. She had been well-fixed financially, and this left her independent. She made her son the active manager for the place, and she was a dancing teacher there. Her son, Sam Gillard, after work would invite us to accompany him and his girl to some of the downtown restaurants, where he would introduce us as his romping, stomping band. At the same time, he built a radio station, WLTH, and made Jack Stanley the manager. Stanley spoke very correct English, and he often invited us to early morning parties. Quite often folks would meet us on the early morning shift.

The whole tour had to be booked from Bangor through northern Maine. Up in Aroostook County, where they planted the potatoes, we opened on a dream date at Lew's Place. We were such a big hit that they kept open until 3 A.M.

During the winter of 1927 we went back into the Strand Danceland in Brooklyn. At Christmastime, Julius "Geechie" Fields, our trombonist, was sick, so he sent Fernando Arbello in his place. Arbello was fresh off the boat from Cuba, where he had been playing with the Havana Symphony Orchestra. In the spring, Fields returned, but his condition was worse, and he collapsed and was put back to bed. We went to Maine and he went with us but, after a few weeks, he quit at his wife's insistence and went home. I think that was the end of his playing days, as I never heard from him again. I made some inquiries and was told that he was a sporting trainer, so this closed the musical career of Julius Fields.

Things happened so fast at that time. We had an unknown celebrity in our midst; he turned out to be named Pete Brown, who was playing with a local band. Pete Brown joined my band in the latter part of 1927 and played all the saxophones with us. He played first alto, a little slow rider, a wonderful saxophonist. He started recording with Clarence Williams, because he was what you'd call "hot property." Pete Brown had a brief but exciting recording career, all of it recorded by Clarence Williams. [*This was one of the few matters that I was able to query with Earle. His reply was that he was not sure of the exact recording dates in 1927 or 1928. He went on to say that possibly the correct date could be confirmed as they printed a publicity sheet immediately afterwards.—D.G.]* Pete Brown was very sensitive and warm with many ideas, he was able to express himself, and great music came out of his alto and tenor playing. He died before gaining his due recognition from the public. It was a great tragedy and real music lost by it. I advise you to get on his bandwagon.

At that time, I had lost two saxophone players, as Allen Jackson and Johnny Russell left to join Billy Kato's Band, so the other chair was taken by Raffael Sanchez on alto and, together with Pete Brown's solid improvisations, we had some outright music.

One night we were playing a colored dance at Charleshurst Ballroom in Salem, Massachusetts, when we were heard by Charles Shribman and given the tour spot that was vacated by Duke Ellington when he went into the Cotton Club. At that time, the Shribman Brothers, Charles and Cy, were the biggest bookers of bands in New England. They booked everything: Paul Whiteman, Fletcher Henderson, McKinney's Cotton Pickers, Rudy Vallee, the Casa Loma, and the great New England territorial band, Cooks Singing Orchestra from Springfield, Massachusetts. They also supplied bands to most of the first-class dance places throughout New England, from the Ritz in Bridgeport, Connecticut, to the Chateau in Bangor, Maine. We took the Duke's place with Shribman, and we held it until Claude Hopkins took our place in 1934.

That summer we were booked into Albany for a colored dance, then on the Saturday we were free. We played a Sunday night dance at a local yacht club, then, with three days free, I went back to New York to find a bass player before we opened in Boston the following Thursday. Road travel is a much better thing today than it was in those days. Then a hundred miles was a long jump; today, it is nothing and is considered a short jump. We used to travel for miles, get off, eat, and go to work the same night. Very few trips were a really long distance; there were long jumps and longer, longer jumps.

The bass player who joined us was Mack Shaw: he had played with Duke Ellington the summer before he came with us. He joined us and worked coast to coast. We used his car for transportation at twenty cents a mile. He had a big old-fashioned Pierce Arrow that all eight of us could get into with instruments and baggage on top and on the sides. Mack was quite a character. He had been gassed during active service in World War I and that was the reason he gave for his drinking to excess; he really could make alcohol disappear. Mack had travelled all over the U.S.A. He was a good liar and storyteller and, during trips between jobs, he could really tell them, as long as he could find drink to oil his pipes on. Before leaving Mack Shaw and his bass, I must say that he was a darn good bass player and his bass was just the thing to fill up many of those holes we had in many places in those arrangements. His brother, Frank Robinson, suggested that Mack was a good man to me. He was a good musician. Even then when he played, they took down and listened to him; he had all of them in the palm of his hand even at that age!

During the winter of 1928, we returned to the Strand Danceland, but from the spring of 1929 to around February or March of 1930 I worked with Bill Benford's Band. I think that Norman Lester preceded me in that band on piano. *[This was confirmed by Tommy Benford, who also added that there were a great many personnel changes within the band.—D.G.]*

Later in 1930, I fronted my own big band in Boston, Massachusetts, during the summer season. It was highlighted by the Labor Day weekend dance with music played by Jacques Renard, who alternated with my band at the Pier Ballroom in Portland, Maine. The ballroom was located over the ocean, and on rough nights the sea shook the walls while the music played.

In those days, the practice of having known leaders front other units was originated around New York City. During the early thirties, two guys in Brooklyn opened a band-booking office in the town and started booking well-known colored bands. The deal called for the leaders to accept the contract to appear and direct the band for a couple of hours, and, if he had a steady job, he could return to that.

In the fall of 1930 a fellow who had worked with me the previous summer as manager for the Shribman Brothers came to New York. Then, about a few weeks after Christmas, he called me and said that he had a good job for us in Ohio. On February 23, we met in the Penn Station at 10 p.m., a Tuesday night. We finally took off in an old bus and eventually arrived on Friday night. We opened the next night at the Palm Grove in Cincinnati and did a six-week contract. We had Henry Mason, Johnny Muse, and a fellow called Ted Barnet (he was later replaced by Albert Snaer) on trumpets; Nat Story, trombone; Seaton "Jew" Harrington, Noel Klukies, and Ernest Purce, saxes; Jesse Scott, bass; Harry Holt (replaced by Arnold Canty), guitar and vocal; C. Dusty Neale, drums and vocal; and myself on piano, leading and doing some vocals.

After those six weeks, my band returned to New York and auditioned for the Savoy Ballroom job. At the same time we were working at the Saratoga Club but looking for another job as the job we had was not paying off regularly. So the Savoy gave us a few gigs to tide us over.

Our first gig was with Cab Calloway at Penn University. The night was a big success. Cab gave a big performance, he was at his jiviest, and he gave a good report to the Savoy, who booked us, so the Jimmy Evans/Tommy Ford Office invited us to sign a contract with their office giving us a number of weekend gigs after we finished our four months job in the Savoy Ballroom. We had opened there from May 22 until Labor Day; after that we hit the road again.

During the summer run we were out for ten days while the great Luis Russell band made a special holiday run. After that we returned to the Home of Happy Feet, the Savoy.

When we came out for the Luis Russell run on July 3, we hit the road to back up Cab Calloway for two nights in Shamokin, Pennsylvania. Cab came in from a date in Chicago. The gig was a big deal for him, something like a couple of thousand bucks, which back in those times [July 1931] was big. A couple of months later, Cab paid us the supreme compliment. A number we had, called "Ain't That Religion," was played by his band and his arrangement was the same as a special arrangement that we had made!

The fall season found my band working on a Saturday as Cab's band, the next as Noble Sissle's, another time as Don Redman's, and one Saturday night as the three mentioned above plus Fletcher Henderson's, all four in one night, due to the idea of many bands, and many Saturday and weekend club dances where there was quite a bit of this kind of work. If you had a few bucks you could easily use some kind of name and give a dance. All you needed was the money to pay for the hall and the band's pay in advance, the rest was nothing. The more popular the groups were, the less you needed. Some of them didn't have to pay the bands in advance. Needless to say, there were a few that the bookers got stung with, but most of them paid off even if they lost money.

During the middle thirties, I was married and had settled in New York City and was raising a family, working locally and working as a subcontractor for a number of name bands. From the spring of 1932 to the end of April 1933, I led my own band at the Rose Danceland in New York. The personnel was Eddie Allen, Billy Douglas, and John Brown, trumpets; Allen Jackson and Cecil Scott, reeds; Arnold Canty, guitar; Frank Smith, tuba; Paul Barbarin, drums (he was replaced by Tommy Curtis); and myself on piano.

In the summer of 1933, I took my band up to Boston and in the latter part of that year Percy Nelson and his band, under my direction, were resident at the Bond Hotel in Hartford, Connecticut. I was with them until I came back to New York City to lead my own resident house band at the Melody Lane and later at Remy's Ballroom.

I was working at Remy's on 65th Street and Broadway, where I was with a small band and rehearsing a big band. We were quite happy about the future. John Hammond was interested in us and there was talk of the band going on a Southern tour and Billie Holiday going with us. It looked like the break that I had hoped for in a long time. Needless to say, it didn't come through, and, at the last minute, they put Billie with Basie. So I stayed on my dancehall job at 23rd Street and worked there another year. Freddie Skerritt was third alto in the band with Allen Jackson on first and Charles Frazier on tenor. Bobby Woodlen was playing on the small job I had at Remy's and for several at the 23rd Street location too.

In 1938, I made a trip to South America with the Baron Lee band. Back in New York in October 1938, I played in the pit band for the Blackbirds Show. Lena Horne was the star of the show, and musically this was the best band that I ever worked with. We had Leonard Davis, Robert "Cookie" Mason, and Sidney De Paris, trumpets; Weldon Hurd and Billy Kato, trombones; George James, Eddie Campbell, H. Thompson, and Charles Frazier, reeds; myself and Nat Stokes, piano; Hayes Alvis, bass; and A.G. Godley, drums; plus a string section. This show ended in the spring of 1939.

Figure 18. Undated photograph of pianist and bandleader Earle Howard.

Then in the summer of 1940, I was with Leon Abbey and his orchestra at the Apollo Theatre. After this I began working as a solo entertainer. In 1951, I came to Europe and opened in December of that year at the Chikita in Berne, Switzerland. I spent a great deal of my time in Switzerland, and two months of every year from 1952 until 1958, I was resident at the Atlantis in Basle.

I also played the Metro Bar and the Africana, both in Zurich. Throughout the fifties, I played in most of Europe. I made my home in Sweden for many years, but I now live in Italy.

It was great fun while it lasted and if I had the chance to do it again I would do so gladly. I have no regrets, nothing but pleasant memories of a lifetime spent in the music business. Those were the days.

Herbie "Kat" Cowens

[Herbert Cowens was born in Dallas, Texas, on May 24, 1904. His was a musical family: his two brothers played drums, one sister was a dancer, and the other sister was a singer. He started work as a shoeshine boy, then later started dancing in the streets. The money he earned as a street dancer enabled him to buy his first set of drums.

He could not start playing with any jazz bands until after he had finished school. Upon leaving high school in 1922, he started playing professionally. Until 1926, Herbie Cowens played with the local Dallas jazz and vaudeville show bands. The first jazz band he played with was The Satisfied Five, then he joined "Frenchy" Polite Christian's New Orleans Jazz Band and later worked with Charlie Dixon's Jazzlanders. When he was old enough to leave Dallas, he headed to New York with the Shake Your Feet Company, which played the Lafayette Theater during Christmas of 1926.

What follows is an attempt to place Herbie Cowens's musical career into chronological order in his own words.—D. G.]

At the end of 1926, I was touring with Caramouche & Cleo Mitchell's Shake Your Feet Company (Mrs. Pearl Jones, piano and leader; R. H. Smith, director; Sylvester Lewis and Walter Young, trumpets; Harry Walker and Charles Wilkerson, saxophones; and others) on the T.O.B.A. circuit. We came back to New York City, after most of 1927 had elapsed, and the first band that I played with on arriving back was that led by trombonist Doc Crawford. He is a great musician and one of the deserving ones from those early days.

When I had been with the Shake Your Feet Company, I had been approached by Jimmie Cooper about joining his show, and by August of 1927 I was featured with Eddie Heywood's Kansas City Black Birds in Jimmie Cooper's Black And White Revue.

Eddie Heywood was the pianist, arranger, and director; James White played cornet; Edward Alexander, saxophone; Levi Mulligan, trombone; and Clarence Phillips, banjo.

I was billed as the "World's Greatest Jazz Drummer," although I did not think I was, but Jimmie Cooper said I was, so as he was the boss that was the way it stayed. *[The Revue played at Waldron's Casino in Boston opening on Saturday, August 27, and the week of August 29, 1927.—D. G.]* We played the Columbia Burlesque Circuit and while we were with the show, I made some recordings with Eddie Heywood *[two sessions took place on September 19 and 21, 1927, in New York City—D. G.]* In early October, we played the Palace Theater, Fayette Street, Baltimore, with Butterbeans and Susie as the featured attractions.

In 1928, I had a band by the name of The Royal Garden Orchestra. We had been playing dance dates, then we were hired by the owner of the Checker Club at 2493 Seventh Avenue in Harlem for his establishment. We were advertised as Herbie Cowens and his Chicago Checker Orchestra.

[Clyde Bernhardt, who was also in Herbie's Chicago Checker Orchestra, said that they had also played at the Audubon Ballroom and, according to him, the band included Ray Carn, first trumpet; Bill Lewis, second trumpet and solo; Eric Brown, first saxophone and clarinet; Castor McCord, tenor saxophone; and Joe McCord, third alto saxophone. He could not recall the names of the pianist, bassist, or banjo player, but both Sam Allen, piano, and John Brown, violin and banjo, are known to have played with Herbert Cowens in September, 1928, so they could be two of the unknown musicians.—D. G.]

After that engagement was finished, we played a big dance at the Rockland Palace at West 155th and 8th Avenue on October 19, 1928. On that date, we were advertised as Herbie Cowens and his Royal Garden Orchestra. We were a ten-piece band. We also played the Cotton Club as a relief band when Duke Ellington and the Cotton Club Show was out playing a benefit or a gig. They also used to have club dates and political dates in the early part of the evening, and we would play until they came to the club to do the shows.

Just earlier than that, I played in a Mae West show with Dave Nelson called *Pleasure Man*. The show was tried out in the Bronx before opening at the Biltmore Theatre on October 1, 1928. Anyway, the show was stopped by the police, who took some of the performers down to the station in a paddy wagon. I don't remember too much about the happenings; it was too short an engagement. *[According to one report, the show, which was produced by Carl Reed, played only three performances. Mae West was furious; she said her play had been dealt "a blow below the belt"!—D. G.]*

I was with Billy Fowler's Band from the start of it in 1929 until he left the States to go to Spain. Doc Crawford, trombone, Jack Butler, trumpet, and Eddie Gibbs, banjo, were also in that orchestra. Doc Crawford took over the leadership of the band and, with a few changes in personnel, we played mostly dance places like the Rose Danceland at 125th Street and Seventh Avenue and the Strand Roof Ballroom on Broadway, as well as the Rosemont Ballroom in Brooklyn.

During this period, I also worked with trumpeter June Clark at the Tango Palace, a dancing school. We left there and went to the Bluebird Dancing School, but later returned to the Tango Palace with a small five-piece band. I left them while they were still at the Tango Palace.

Lucky Millinder came to New York from Chicago, around October 1931, with his band, which broke up, and Millinder took over Doc Crawford's band. Then we went out and played a long line of R.K.O. (Radio-Keith-Orpheum) dates for Roger Wolfe Kahn, who also led a fine White band. We played all the Harlem theaters in New York (Lafayette, Lincoln, Alhambra, Harlem Opera House, and the Apollo).

I joined Eubie Blake's Concert Orchestra, but as we were going to Chicago to play the Illinois Theater during the Chicago World's Fair of 1933, Eubie changed our name to the Shuffle Along Orchestra: Eubie Blake, piano; Alfred Brown, first trumpet; Henry Walton, second trumpet; Shad Collins, third trumpet; William Bradley, trombone; Norman Thornton, James Robinson, and Lester Boone, saxes; Lorenzo Cauldwell, violin and piano; and Eddie Gibbs, guitar. *[Charles Vernon on trombone and tuba, who was also in the personnel according to most sources, was the only person Herbie did not identify.—D. G.]* The show starred Mantan Moreland, Edith Wilson, Flournoy Miller, and others, and we also went on the theater circuit with it, until the early part of 1934.

I was with Ferman Tapps in Small's Paradise in 1936. It was

when I was playing with his group that I married my wife, Rubye, on July 26 of that year.

In the summer of 1937, I worked with Charlie Johnson's Original Paradise Orchestra at the Paradise Club, North Illinois and Baltic Avenues in Atlantic City. Trumpeter Henry Goodwin was also with us in that band, as was Leonard Davis, trumpet; Sidney De Paris, trumpet; Ben Witted, alto saxophone; and Benny Waters, tenor saxophone. I don't remember us having a night off.

Around that period, I worked with Charlie "Fat Man" Turner at a ballroom at Seventh Avenue and 53rd Street. After that date, we played for the opening of the West End Theater on 125th Street in Harlem. Later, in the spring of 1938, we went out on a tour in a show with Buck and Bubbles. Fats Waller wanted Charlie Turner to go on the road with him, as Fats' band. We rehearsed at the Savoy getting set for Fats. I had already played some dates with Fats on gigs, but I did not want to go on the road with him, so I gave my job to Arnold "Scrippy" Boling. Instead, I left and went to Washington, D.C., with Fess Williams to play the Howard Theater.

I made some recordings with vocalist Jack Meredith at my own expense around this time. We had Merrill "Step" Stepter, trumpet; William "Sonny" Jordan, alto sax; Edgar "Spider" Courance, tenor sax; Tommy Fulford, piano; and Ernest "Bass" Hill, bass. Jack Meredith later made two trips to the Far East with me in 1945 and 1948 and then moved to Albany, New York.

At the end of 1938, I replaced Cozy Cole in Stuff Smith's group. In 1939, we played at the LaSalle Hotel Blue Fountain Room, Chicago, and the Off Beat Club, 222 North State Street, Chicago. In 1940 we were at the Hickory House on 52nd Street, New York City; the Sherman Hotel in Chicago; and the Hollywood Onyx Club in Los Angeles. Stuff Smith, violin; Jonah Jones, trumpet; George Clark, tenor saxophone; Eric "Sneeze" Henry, piano; John Brown, bass; and Luke Stewart, guitar, played those dates.

Stuff Smith was disbanding his band and Fletcher Henderson, after leaving Benny Goodman, was organizing his own band, around January 1941. Jonah Jones had already promised Fletcher that he would come in and join them, and as Fletcher needed a drummer, Jonah recommended me. Fletcher contacted me and I was offered the job; that was how I came to join them at the Roseland Ballroom. Later, in that same year, I went into the recording studios on two occasions. The first time, I was a member of pianist Eddie Heywood's band when I recorded with Billie Holiday.

Then I was at the Decca recording studios with Sammy Price, piano; Chester Boone, trumpet; Skippy Williams, tenor saxophone; Ed Morant, trombone; Don Stovall, alto saxophone and arranger; and Ernest "Bass" Hill, bass. *[Note: Floyd Brady is listed as the trombonist for this session.—D. G.]*

I worked with Bill Robinson's *Hot From Harlem* show and Billy Butler's Swing Phonic Orchestra before going with Garvin Bushell to Philadelphia. At the end of 1942, I joined Alfred Lunt and Lynn Fontanne's Broadway show, *The Pirate*, which opened at the Martin Beck Theatre on November 25, 1942; it was set in a West Indies village. Emilio Denti from Paris, trumpet and vocals; John Dixon, Doc Cheatham, trumpets; Emmett Matthews, soprano saxophone; Wilbur De Paris, trombone; Eddie Gibbs, guitar; John Brown, bass; and besides myself on drums, there was Max Rich on snare drums. Juanita Hall was also in the cast.

From 1943 to 1971, I was involved in tours with the U.S.O. We made three trips to Vietnam between 1965 and 1971. It was while making one of those tours, back in 1946 in Manila, that I was in a big car accident and I had my right arm almost torn off. The army doctors saved my arm and told me to take it easy for a year, and I did exactly what they had advised me to do.

In the late seventies, I was still leading my own group, and we held regular rehearsals at the New Amsterdam Music Association club. Bernard Flood, trumpet; Carl Frye, alto saxophone and clarinet; Johnny Russell, tenor saxophone; Andrew "Mule" Maize, piano; and John Brown, bass, joined me in this group.

Then in August of 1979, I left New York City and returned to Dallas. I absolutely refused to see New York go to the unlawful elements, so I left and remembered when it was really the greatest city in all ways. I think I know it will survive, but I want to remember it, as it was.

I can recall those Depression days when I lived for two weeks with only rice and tea as food, but nobody knew it, because the less money you had, the sharper you were dressed. I washed and ironed my white shirt every night, shined my shoes, and pressed my pants, and came out the next day looking like a fashion plate or a mannequin.

On my return to Dallas, I have continued to remain active musically and have worked with the Sophisticated Jazz outfit and currently still play with the Legendary Revelations. Work is not too plentiful in Dallas for jazz musicians like myself, and it would be great if there was a club where the senior citizen musicians could play every night if they wanted to. Dallas has not changed that much since the early twenties when I started my career. I could barely make a living then, and it's the same way now. *[Written in 1989—D. G.]*

Selected Discography

All of these recordings were currently available when this book was published, but subsequently some of them may no longer be in catalogue. All can be obtained from specialist jazz stores in the U.S. and Canada.

EDDIE DAWSON
Herb Morand, 1949   American Music AMCD-9

AUGUST LANOIX
Peter Bocage With The Love/Jiles   OJC-CD1835
     Ragtime Orchestra

EMMANUEL PAUL
Emanuel Paul's International Jazz   GHB BCD-20
     Band Vol. 1
Emanuel Paul's International Jazz   GHB BCD-21
     Band Vol. 2

KID THOMAS
Kid Thomas & His Algiers   OJC-CD1833
     Stompers
Kid Thomas Valentine In   GHB BCD 296
     California

KID SHEIK
Kid Sheik's Swingsters   American Music AMCD-91
Kid Sheik in Cleveland & Boston   American Music AMCD-69

LIZZIE MILES
Lizzie Miles   American Music AMCD-73

GEORGE GUESNON
George Lewis with George   American Music AMCD-59
     Guesnon: Endless The Trek
George Guesnon   American Music AMCD-87

EMANUEL SAYLES

The Louis Cottrell Trio—Bourbon Street	OJC-CD1836
Emanuel Sayles With Barry Martyn's Band	GHB BCD-359

FLOYD CAMPBELL

Jazz in St. Louis 1924/27	Timeless Historical CBC 1-036 (Netherlands)

JASPER TAYLOR

Jimmy O'Bryant Vol. 1.	RST 1518 (Austria)

CURTIS JONES

Curtis Jones 1937/41	Blue Archives 158312
The Bluesville Years Vol. 4 In The Key Of Blues	Prestige PRCD 9908-2

FLOYD "CANDY" JOHNSON

Candy's Mood	Black & Blue BB 884-2 (France)

BILL DILLARD

Dickie Wells 1927/43	Classics 937 (France)

CHARLES I. WILLIAMS

Ruth Brown—The Songs Of My Life	Fantasy FCD 96665-2

LESLIE JOHNAKINS

Billie Holiday—The Complete Decca Recordings	MCA/GRP 2-601
Buddy Johnson 1939/42	Classics 884 (France)

FREDDIE SKERRITT

Edgar Hayes Orchestra 1937/38	Classics 730 (France)
Fats Waller—The Middle Years 1936/38	Bluebird 0786-66083-2

ROGER BOYD

The Chronological Blanche Calloway 1925/35	Classics 783 (France)

GEORGE HANCOCK
The Dinah Washington Story   Mercury 514841-2

GREELY WALTON
Louis Armstrong—Rhythm Saved   GRP GRD-602
   The World
The Luis Russell Collection 1926/   Collectors Classics COCD-7
   34   (Denmark)

JOSH WHITE
Josh White—Blues Singer   Columbia/Legacy CK 67001

MEMPHIS SLIM
The Real Folk Blues   MCA MCD 09270
The Bluesville Years Vol. 3   Prestige 9907-2
Beale Street Get-Down

Index

243

About the Author

David Griffiths has been contributing a weekly jazz column to the *South Wales Evening Post* since the mid-1980s. His articles have also appeared in *Storyville, The Mississippi Rag,* and *Jazz Journal.* He lives in Swansea, Wales.